90014

ROBIN J. WILSON *studied at Oxford University, University of Pennsylvania, and Massachusetts Institute of Technology. He is currently Senior Lecturer in Mathematics at the Open University. He has written and edited a number of books on mathematics and music, including* Introduction to Graph Theory, Graph Theory 1736–1936 *(with N. L. Biggs and E. K. Lloyd),* Selected Topics in Graph Theory 1, 2, 3 *(with L. W. Beineke),* Let Newton Be! *(with J. Fauvel, R. Flood, and M. Shortland), and* Gilbert and Sullivan: The D'Oyly Carte Years *(with F. Lloyd). He was awarded a Lester Ford award in 1975 for outstanding expository writing and is to be featured in* Mathematical People II *(edited by D. Albers, G. Alexanderson, and C. Reid).*

JOHN J. WATKINS, *Associate Professor and Chair of Mathematics at Colorado College, works in both commutative ring theory and graph theory. He studied at Oberlin College and taught mathematics in Ghana as a Peace Corps Volunteer before receiving his doctorate from the University of Kansas. In addition to mountain climbing and skiing, his interests include music and the history of mathematics. He is currently working on a book on commutative rings.*

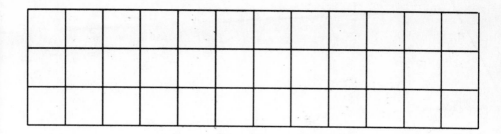

GRAPHS
AN INTRODUCTORY APPROACH

A First Course in Discrete Mathematics

ROBIN J. WILSON
The Open University

JOHN J. WATKINS
Colorado College

Based on The Open University course *Graphs, Networks and Design*

WILEY

John Wiley & Sons, Inc.

New York ■ Chichester ■ Brisbane ■ Toronto ■ Singapore

Library of Congress Cataloging-in-Publication Data

Wilson, Robin J.
    Graphs: an introductory approach : a first course in discrete
mathematics / Robin J. Wilson, John J. Watkins.
        p.   cm.

    "Based on The Open University course Graphs, Networks and
Design."
    Bibliography: p.
    Includes index.

    1. Graph theory. I. Watkins, John J.   II. Title.
QA166, W54 1989
511'.5--dc20   89-34111
                                                                                    CIP

Printed in Singapore.

10 9 8 7 6 5 4 3

"This book is based upon The Open University course TM361: *Graphs, Networks and Design*, first published in 1981. Material is reproduced by permission of The Open University."

PREFACE

In recent years, there has been a significant movement away from traditional calculus courses and toward courses on discrete mathematics. The impetus for this has undoubtedly been due in part to the increasing importance of the computer, and the consequence has been a proliferation of courses and books entitled *Discrete Mathematics, Finite Mathematics, Mathematics for Computer Science,* and other similar titles.

It is an unfortunate feature of some of these courses that a large number of different topics are covered at a superficial level, leaving the student frustrated and confused and having little understanding of the underlying reasons for introducing so many seemingly unrelated areas. Our experience is that students benefit more from an introductory course based in just one area, chosen so as to link in with other subjects whenever the instructor considers it appropriate to do so. Graph theory is an ideal topic for such an introductory course—it is fun, students enjoy it, they can 'get their hands dirty' drawing pictures, and it is an excellent stepping stone towards a wide range of courses in mathematics and computer science.

This book arose out of a British Open University course on *Graphs, Networks and Design,* which first appeared in 1981 and has been presented every year since then. It has regularly attracted over 500 students per year, with the result that several thousand students have successfully completed the course. In addition, various drafts of this book have been used at Colorado College since 1984 in a freshman/sophomore level course.

The original course·was written by a team of Open University mathematicians and technologists. Those who contributed most to the material in this book were Joan Aldous, Keith Cavanagh, Alan Dolan, Stanley Fiorini, Yin-Seong Ho, Fred Holroyd, Roy Nelson, Joe Rooney, Richard Scott, and Robin Wilson. Others who contributed valuable assistance are Marlow Anderson, Rosemary Bailey, Chris Bissell, Amanda Chetwynd, Chris Earl, Lionel March, Michael Martin, Carole Mills, John Stratford, and Michelle Wemple.

As with other Open University courses, *Graphs, Networks and Design* consists mainly of correspondence material, supported by audio-cassette tapes and BBC television programs which are broadcast throughout Britain. Having produced this material, the course team felt that parts of it would be ideally suited to the classroom situation, and could successfully be converted into book form appropriate for an international audience.

The first of these books, on *Graphs,* is presented here. A companion volume, on *Networks,* is currently being prepared by A. K. Dolan and J. Aldous. Each book is self-contained, and is suitable for a semester course on discrete mathematics in the first or second year of an American college or university. Since the approach, terminology, and notation are the same for both books, an instructor wishing to teach both graphs and networks will find that the two books can be used concurrently.

This book is divided into two parts. Part I contains the basic definitions relating to graphs and digraphs, together with a large number of examples and applications. Part II contains a number of different topics from which an instructor can select depending upon the length of the course. The choice of material to be covered will depend on the instructor's particular aims and time constraints. As a rough guide, an instructor interested in the 'purer' aspects of the subject may wish to concentrate mainly on Chapters 1–3, 6 and 7, and 10–13, whereas an instructor interested in applications may prefer to cover Chapters 1–5 and 8–10. In any case, it would be preferable to cover the material in Part I fairly quickly, and to proceed to Part II as soon as practicable; it is not necessary to cover all of the applications in Chapters 3 and 5. An appendix on methods of proof appears at the end of Part I, after Chapter 5.

An important part of learning graph theory is problem-solving, and for this reason we have included a large number of problems at the end of each chapter. Many of these are routine exercises, designed to test understanding of the material in the text, but some are more challenging and less routine; these latter problems are marked with a dagger (†). Several problems are answered in full at the end of the book; these problems are marked with an encircled star ✪.

ROBIN J. WILSON
JOHN J. WATKINS

CONTENTS

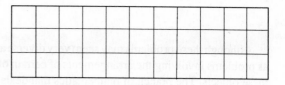

PART I

INTRODUCTION

Here are just a few of the many problems you will encounter in this book.

a. Suppose you are stuck in the middle of a maze. Is there a foolproof method for finding your way out again?

b. If you wanted to drive from New York to San Francisco, how would you find the shortest route?

c. If you try to color a map of the United States in such a way that neighboring states are assigned different colors, you will find that only four colors are necessary; is this true for all maps, or are there maps that need more colors?

d. How many chemical molecules are there with the formula C_6H_{14}?

e. What is the best way of bracing a given plane framework to make it rigid?

Although these problems may seem very diverse at first sight, they can all be expressed as problems involving the arrangements of certain objects and the relationships between these objects. The branch of mathematics that deals with such arrangement problems is known as *graph theory*; the development of this subject is one of the two main themes of this book. By developing general methods for tackling problems of this kind, we shall show not only how to solve such problems, but also how to spot the connections between problems which may appear at first sight to have little in common. By understanding the underlying reasons for these connections, you will gradually gain further insight into the nature of the original problems and their solutions.

Several of the problems we examine in this book arise from important practical problems in technology and the sciences. Indeed, much of the impetus to the subject in the last few years has arisen out of the need to solve particular problems in industry. By applying the kind of techniques discussed in this book to industrial problems involving network analysis or operations research, it has been possible to make substantial savings in time or money. In view of this, it is important to be able to represent these problems in graph-theoretical terms, and this brings us to the other main theme of the book—*mathematical modeling.*

The modeling process involves formulating a problem in such a way that it can be attacked by the techniques of graph theory. This is not always easy; the way in which the modeling is carried out, and the degree to which the mathematical model accurately represents the original problem, varies considerably from problem to problem. Throughout the book we emphasize not only the modeling process itself, but also its limitations.

The two main themes of the book are the development of graph theory as a subject in its own right, and the modeling of problems. For the mathematician the primary interest may well be the former, whereas for the technologist the problems themselves may well provide the main interest. In writing this book we have tried to integrate these two approaches, since we believe that, in this subject, theory and practice are too interrelated to be separated successfully. The historical development of the subject has arisen out of the joint efforts of mathematicians and practitioners, with great benefit to both. The mathematical ideas have been used to tackle practical problems, which, in turn, have given rise to new mathematical ideas, and so on. These mathematical ideas have often proved more interesting than the problems that gave rise to them, and are now studied in their own right.

In view of the above comments, it is our hope that the book will prove to be of interest to technologists, scientists, and mathematicians. For the mathematician this book provides an opportunity to see real mathematics in action solving worthwhile problems, whereas for the technologist and scientist this book shows the importance and usefulness of developing a mathematical framework which can be used to interrelate different problems and provide means for solving them. The subject you are about to embark on is a very exciting one, both in its underlying mathematical structure and in its applications in present-day science and technology. Although its roots go back a long time, it is a very modern subject in which substantial advances are being made all the time. It is likely to play an ever-increasing role in the years to come, and this book is designed to give you the necessary background to understand these future developments.

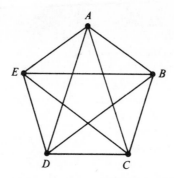

We begin Part I with an introduction to graphs and digraphs. Here the word *graph* refers to a diagram of points interconnected by lines, as shown above, rather than to a picture representing a function. The interconnections between points may refer to bonds between atoms in a chemical molecule, wires between terminals in an electrical network, roads between towns on a map, and so on. *Digraphs* (short for "directed graphs") are like graphs, except that each line has a direction indicated by an arrow, and may be used, for example, to represent one-way road systems.

We discuss the properties of graphs and digraphs and describe a number of applications, including the use of graph theory in chemistry, genetics, and music, and the use of digraphs in linguistics, control theory, and the social sciences.

CHAPTER 1

WHAT IS A GRAPH?

1.1 INTRODUCTION

In this chapter we describe a number of situations which can be represented by graphs. These include chemical molecules, architectural floor plans, and electrical networks. In order to investigate such situations, we need to study graphs in some detail. We start by introducing some basic concepts and terminology which will be needed for this investigation.

In order to introduce the idea of a graph, we consider the following examples.

Route Maps

The following diagram is a map of the central part of the London Underground. Like all maps, it does not represent every feature of the city in question, but only those of relevance to the people who use it. In the case of the London Underground map, the exact geographical locations of the stations are unimportant. What is important, however, is the way in which the various stations are interconnected, so that a passenger can plan a route from one station to another. The map is simply a diagrammatic way of indicating how the stations are interconnected.

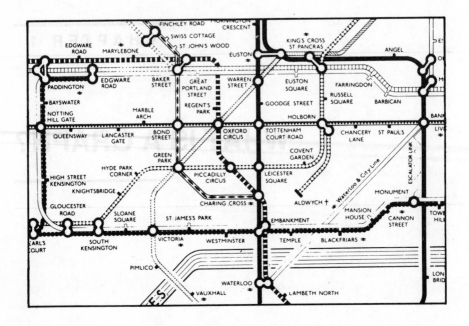

Chemical Molecules

A chemical molecule consists of a number of atoms linked by chemical bonds. For example, a molecule of water (H_2O) consists of an oxygen atom bonded to two hydrogen atoms, and may be represented by the diagram

$$H—O—H$$

More complicated examples are given by the molecules of methane (CH_4), ethanol (C_2H_5OH) and ethene (C_2H_4), that may be represented by the diagrams

methane   **ethanol**   **ethene**

Pictures of this sort are often called *structural diagrams*. Note that they do not give us any information about how the atoms are aligned in space; for example, the hydrogen atoms of methane do not lie in a plane, but are situated at the vertices of a regular tetrahedron with the carbon atom at the center. In spite of this, such diagrams are extremely useful in telling us how the various atoms are connected, and we can obtain a lot of information about the chemical behavior of a molecule by studying its structural diagram.

Architectural Floor Plans

The plan of the lower floor of a house is represented by

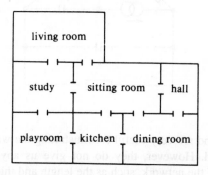

For small plans like this, such a diagram is very convenient for showing which rooms have mutual access, but for large plans a less cumbersome representation is useful. One such representation is to draw the rooms as small solid circles

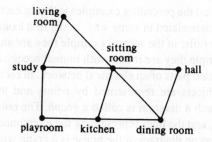

Such diagrams are known to architects as *circulation diagrams,* because of their use in analyzing the movements of people in large buildings. In particular, they have been used in the designing of airports, and in planning the layout of supermarkets. Such diagrams are useful in representing the connections between the various rooms, but they do not give us any information about the size or shape of the rooms.

Electrical Networks

The following diagram represents an electrical network containing two resistors, two capacitors, two inductors, and voltage and current generator elements:

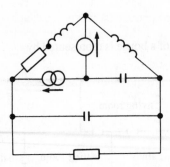

Diagrams of this kind are very useful for illustrating the way in which parts of the network are connected. However, they do not give us any information about the geometrical features of the network, such as the length and thickness of each wire and its position in space.

1.2 THE DEFINITION OF A GRAPH

The common feature in all the preceding examples is that in each case we have a system of 'objects' which are interrelated in some way. In the first example the objects are stations interconnected by rails; in the second example they are atoms linked by chemical bonds; in the third example they are rooms with mutual access; and in the fourth example they are interconnected parts of an electrical network. In each case we can draw a diagram in which the objects are represented by points and the interconnections are represented by lines. Such a diagram is called a *graph*. The points representing the objects are called *vertices,* and the lines representing the interconnections are called *edges*. For example, the circulation diagram of the house is a graph with seven vertices (corresponding to the playroom, kitchen, hall, etc.) and ten edges (corresponding to the interconnections between these rooms).

We can formalize these ideas as follows:

TEMPORARY DEFINITION. *A* **graph** *is a diagram consisting of points, called* **vertices***, joined together by lines, called* **edges***; each edge joins exactly two vertices.*

In graph theory the terminology is not completely standard; for example, some authors use the term *node* or *point* for what we have called a *vertex,* and *arc or line* for what we have called an *edge*. Any of these choices of terminology is acceptable as long as it is used consistently.

The trouble with the above definition of a graph is that we can use many different diagrams to represent the same interconnections. An example is provided by the **utilities problem,** which we shall solve in Chapter 11. In this problem, we wish to connect three houses, *A, B,* and *C,* to three utilities, *gas, water,* and *electricity.* For safety reasons it is necessary that the various connections should not cross each other. Can the connections be made? The following picture shows how eight of the nine connections can be drawn, but how about the ninth?

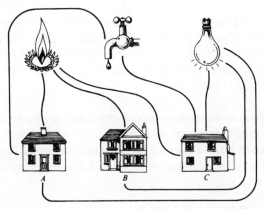

We can represent the connections by means of the following graphs, where the vertices correspond to the three houses and the three utilities. Each of these graphs has six vertices and nine edges, and both graphs convey the same information—the three houses are connected to each of the three utilities, but not to each other. Thus, these two graphs are the same. The utilities problem is that of finding whether there is yet another graph which is the same as these two, but in which no two edges cross.

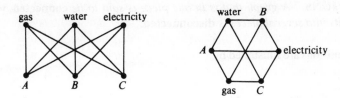

It follows from the above that a graph is determined as soon as we know its vertices, and which edges join which pairs of vertices. Once we have this information, we can draw the graph and, in principle, any picture we draw is as good as any other. In other words, we can describe a graph completely by listing its vertices and edges in any order, and the actual way in which the vertices and edges are drawn is irrelevant. For example, the utilities graph may be described completely by the lists

vertices: *A, B, C, g, w, e*

edges: *Ag, Aw, Ae, Bg, Bw, Be, Cg, Cw, Ce*

We may equally well write these lists in a different order

vertices: w, C, B, e, g, A

edges: $gA, gB, gC, eA, eB, eC, wA, wB, wC$

We can now replace our temporary definition of a graph by one which involves these lists.

DEFINITIONS. *A* **graph** G *consists of a non-empty set of elements, called* **vertices,** *and a list of unordered pairs of these elements, called* **edges.** *The set of vertices of the graph* G *is called the* **vertex-set** *of* G, *denoted by* **V(G),** *and the list of edges is called the* **edge-list** *of* G, *denoted by* **E(G).** *If* v *and* w *are vertices of* G, *then an edge of the form* vw *or* wv *is said to* **join** v *and* w.

We shall continue to use pictures to depict graphs; any such picture is only one of many that can be used to represent the graph.

The definition of a graph allows for the possibility of several edges joining the same pair of vertices, or an edge joining a vertex to itself. The following terminology is useful when discussing such graphs:

DEFINITIONS. *Two or more edges joining the same pair of vertices are called* **multiple edges,** *and an edge joining a vertex to itself is called a* **loop.** *A graph with no loops or multiple edges is called a* **simple graph.**

It is also convenient to distinguish between graphs that are 'in one piece' and those that are not.

DEFINITIONS. *A graph that is in one piece is said to be* **connected,** *whereas one which splits into several pieces is* **disconnected.**

These definitions are illustrated by

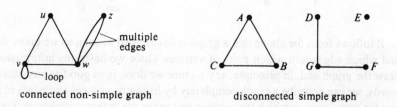

connected non-simple graph   disconnected simple graph

We also need the concept of a *subgraph* of a graph. It is a common feature of both mathematics and technology that we study complicated objects by looking at simpler objects of the same type contained inside them, and these smaller objects are often indicated by the prefix "sub." For example, we study subsets of sets, subsystems of systems, subgroups of groups, and so on. In graph theory we make the following definition.

DEFINITION.   *Let G be a graph with vertex-set* V(G) *and edge-list* E(G). *A* **subgraph**
of G *is a graph all of whose vertices belong to* V(G) *and all of whose edges belong to*
E(G).

For example, if *G* is the connected graph above, where

$$V(G) = \{u,v,w,z\} \text{ and } E(G) \text{ is } (uv, uw, vv, vw, wz, wz),$$

then the following graphs are all subgraphs of *G*:

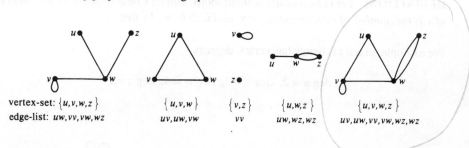

vertex-set: $\{u,v,w,z\}$ $\{u,v,w\}$ $\{v,z\}$ $\{u,w,z\}$ $\{u,v,w,z\}$
edge-list: uw, vv, vw, wz uv, uw, vw vv uw, wz, wz uv, uw, vv, vw, wz, wz

Note that a subgraph of *G* must actually be a graph, and that *G* is regarded as a subgraph
of itself.

1.3 THE DEGREE OF A VERTEX

It is also useful to have a term for the number of edges meeting at a given vertex. Such a
concept occurs, for example, in a road map, where a junction has three or more roads
meeting. It also arises in electrical network theory where we may be interested in the
number of wires at a given terminal, or in architecture where we may be concerned with
the number of rooms accessible from a given one. These situations are illustrated as

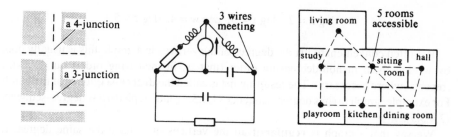

   In chemistry the term *valency* is used to indicate the number of bonds connecting an
atom to its neighbors. For example, in the diagram representing the ethanol molecule,
each carbon atom has valency 4, the oxygen atom has valency 2, and each hydrogen atom
has valency 1. Although some authors extend this chemical use of the word *valency* to
graphs, we shall use the word *degree*.

$$H-\overset{\overset{\displaystyle H}{|}}{\underset{\underset{\displaystyle H}{|}}{C}}-\overset{\overset{\displaystyle H}{|}}{\underset{\underset{\displaystyle H}{|}}{C}}-O-H$$

ethanol

DEFINITION.   *Let* G *be a graph without loops, and let* v *be a vertex of* G. *The* **degree** *of* v *is the number of edges meeting at* v, *and is denoted by* **deg** v.

For example, graph (a) below has vertex-degrees

$$\deg u = 2, \ \ \deg v = 3, \ \ \deg w = 4, \ \ \deg z = 1$$

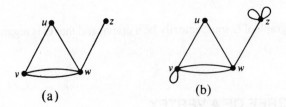

(a)   (b)

Although the degree of a vertex has been defined only for graphs without loops, the definition can easily be extended to graphs with loops. We do this by requiring that each loop contributes 2 to the degree of the corresponding vertex. For example, graph (b) above has vertex-degrees

$$\deg u = 2, \ \ \deg v = 5, \ \ \deg w = 4, \ \ \deg z = 5$$

It is often convenient to list the degrees of the vertices in a graph; this is usually done by writing them in non-decreasing order (that is, in increasing order, but allowing 'repeats' where necessary). The resulting list is called the **degree-sequence** of the graph. For example, graph (a) has degree-sequence (1,2,3,4) and graph (b) has degree-sequence (2,4,5,5).

We say that a graph is **regular** if all the vertices of G have the same degree. In particular, if the degree of each vertex is r, then G is **regular of degree** r. In the following diagram we illustrate some examples of graphs which are regular of degree r, for various values of r:

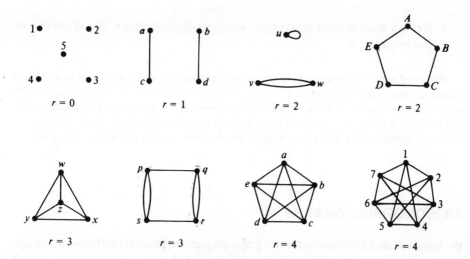

We observe that the last graph above is regular of degree 4 and has seven vertices, and so the sum of the vertex-degrees is 28. We also observe that this graph has 14 edges (seven around the outside heptagon and seven for the inside star). In other words, the sum of the vertex-degrees is exactly twice the number of edges. A corresponding result holds for all graphs, and is sometimes called the *handshaking lemma*.

THE HANDSHAKING LEMMA.   *In any graph, the sum of all the vertex-degrees is equal to twice the number of edges.*

Proof   Since each edge has two ends, it must contribute exactly 2 to the sum of the degrees. The result follows immediately. ☐

Note that this proof is valid even when the graph contains loops, since each loop contributes exactly 2 to the degree of the corresponding vertex.

The name *handshaking lemma* arises from the fact that a graph can be used to represent a group of people shaking hands at a party. In such a graph, the people are represented by the vertices, and an edge is included whenever the corresponding people have shaken hands. With this interpretation, the number of edges represents the total number of handshakes, the degree of a vertex is the number of hands shaken by the corresponding person, and the sum of the degrees is the total number of hands shaken. So the handshaking lemma states simply that the total number of hands shaken is equal to twice the number of handshakes—the reason being, of course, that exactly two hands are involved in each handshake.

There are some important consequences of the handshaking lemma. We leave the proofs to you (see Problem 1.14).

Consequences of the Handshaking Lemma

1. In any graph, the sum of all the vertex-degrees is an even number.
2. In any graph, the number of vertices of odd degree is even.

3. If G is a graph which has n vertices and is regular of degree r, then G has exactly $\frac{1}{2}nr$ edges.

Historical note. The handshaking lemma first appeared (in a different form) in a paper of Leonhard Euler (1707–1783) entitled *Solutio problematis ad geometriam situs pertinentis* (The solution of a problem relating to the geometry of position). This important paper dates from 1736, and is widely regarded as 'the earliest paper in graph theory'. It contains Euler's solution of the celebrated problem of the Königsberg bridges. We shall return to this problem in Chapter 6.

1.4 ISOMORPHIC GRAPHS

We have seen that it is possible for two graph diagrams to look very different, but to represent the same graph. On the other hand, it is possible for two graphs diagrams to look very similar, but to represent different graphs. For example, the diagrams below look very similar, but are clearly not the same graph (since gas and water are joined in the second graph, but not in the first graph).

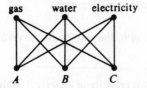
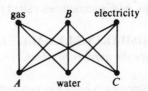

We express this similarity by saying that the graphs represented by these two diagrams are *isomorphic*. This means that we can relabel the vertices in the first graph to get the second one: simply replace *water* by B, and conversely. (The word *isomorphic* derives from the Greek for *same* and *form*.)

Similarly, the graphs represented by the diagrams

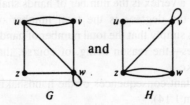

and

are not the same, but are isomorphic, since we can relabel the vertices in the graph G to get the graph H: simply interchange u and z, and v and w. This gives us a one-to-one correspondence between the vertices of G and those of H such that edges in G correspond to edges in H—namely,

$$G: u\ v\ w\ z$$
$$\updownarrow\ \updownarrow\updownarrow\updownarrow\updownarrow$$
$$H: z\ w\ v\ u$$

Note that

the two edges *uv* in *G* correspond to the two edges *zw* in *H*

the edge *uw* in *G* corresponds to the edge *zv* in *H*

the loop at *w* in *G* corresponds to the loop at *v* in *H*

and so on. This leads to the following definition.

DEFINITION.   *Two graphs* G *and* H *are* **isomorphic** *if* H *can be obtained from* G *by relabeling the vertices—that is, if there is a one-to-one correspondence between the vertices of* G *and those of* H, *such that the number of edges joining any pair of vertices in* G *is equal to the number of edges joining the corresponding pair of vertices in* H.

Note that in checking whether or not two graphs are the same, we must check carefully that all the labels on the vertices correspond. However, when checking whether or not two graphs are isomorphic, we can ignore the symbols used to label the vertices, since the vertices can be relabeled as necessary. In view of this, we often drop the labels altogether when they are not relevant to the problem in hand, and say (for example) that the "unlabeled graph"

refers to any of the isomorphic graphs:

It follows that two unlabeled graphs, such as

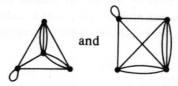

and

are isomorphic if labels can be attached to their vertices so that they become the same graph.

We can summarize the preceding discussion as follows.

Labeled Graphs

These labeled graphs are the same.   These labeled graphs are not the same,
                                                   but are isomorphic.

Unlabeled Graphs

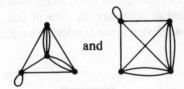

These unlabeled graphs are isomorphic.

In the future, whenever we use the word *graph,* it will be clear whether we are referring to labeled or unlabeled graphs. If there is any possibility of confusion, we shall insert the word *labeled* or *unlabeled,* as appropriate.

1.5 COUNTING GRAPHS

How many chemical molecules are there with formula C_8H_{18}? How many irrigation canal systems are there linking five locations with four canals? How many architectural floor plans are there satisfying certain given properties?

As you will see, we can reduce many such problems to that of determining the number of graphs with a particular property. Since many standard graph-counting problems have been completely solved, we can often use the results to deduce the solution of a problem in which we are interested. We briefly survey the progress made on several graph-counting problems.

Counting Labeled Graphs

When counting labeled graphs, we distinguish between labeled graphs which are not isomorphic, but not between isomorphic graphs—we sometimes express this by saying that the graphs are counted *up to isomorphism*. For example, there are just eight non-isomorphic labeled simple graphs with three vertices.

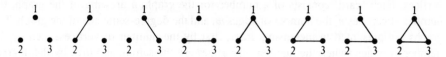

The problem of determining the number of labeled simple graphs with n vertices is easy to solve. By consequence 3 of the handshaking lemma, there are $\frac{1}{2} n(n-1)$ possible edges, and each may be either present or absent (a choice of two possibilities); thus, the required number is $2^{n(n-1)/2}$. The following table lists the number of labeled simple graphs with n vertices, for $n \le 8$:

n	1	2	3	4	5	6	7	8
labeled graphs	1	2	8	64	1024	32768	2097152	268435456

Counting Unlabeled Graphs

When counting unlabeled graphs, we distinguish only between graphs which are not isomorphic. For example, there are just four non-isomorphic unlabeled simple graphs with three vertices.

One can quickly determine the number of simple graphs with at most six vertices and any given number of edges or degree-sequence. For larger numbers of vertices, listing all possible graphs soon becomes impracticable, and it is necessary to find some other way of counting them. In 1935 George Pólya obtained a general formula from which one can calculate the number of unlabeled graphs with any given number of vertices and edges. Pólya's methods have since been applied to several other graph-counting problems, and formulas have been obtained for the number of connected graphs or regular graphs with any given number of vertices. The table lists the number of unlabeled simple graphs of various types with n vertices, for $n \le 8$.

n	1	2	3	4	5	6	7	8
graphs	1	2	4	11	34	156	1044	12346
connected graphs	1	1	2	6	21	112	853	11117
regular graphs	1	2	2	4	3	8	6	20

In general, counting problems for unlabeled graphs are much harder to solve than their analogs for labeled graphs. In fact, there are certain types of graph for which the latter problem has been solved while the former problem remains unsolved.

1.6 THE GRAPH CARDS

To conclude this chapter we present the 208 unlabeled simple graphs with at most six vertices. Each 'card' consists of a number for the graph, a drawing of the graph, the number of vertices n, the number of edges m, and the degree-sequence of the graph. The graphs are presented in increasing order, first by the number of vertices, then by the number of edges (when the number of vertices are the same), and then by the degree-sequence (when the numbers of vertices and edges are the same).

GRAPH CARDS

1
$n = 1$
$m = 0$
$d = (0)$

2
$n = 2$
$m = 0$
$d = (0,0)$

3
$n = 2$
$m = 1$
$d = (1,1)$

4
$n = 3$
$m = 0$
$d = (0,0,0)$

5
$n = 3$
$m = 1$
$d = (0,1,1)$

6
$n = 3$
$m = 2$
$d = (1,1,2)$

7
$n = 3$
$m = 3$
$d = (2,2,2)$

8
$n = 4$
$m = 0$
$d = (0,0,0,0)$

9
$n = 4$
$m = 1$
$d = (0,0,1,1)$

10
$n = 4$
$m = 2$
$d = (0,1,1,2)$

11
$n = 4$
$m = 2$
$d = (1,1,1,1)$

12
$n = 4$
$m = 3$
$d = (0,2,2,2)$

13
$n = 4$
$m = 3$
$d = (1,1,1,3)$

14
$n = 4$
$m = 3$
$d = (1,1,2,2)$

15
$n = 4$
$m = 4$
$d = (1,2,2,3)$

16
$n = 4$
$m = 4$
$d = (2,2,2,2)$

17
$n = 4$
$m = 5$
$d = (2,2,3,3)$

18
$n = 4$
$m = 6$
$d = (3,3,3,3)$

19
$n = 5$
$m = 0$
$d = (0,0,0,0,0)$

20
$n = 5$
$m = 1$
$d = (0,0,0,1,1)$

21
$n = 5$
$m = 2$
$d = (0,0,1,1,2)$

22
$n = 5$
$m = 2$
$d = (0,1,1,1,1)$

23
$n = 5$
$m = 3$
$d = (0,0,2,2,2)$

24
$n = 5$
$m = 3$
$d = (0,1,1,1,3)$

25
$n = 5$
$m = 3$
$d = (0,1,1,2,2)$

26
$n = 5$
$m = 3$
$d = (1,1,1,1,2)$

27
$n = 5$
$m = 4$
$d = (0,1,2,2,3)$

28
$n = 5$
$m = 4$
$d = (0,2,2,2,2)$

29
$n = 5$
$m = 4$
$d = (1,1,1,1,4)$

30
$n = 5$
$m = 4$
$d = (1,1,1,2,3)$

31
$n = 5$
$m = 4$
$d = (1,1,2,2,2)$

32
$n = 5$
$m = 4$
$d = (1,1,2,2,2)$

33
$n = 5$
$m = 5$
$d = (0,2,2,3,3)$

34
$n = 5$
$m = 5$
$d = (1,1,2,2,4)$

35
$n = 5$
$m = 5$
$d = (1,1,2,3,3)$

36

$n = 5$
$m = 5$
$d = (1,2,2,2,3)$

37

$n = 5$
$m = 5$
$d = (1,2,2,2,3)$

38

$n = 5$
$m = 5$
$d = (2,2,2,2,2)$

39

$n = 5$
$m = 6$
$d = (0,3,3,3,3)$

40

$n = 5$
$m = 6$
$d = (1,2,2,3,4)$

41

$n = 5$
$m = 6$
$d = (1,2,3,3,3)$

42

$n = 5$
$m = 6$
$d = (2,2,2,2,4)$

43

$n = 5$
$m = 6$
$d = (2,2,2,3,3)$

44

$n = 5$
$m = 6$
$d = (2,2,2,3,3)$

45

$n = 5$
$m = 7$
$d = (1,3,3,3,4)$

46

$n = 5$
$m = 7$
$d = (2,2,2,4,4)$

47

$n = 5$
$m = 7$
$d = (2,2,3,3,4)$

48

$n = 5$
$m = 7$
$d = (2,3,3,3,3)$

49

$n = 5$
$m = 8$
$d = (2,3,3,4,4)$

50

$n = 5$
$m = 8$
$d = (3,3,3,3,4)$

51

$n = 5$
$m = 9$
$d = (3,3,4,4,4)$

52

$n = 5$
$m = 10$
$d = (4,4,4,4,4)$

53

$n = 6$
$m = 0$
$d = (0,0,0,0,0,0)$

54

$n = 6$
$m = 1$
$d = (0,0,0,0,1,1)$

55

$n = 6$
$m = 2$
$d = (0,0,1,1,1,1)$

56

$n = 6$
$m = 2$
$d = (0,0,0,1,1,2)$

57

$n = 6$
$m = 3$
$d = (0,0,0,2,2,2)$

58

$n = 6$
$m = 3$
$d = (0,0,1,1,1,3)$

59

$n = 6$
$m = 3$
$d = (0,0,1,1,2,2)$

60

$n = 6$
$m = 3$
$d = (0,1,1,1,1,2)$

61

$n = 6$
$m = 3$
$d = (1,1,1,1,1,1)$

62

$n = 6$
$m = 4$
$d = (0,0,1,2,2,3)$

63

$n = 6$
$m = 4$
$d = (0,0,2,2,2,2)$

64

$n = 6$
$m = 4$
$d = (0,1,1,1,1,4)$

65

$n = 6$
$m = 4$
$d = (0,1,1,1,2,3)$

66

$n = 6$
$m = 4$
$d = (0,1,1,2,2,2)$

67

$n = 6$
$m = 4$
$d = (0,1,1,2,2,2)$

68

$n = 6$
$m = 4$
$d = (1,1,1,1,1,3)$

69

$n = 6$
$m = 4$
$d = (1,1,1,1,2,2)$

70

$n = 6$
$m = 4$
$d = (1,1,1,1,2,2)$

71

$n = 6$
$m = 5$
$d = (0,0,2,2,3,3)$

72

$n = 6$
$m = 5$
$d = (0,1,1,2,2,4)$

73

$n = 6$
$m = 5$
$d = (0,1,1,2,3,3)$

74

$n = 6$
$m = 5$
$d = (0,1,2,2,2,3)$

75

$n = 6$
$m = 5$
$d = (0,1,2,2,2,3)$

76

$n = 6$
$m = 5$
$d = (0,2,2,2,2,2)$

77

$n = 6$
$m = 5$
$d = (1,1,1,1,1,5)$

78

$n = 6$
$m = 5$
$d = (1,1,1,1,2,4)$

79

$n = 6$
$m = 5$
$d = (1,1,1,1,3,3)$

80

$n = 6$
$m = 5$
$d = (1,1,1,2,2,3)$

81

$n = 6$
$m = 5$
$d = (1,1,1,2,2,3)$

82

$n = 6$
$m = 5$
$d = (1,1,1,2,2,3)$

83

$n = 6$
$m = 5$
$d = (1,1,2,2,2,2)$

84

$n = 6$
$m = 5$
$d = (1,1,2,2,2,2)$

85

$n = 6$
$m = 5$
$d = (1,1,2,2,2,2)$

86

$n = 6$
$m = 6$
$d = (0,0,3,3,3,3)$

87

$n = 6$
$m = 6$
$d = (0,1,2,2,3,4)$

88

$n = 6$
$m = 6$
$d = (0,1,2,3,3,3)$

89

$n = 6$
$m = 6$
$d = (0,2,2,2,2,4)$

90

$n = 6$
$m = 6$
$d = (0,2,2,2,3,3)$

91

$n = 6$
$m = 6$
$d = (0,2,2,2,3,3)$

92

$n = 6$
$m = 6$
$d = (1,1,1,2,2,5)$

93

$n = 6$
$m = 6$
$d = (1,1,1,2,3,4)$

94

$n = 6$
$m = 6$
$d = (1,1,1,3,3,3)$

95

$n = 6$
$m = 6$
$d = (1,1,2,2,3,3)$

96

$n = 6$
$m = 6$
$d = (1,1,2,2,2,4)$

97

$n = 6$
$m = 6$
$d = (1,1,2,2,2,4)$

98

$n = 6$
$m = 6$
$d = (1,1,2,2,3,3)$

99

$n = 6$
$m = 6$
$d = (1,1,2,2,3,3)$

100

$n = 6$
$m = 6$
$d = (1,1,2,2,3,3)$

101

$n = 6$
$m = 6$
$d = (1,1,2,2,3,3)$

102

$n = 6$
$m = 6$
$d = (1,2,2,2,2,3)$

103

$n = 6$
$m = 6$
$d = (1,2,2,2,2,3)$

104

$n = 6$
$m = 6$
$d = (1,2,2,2,2,3)$

105

$n = 6$
$m = 6$
$d = (2,2,2,2,2,2)$

106

$n = 6$
$m = 6$
$d = (2,2,2,2,2,2)$

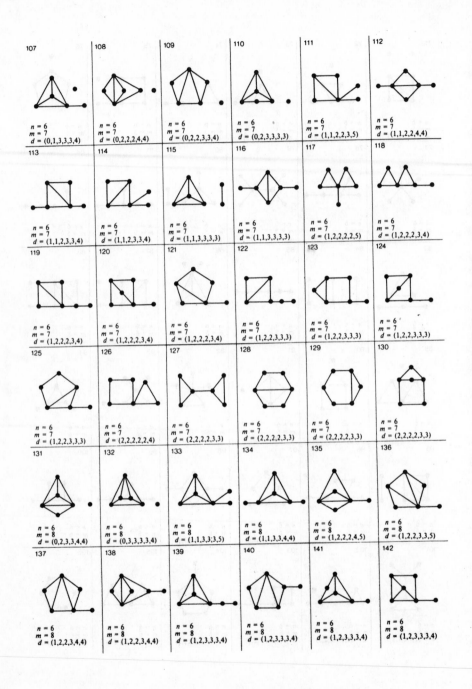

107

$n = 6$
$m = 7$
$d = (0,1,3,3,4)$

108

$n = 6$
$m = 7$
$d = (0,2,2,2,4,4)$

109

$n = 6$
$m = 7$
$d = (0,2,2,3,3,4)$

110

$n = 6$
$m = 7$
$d = (0,2,3,3,3,3)$

111

$n = 6$
$m = 7$
$d = (1,1,2,2,3,5)$

112

$n = 6$
$m = 7$
$d = (1,1,2,2,4,4)$

113

$n = 6$
$m = 7$
$d = (1,1,2,3,3,4)$

114

$n = 6$
$m = 7$
$d = (1,1,2,3,3,4)$

115

$n = 6$
$m = 7$
$d = (1,1,3,3,3,3)$

116

$n = 6$
$m = 7$
$d = (1,1,3,3,3,3)$

117

$n = 6$
$m = 7$
$d = (1,2,2,2,2,5)$

118

$n = 6$
$m = 7$
$d = (1,2,2,2,3,4)$

119

$n = 6$
$m = 7$
$d = (1,2,2,2,3,4)$

120

$n = 6$
$m = 7$
$d = (1,2,2,2,3,4)$

121

$n = 6$
$m = 7$
$d = (1,2,2,2,3,4)$

122

$n = 6$
$m = 7$
$d = (1,2,2,3,3,3)$

123

$n = 6$
$m = 7$
$d = (1,2,2,3,3,3)$

124

$n = 6$
$m = 7$
$d = (1,2,2,3,3,3)$

125

$n = 6$
$m = 7$
$d = (1,2,2,3,3,3)$

126

$n = 6$
$m = 7$
$d = (2,2,2,2,2,4)$

127

$n = 6$
$m = 7$
$d = (2,2,2,2,3,3)$

128

$n = 6$
$m = 7$
$d = (2,2,2,2,3,3)$

129

$n = 6$
$m = 7$
$d = (2,2,2,2,3,3)$

130

$n = 6$
$m = 7$
$d = (2,2,2,2,3,3)$

131

$n = 6$
$m = 8$
$d = (0,2,3,3,4,4)$

132

$n = 6$
$m = 8$
$d = (0,3,3,3,3,4)$

133

$n = 6$
$m = 8$
$d = (1,1,3,3,3,5)$

134

$n = 6$
$m = 8$
$d = (1,1,3,3,4,4)$

135

$n = 6$
$m = 8$
$d = (1,2,2,2,4,5)$

136

$n = 6$
$m = 8$
$d = (1,2,2,3,3,5)$

137

$n = 6$
$m = 8$
$d = (1,2,2,3,4,4)$

138

$n = 6$
$m = 8$
$d = (1,2,2,3,4,4)$

139

$n = 6$
$m = 8$
$d = (1,2,3,3,3,4)$

140

$n = 6$
$m = 8$
$d = (1,2,3,3,3,4)$

141

$n = 6$
$m = 8$
$d = (1,2,3,3,3,4)$

142

$n = 6$
$m = 8$
$d = (1,2,3,3,3,4)$

143
$n = 6$
$m = 8$
$d = (1,3,3,3,3,3)$

144
$n = 6$
$m = 8$
$d = (2,2,2,2,3,5)$

145
$n = 6$
$m = 8$
$d = (2,2,2,2,4,4)$

146
$n = 6$
$m = 8$
$d = (2,2,2,2,4,4)$

147
$n = 6$
$m = 8$
$d = (2,2,2,3,3,4)$

148
$n = 6$
$m = 8$
$d = (2,2,2,3,3,4)$

149
$n = 6$
$m = 8$
$d = (2,2,2,3,3,4)$

150
$n = 6$
$m = 8$
$d = (2,2,2,3,3,4)$

151
$n = 6$
$m = 8$
$d = (2,2,3,3,3,3)$

152
$n = 6$
$m = 8$
$d = (2,2,3,3,3,3)$

153
$n = 6$
$m = 8$
$d = (2,2,3,3,3,3)$

154
$n = 6$
$m = 8$
$d = (2,2,3,3,3,3)$

155
$n = 6$
$m = 9$
$d = (0,3,3,4,4,4)$

156
$n = 6$
$m = 9$
$d = (1,2,3,3,4,5)$

157
$n = 6$
$m = 9$
$d = (1,2,3,4,4,4)$

158
$n = 6$
$m = 9$
$d = (1,3,3,3,3,5)$

159
$n = 6$
$m = 9$
$d = (1,3,3,3,4,4)$

160
$n = 6$
$m = 9$
$d = (1,3,3,3,4,4)$

161
$n = 6$
$m = 9$
$d = (2,2,2,2,5,5)$

162
$n = 6$
$m = 9$
$d = (2,2,2,3,4,5)$

163
$n = 6$
$m = 9$
$d = (2,2,2,4,4,4)$

164
$n = 6$
$m = 9$
$d = (2,2,3,3,3,5)$

165
$n = 6$
$m = 9$
$d = (2,2,3,3,3,5)$

166
$n = 6$
$m = 9$
$d = (2,2,3,3,4,4)$

167
$n = 6$
$m = 9$
$d = (2,2,3,3,4,4)$

168
$n = 6$
$m = 9$
$d = (2,2,3,3,4,4)$

169
$n = 6$
$m = 9$
$d = (2,2,3,3,4,4)$

170
$n = 6$
$m = 9$
$d = (2,2,3,3,4,4)$

171
$n = 6$
$m = 9$
$d = (2,3,3,3,3,4)$

172
$n = 6$
$m = 9$
$d = (2,3,3,3,3,4)$

173
$n = 6$
$m = 9$
$d = (2,3,3,3,3,4)$

174
$n = 6$
$m = 9$
$d = (3,3,3,3,3,3)$

175
$n = 6$
$m = 9$
$d = (3,3,3,3,3,3)$

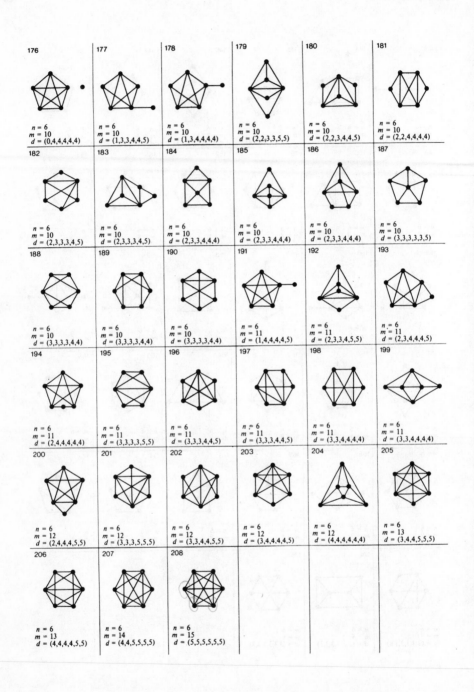

176
$n = 6$
$m = 10$
$d = (0,4,4,4,4,4)$

177
$n = 6$
$m = 10$
$d = (1,3,3,4,4,5)$

178
$n = 6$
$m = 10$
$d = (1,3,4,4,4,4)$

179
$n = 6$
$m = 10$
$d = (2,2,3,3,5,5)$

180
$n = 6$
$m = 10$
$d = (2,2,3,4,4,5)$

181
$n = 6$
$m = 10$
$d = (2,2,4,4,4,4)$

182
$n = 6$
$m = 10$
$d = (2,3,3,3,4,5)$

183
$n = 6$
$m = 10$
$d = (2,3,3,3,4,5)$

184
$n = 6$
$m = 10$
$d = (2,3,3,4,4,4)$

185
$n = 6$
$m = 10$
$d = (2,3,3,4,4,4)$

186
$n = 6$
$m = 10$
$d = (2,3,3,4,4,4)$

187
$n = 6$
$m = 10$
$d = (3,3,3,3,3,5)$

188
$n = 6$
$m = 10$
$d = (3,3,3,3,4,4)$

189
$n = 6$
$m = 10$
$d = (3,3,3,3,4,4)$

190
$n = 6$
$m = 10$
$d = (3,3,3,3,4,4)$

191
$n = 6$
$m = 11$
$d = (1,4,4,4,4,5)$

192
$n = 6$
$m = 11$
$d = (2,3,3,4,5,5)$

193
$n = 6$
$m = 11$
$d = (2,3,4,4,4,5)$

194
$n = 6$
$m = 11$
$d = (2,4,4,4,4,4)$

195
$n = 6$
$m = 11$
$d = (3,3,3,3,5,5)$

196
$n = 6$
$m = 11$
$d = (3,3,3,4,4,5)$

197
$n = 6$
$m = 11$
$d = (3,3,3,4,4,5)$

198
$n = 6$
$m = 11$
$d = (3,3,4,4,4,4)$

199
$n = 6$
$m = 11$
$d = (3,3,4,4,4,4)$

200
$n = 6$
$m = 12$
$d = (2,4,4,4,5,5)$

201
$n = 6$
$m = 12$
$d = (3,3,3,5,5,5)$

202
$n = 6$
$m = 12$
$d = (3,3,4,4,5,5)$

203
$n = 6$
$m = 12$
$d = (3,4,4,4,4,5)$

204
$n = 6$
$m = 12$
$d = (4,4,4,4,4,4)$

205
$n = 6$
$m = 13$
$d = (3,4,4,5,5,5)$

206
$n = 6$
$m = 13$
$d = (4,4,4,4,5,5)$

207
$n = 6$
$m = 14$
$d = (4,4,5,5,5,5)$

208
$n = 6$
$m = 15$
$d = (5,5,5,5,5,5)$

PROBLEMS

Here, and throughout the book, ❂ indicates that a full solution is given at the end of the book.

The Definition of a Graph

❂**1.1.** Write down the vertex-set and edge-list of each of the following graphs:

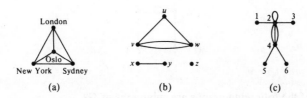

(a)   (b)   (c)

1.2. Write down the vertex-set and edge-list of each of the following graphs:

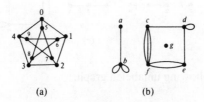

(a)   (b)

❂**1.3.** Draw the graphs given by the following lists:

(a) vertex-set: {□, ○, ◇, △}
   edge-list: □○, ○◇, ○△, ◇△
(b) vertex-set: {A, B, C, D}
   edge-list: (none)
(c) vertex-set: {1, 2, 3, 4, 5, 6, 7, 8}
   edge-list: 12, 22, 23, 34, 34, 35, 67, 68, 78

❂**1.4.** Consider the following graphs:

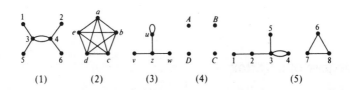

(1)   (2)   (3)   (4)   (5)

Which of these graphs (a) contain multiple edges? (b) contain a loop? (c) are simple? (d) are connected?

1.5.   Draw graphs G_1, G_2, G_3, and G_4, each with five vertices and eight edges, satisfying the following conditions:

G_1 is a simple graph;

G_2 is a non-simple graph containing no loops;

G_3 is a non-simple graph containing no multiple edges;

G_4 is a non-simple graph containing both loops and multiple edges.

1.6.   Let G be the following labeled graph:

Which of the following graphs are subgraphs of G?

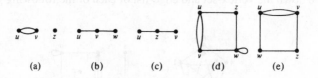

    (a)   (b)   (c)   (d)   (e)

1.7.   Let G be the following unlabeled graph:

Which of the following graphs are subgraphs of G?

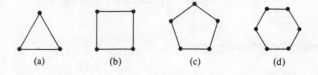

    (a)   (b)   (c)   (d)

The Degree of a Vertex

1.8.   For each of the following graphs, write down

    a.   the degrees of all the vertices;

    b.   the degree-sequence.

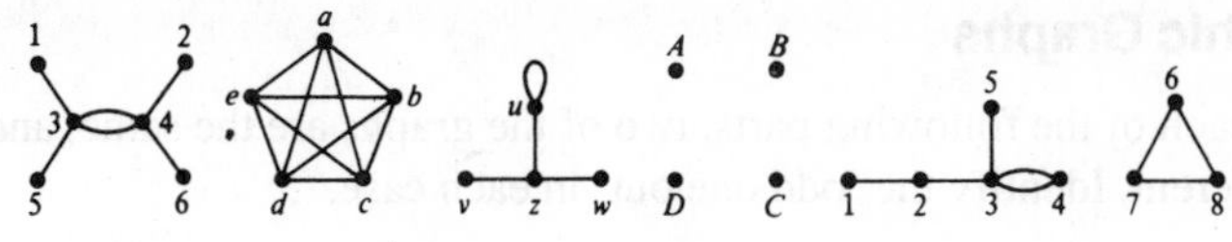

(1) (2) (3) (4) (5)

1.9. a. Let G be a graph with four vertices and degree-sequence (1,2,3,4). Write down the number of edges of G, and construct such a graph.

b. Are there any simple graphs with four vertices and degree-sequence (1,2,3,4)?

1.10. a. Draw a simple connected graph with eight vertices and degree-sequence (1,1,2,3,3,4,4,6).

b. Draw a simple connected graph with eight vertices and degree-sequence (3,3,3,3,3,5,5,5).

✪1.11. a. Write down the degree-sequence of each of the following graphs:

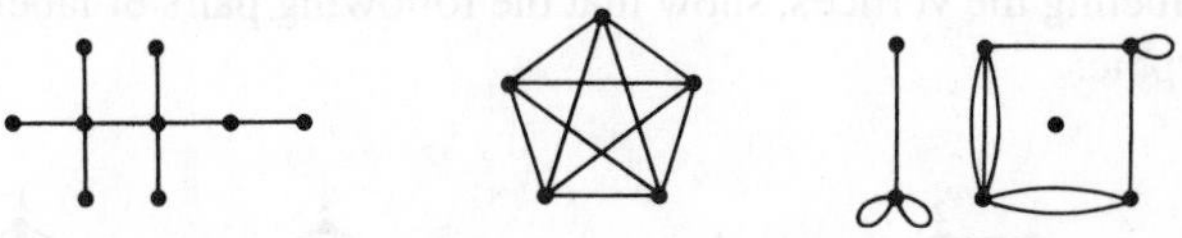

(a) (b) (c)

b. Verify the handshaking lemma for each of the graphs in (a).

✪1.12. Verify consequence 3 of the handshaking lemma for each of the following regular graphs:

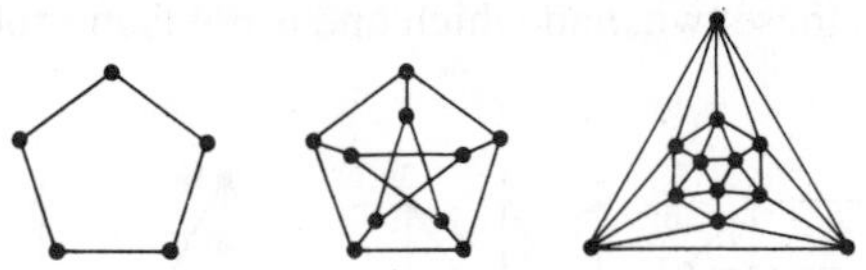

(a) (b) (c)

1.13. Prove that there is no graph with seven vertices that is regular of degree 3.

✪1.14. Prove the three consequences of the handshaking lemma.

1.15. Prove that, if G is a simple graph with a least two vertices, then G has two or more vertices of the same degree.

Isomorphic Graphs

○1.16. In each of the following parts, two of the graphs are the same, and the third is different. Identify the 'odd one out' in each case.

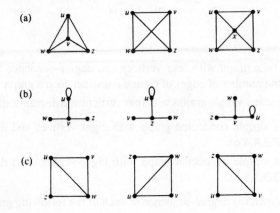

○1.17. By relabeling the vertices, show that the following pairs of labeled graphs are isomorphic:

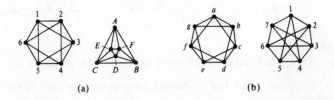

(a)   (b)

○1.18. Of the following four labeled graphs, which two are the same, which one is isomorphic to these two, and which one is not isomorphic to any of the others?

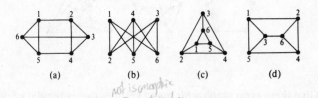

(a)   (b)   (c)   (d)

1.19. By suitably labeling the vertices, show that the following unlabeled graphs are isomorphic:

1.20. Show that the following unlabeled graphs are not isomorphic:

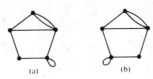

(a)   (b)

○1.21. Are the following two graphs isomorphic?

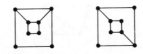

1.22. Are the following two graphs isomorphic?

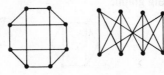

1.23. a. Draw two non-isomorphic regular graphs with 8 vertices and 12 edges.
b. Draw two non-isomorphic regular graphs with 10 vertices and 20 edges.

1.24. Classify each of the following statements as true or false:

a. If G and H are isomorphic graphs, then they have the same number of vertices and the same number of edges.

b. If G and H have the same number of vertices and the same number of edges, then they are isomorphic.

c. If G and H are isomorphic graphs, then they have the same degree-sequence.

d. If G and H have the same degree-sequence, then they are isomorphic.

The Graph Cards

○1.25. Locate the graph cards that depict the following graphs:

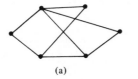
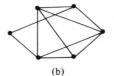

(a)   (b)

1.26. Locate the graph cards that depict the following graphs:

(a)   (b)   (c)

1.27. Let G be the following graph:

Which three of the following graph cards depict subgraphs of G?

a. number 18;   c. number 37;   e. number 46;

b. number 34;   d. number 44;   f. number 50.

1.28. Let G be the following graph:

Which two of the following graph cards depict subgraphs of G?

a. number 45;   c. number 84;   e. number 126;

b. number 50;   d. number 117;   f. number 128.

1.29. Use the graph cards to find how many simple graphs there are with

a. five vertices, six edges, and degree-sequence (2,2,2,3,3);

b. six vertices, seven edges, and degree-sequence (1,2,2,2,3,4);

c. six vertices and degree-sequence (2,2,2,2,2,2);

d. six vertices and degree-sequence (3,3,3,3,3,3).

1.30. a. Without looking at the graph cards, draw all unlabeled simple graphs with four vertices (up to isomorphism). Check your answer with the graph cards.

b. How many of these are regular?

1.31. Using your graph cards, determine the number of connected simple graphs with five and six vertices, and check your answers with the table on page 17.

CHAPTER 2

DEFINITIONS AND EXAMPLES

In Chapter 1 you saw how a graph can be used to depict the relationships between certain objects; you simply represent the objects by vertices, and the relationships by edges joining the vertices. In order to investigate such relationships more deeply, we need to study the theory of graphs in greater detail. To this end, we now introduce some useful terminology which will be needed in what follows.

2.1 ADJACENCY AND INCIDENCE

Since graph theory is primarily concerned with interconnections between objects, we shall need some terminology which tells us when certain vertices and edges occur next to each other in a graph. This terminology applies to all graphs, and can be used equally well for wires connecting terminals in an electrical network, bonds connecting atoms in a chemical molecule, or roads connecting towns on a road map.

DEFINITIONS. *Let* v *and* w *be vertices of a graph. If* v *and* w *are joined by an edge* e, *then* v *and* w *are said to be* **adjacent**. *Moreover,* v *and* w *are said to be* **incident with** e, *and* e *is said to be* **incident with** v **and** w.

v e w

v and w are *adjacent;*
v and w are *incident* with e;
e *is incident* with v and w.

You have already seen two ways of representing a graph—as a diagram consisting of points joined by lines, and as a set of vertices and a list of edges. The pictorial representation is useful in many situations, especially when we wish to examine the structure of the graph as a whole, but its value diminishes as soon as we need to describe large or complicated graphs. For example, if we wish to store a large graph in a computer, then a pictorial representation may well be unsuitable, and some other method would then be necessary.

One possibility is to store the set of vertices and the list of edges; this method is often used in practice, especially when the graph is 'sparse'—that is, it has a lot of vertices but relatively few edges. Another method is to take each vertex in turn and list those vertices that are adjacent to it. By joining each vertex to its 'neighbors', we can easily reconstruct the graph. Yet another method is to draw up a table indicating the pairs of vertices that are adjacent, or a table indicating which vertices are incident with which edges.

Each of these methods has its advantages, but the last one is particularly useful in a number of practical applications. In this method, we represent a graph by a rectangular array of numbers, called a *matrix;* a matrix with k rows and l columns is called a $k \times l$ *matrix.* Such matrices lend themselves to mechanical manipulation, and in several applications of graph theory they yield the most natural way of formulating a given problem. There are various types of matrices that can be used to specify a given graph. Here we describe the most important ones—the *adjacency matrix* and the *incidence matrix.* For simplicity, we restrict our attention to graphs without loops.

The Adjacency Matrix

Consider the following example

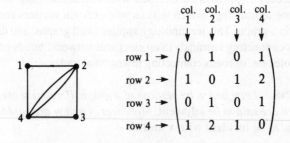

On the left-hand side we have a graph with *four vertices,* and on the right-hand side we have a 4 × 4 *matrix.* The numbers appearing in the matrix refer to the number of edges joining the corresponding vertices in the graph. For example,

vertices 1 and 2 are joined by 1 edge, so 1 appears in row 1 column 2 and in
  row 2 column 1

vertices 2 and 4 are joined by 2 edges, so 2 appears in row 2 column 4 and in
  row 4 column 2

vertices 1 and 3 are joined by 0 edges, so 0 appears in row 1 column 3 and in
  row 3 column 1

Note that every entry on the main (top-left to bottom-right) diagonal is 0, since the graph
has no loops. Note also that the matrix is symmetrical about this main diagonal.
   We can generalize this idea as follows.

DEFINITION. *Let G be a graph without loops, with* n *vertices labeled 1,2,3,...,n.
The* **adjacency matrix M(G)** *is the* n × n *matrix in which the entry in row* i *and column* j
is the number of edges joining the vertices i *and* j.

The Incidence Matrix

Whereas the adjacency matrix of a graph involves the adjacency of vertices, the
incidence matrix involves the incidence of vertices and edges. To see what is involved,
consider the following example; we have circled the labels of the vertices to distinguish
them from the labels of the edges.

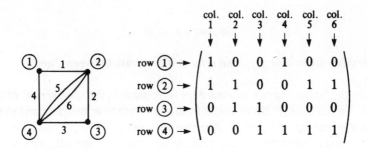

On the left-hand side we have a graph with *four vertices* and *six edges,* and on the right-
hand side we have a 4 × 6 *matrix.* Each of the numbers appearing in the matrix is either 1
or 0, depending on whether or not the corresponding vertex and edge are incident with
each other. For example,

   vertex ① is incident with edge 4,   so 1 appears in row 1 column 4

   vertex ② is not incident with edge 4,   so 0 appears in row 2 column 4

   We can generalize this idea, as follows.

DEFINITION. *Let G be a graph without loops, with* n *vertices labeled* ①,②,③,..., n
and m *edges labeled 1,2,3,...,* m. *The* **incidence matrix I(G)** *is the* n × m *matrix in which
the entry in row* i *and* column j *is* 1 *if.vertex* i *is incident with edge* j, *and* 0 *otherwise.*

Note that the incidence matrix depends on the particular way that the vertices and edges are labeled. We obtain one incidence matrix from another by interchanging rows (corresponding to relabeling the vertices) and columns (corresponding to relabeling the edges).

2.2 PATHS AND CYCLES

Many of the applications of graph theory involve 'getting from one vertex to another' in a graph. For example, how can you find the shortest route between one London Underground station and another? Other examples include the routing of a telephone call between one subscriber and another, the flow of current between two terminals of an electrical network, and the tracing of a maze. Our aim in this section is to make this idea precise by means of some definitions. We start by defining a *walk* in a graph.

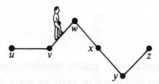

DEFINITION.   *A* **walk of length** k *in a graph* G *is a succession of* k *edges of* G *of the form*

$$uv, vw, wx, ..., yz$$

We denote this walk by uvwx...yz, *and refer to it as a* **walk between** u **and** z.

Note that the 'second vertex' of each edge is the same as the 'first vertex' of the next. Intuitively, we can think of this as a walk from u to v, then to w, then to x, and so on, until we eventually end up at vertex z. Alternatively, since the edges have no specified direction, we can think of it as a walk from z to y and so on, eventually, to x, w, v, and u. Thus we can also denote this walk by $zy...xwvu$, and refer to it as a **walk between z and u.**

We do not require all the edges or vertices in a walk to be different. For example, in the following graph

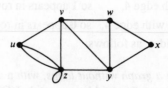

$uvwxywvzzy$ is a *walk of length 9* between u and y, which includes the edge vw twice, and the vertices v, w, y, and z twice. This leads to the following definitions.

DEFINITIONS. *If all the edges (but not necessarily all the vertices) of a walk are different, then the walk is called a* **trail**. *If, in addition, all the vertices are different, then the trail is called a* **path**.

In the above diagram, the walk *vzzywxy* is a *trail* which is not a path (since the vertices *y* and *z* both occur twice), whereas the walk *vwxyz* has no repeated vertices, and is therefore a *path*. Note that a walk such as *uzvuz* is also a trail, as long as the two occurrences of *uz* refer to the two different edges joining *u* and *z*.

It is also useful to have special terms for those walks or trails which start and finish at the same vertex.

DEFINITIONS. *A* **closed walk** *in a graph* G *is a succession of edges of* G *of the form*

$$uv, vw, wx, ..., yz, zu$$

If all of these edges are different, then the walk is called a **closed trail**. *If, in addition, the vertices u,v,w,x,...,y,z are all different, then the trail is called a* **cycle**.

In the above graph, the closed walk *uvwyvzu* is a *closed trail* which is not a cycle (since the vertex *v* occurs twice), whereas the closed trails *zz*, *vwxyv*, and *vwxyzv* are all *cycles*. A cycle of length three, such as *vwyv* or *wxyw*, is called a **triangle**, for obvious reasons. In describing closed walks, we can allow any vertex to be the starting vertex. For example, the triangle *vwyv* can equally well be described by the letters *wyvw* or *yvwy* or (since the direction is immaterial) by *ywvy*, *vywv*, or *wvyw*.

We can use the concept of a path to explain exactly what is meant by a *connected graph*. Recall from Chapter 1 that a graph is connected if it is 'in one piece'. For example, the following graph is not connected, but can be split into four connected pieces.

The observation that there is a path between *x* and *y* (which lie in the same piece), but not between *u* and *y* (which lie in different pieces), leads to the following definitions.

DEFINITIONS. *A graph* G *is* **connected** *if there is a path in* G *between any given pair of vertices, and* **disconnected** *otherwise. Every disconnected graph can be split up into a number of connected subgraphs, called* **components**.

2.3 EXAMPLES OF GRAPHS

We now introduce some important types of graphs. You should make sure you are familiar with them since they will appear frequently, both in applications and as examples.

Complete Graphs

A **complete graph** is a graph in which every two distinct vertices are joined by exactly one edge. The complete graph with n vertices is denoted by K_n. Note that, apart from K_4, we usually draw the vertices of K_n in the form of a regular polygon.

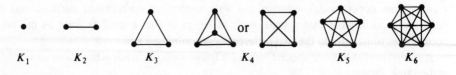

The graph K_n is regular of degree $n - 1$, and therefore has $\frac{1}{2}n(n - 1)$ edges, by consequence 3 of the handshaking lemma.

Null Graphs

A **null graph** is a graph containing no edges. The null graph with n vertices is denoted by N_n.

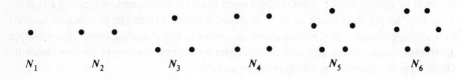

Note that N_n is regular of degree 0.

Cycle Graphs

A **cycle graph** is a graph consisting of a single cycle. The cycle graph with n vertices is denoted by C_n.

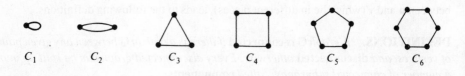

Note that C_n is regular of degree 2, and has n edges.

Path Graphs

A **path graph** is a graph consisting of a single path. The path graph with n vertices is denoted by P_n.

$$P_1 \quad P_2 \quad P_3 \quad P_4 \quad P_5 \quad P_6$$

Note that P_n has $n-1$ edges, and can be obtained from the cycle graph C_n by removing any edge.

Bipartite Graphs

Of particular importance in applications are the bipartite graphs. A **bipartite graph** is a graph whose vertex-set can be split into sets A and B in such a way that each edge of the graph joins a vertex in A to a vertex in B. We can distinguish the vertices in A from those in B by drawing the former in black and the latter in white, so that each edge is incident with a black vertex and a white vertex. Some examples of bipartite graphs are

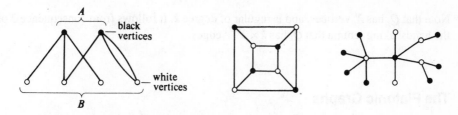

A **complete bipartite graph** is a bipartite graph in which each black vertex is joined to each white vertex by exactly one edge. The complete bipartite graph with r black vertices and s white vertices is denoted by $K_{r,s}$. A complete bipartite graph of the form $K_{1,s}$ is called a **star graph**. Some examples of complete bipartite graphs are

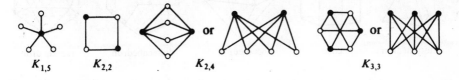

$$K_{1,5} \quad K_{2,2} \quad K_{2,4} \quad \text{or} \quad \quad K_{3,3} \quad \text{or}$$

Note that $K_{r,s}$ has $r + s$ vertices (r vertices of degree s, and s vertices of degree r), and rs edges. Note also that $K_{r,s} = K_{s,r}$; it is usual, but not necessary, to put the smaller of r and s first.

Cube Graphs

Of particular interest among the bipartite graphs are the cube graphs. These graphs have important applications in coding theory, and may be constructed by taking as vertices all binary words (sequences of 0s and 1s) of a given length and joining two of these vertices if the corresponding binary words differ in just one place. The graph obtained in this way from the binary words of length k is called the **k-cube** (or *k-dimensional cube*), and is denoted by Q_k.

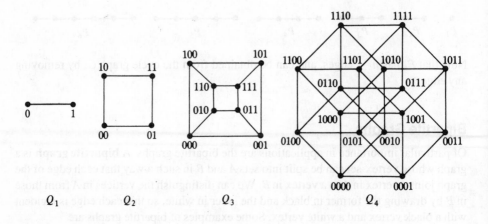

Q_1 Q_2 Q_3 Q_4

Note that Q_k has 2^k vertices, and is regular of degree k. It follows from consequence 3 of the handshaking lemma that Q_k has $k \times 2^{k-1}$ edges.

The Platonic Graphs

The following five regular solids are known as the *Platonic solids:*

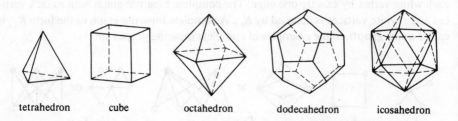

tetrahedron   cube   octahedron   dodecahedron   icosahedron

We can regard the vertices and edges of each solid as the vertices and edges of a graph. The resulting five graphs are known as the **Platonic graphs**, and are often drawn as

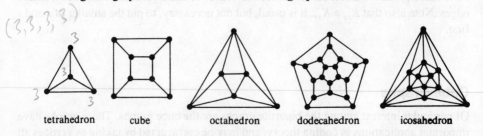

tetrahedron   cube   octahedron   dodecahedron   icosahedron

A Platonic graph is obtained by projecting the corresponding solid on to a plane. Alternatively, it is the view you get when you look at a wire model of the solid from a point near the middle of one of the faces. The name *Platonic* arises from the fact that these solids were mentioned in Plato's *Timaeus*.

The Petersen Graph

. Our next example is a famous graph which has already appeared in the Problems of Chapter 1. It is known as the **Petersen graph**, and has several interesting properties which you will discover as you progress through the book. The Petersen graph may be drawn in various ways, two of which are shown here

Julius Petersen (1839–1910) was a Danish mathematician, who discussed the graph named after him in a paper of 1898.

Trees

A connected graph which contains no cycles is called a **tree**. Some examples of trees are as follows; the tree on the right is particularly well known for its bark!

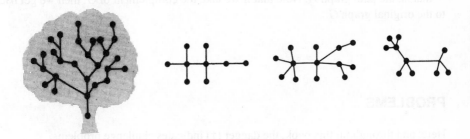

If G is a connected graph, then a **spanning tree** in G is a subgraph of G which includes every vertex of G and is also a tree. For example, a graph and three of its spanning trees are

| a graph G | spanning tree | spanning tree | spanning tree |

The number of spanning trees in a graph can be very large. For example, the Petersen graph has no fewer than 2000 different spanning trees.

Unions and Complements

There are several operations we can perform on graphs in order to form new ones. The simplest of these is to form their **union**, which is the graph whose components are the individual graphs. For example, the null graph N_n is the union of n copies of N_1, and the graph

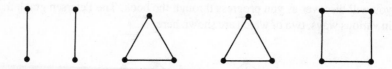

is the union of two copies of K_2, two copies of K_3, and one copy of $K_{2,2}$.

Finally, if G is a simple graph, we form its **complement** $\overline{G}$ by taking the vertex-set of G and joining two vertices by an edge whenever they are not joined in G. For example, the complement of K_n is N_n, and the complement of

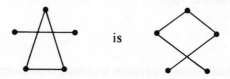

—that is, the path graph P_5. Note that if we take the complement of $\overline{G}$, then we get back to the original graph G.

PROBLEMS

Here, and throughout this book, the dagger (†) indicates challenge problems.

Adjacency and Incidence

❂2.1   Consider the following graph:

Classify each of the following statements as *true* or *false:*

a. u and z are adjacent;   e. u is incident with c;

b. v and z are adjacent;   f. b is incident with d;

c. d and z are adjacent;   g. e is incident with w;

d. v is incident with d;   h. v is incident with f.

2.2. Consider the following graph:

Classify each of the following statements as *true* or *false:*

a. *e* is incident with *u*;   c. *a* is incident with *e*;

b. *c* is adjacent to *x*;   d. *w* is adjacent to *v*.

2.3. Match up each of the following graphs with its adjacency matrix and incidence matrix:

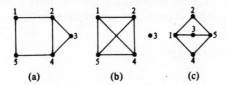

    (a)   (b)   (c)

Adjacency matrices.

$$\begin{pmatrix} 0 & 1 & 0 & 0 & 1 \\ 1 & 0 & 1 & 1 & 0 \\ 0 & 1 & 0 & 1 & 0 \\ 0 & 1 & 1 & 0 & 1 \\ 1 & 0 & 0 & 1 & 0 \end{pmatrix} \quad \begin{pmatrix} 0 & 1 & 1 & 1 & 0 \\ 1 & 0 & 0 & 0 & 1 \\ 1 & 0 & 0 & 0 & 1 \\ 1 & 0 & 0 & 0 & 1 \\ 0 & 1 & 1 & 1 & 0 \end{pmatrix} \quad \begin{pmatrix} 0 & 1 & 0 & 1 & 1 \\ 1 & 0 & 0 & 1 & 1 \\ 0 & 0 & 0 & 0 & 0 \\ 1 & 1 & 0 & 0 & 1 \\ 1 & 1 & 0 & 1 & 0 \end{pmatrix}$$

Incidence matrices.

$$\begin{pmatrix} 1 & 0 & 0 & 1 & 1 & 0 \\ 1 & 1 & 0 & 0 & 0 & 1 \\ 0 & 0 & 0 & 0 & 0 & 0 \\ 0 & 1 & 1 & 0 & 1 & 0 \\ 0 & 0 & 1 & 1 & 0 & 1 \end{pmatrix} \quad \begin{pmatrix} 1 & 1 & 1 & 0 & 0 & 0 \\ 1 & 0 & 0 & 1 & 0 & 0 \\ 0 & 1 & 0 & 0 & 1 & 0 \\ 0 & 0 & 1 & 0 & 0 & 1 \\ 0 & 0 & 0 & 1 & 1 & 1 \end{pmatrix} \quad \begin{pmatrix} 1 & 0 & 0 & 0 & 0 & 1 \\ 1 & 1 & 0 & 1 & 0 & 0 \\ 0 & 1 & 1 & 0 & 0 & 0 \\ 0 & 0 & 1 & 1 & 1 & 0 \\ 0 & 0 & 0 & 0 & 1 & 1 \end{pmatrix}$$

2.4. Write down the adjacency matrices of the graphs

         ✪(a)   (b)

2.5.   Draw the graphs whose adjacency matrices are

$$\begin{pmatrix} 0 & 2 & 0 & 1 & 1 \\ 2 & 0 & 0 & 1 & 1 \\ 0 & 0 & 0 & 0 & 0 \\ 1 & 1 & 0 & 0 & 2 \\ 1 & 1 & 0 & 2 & 0 \end{pmatrix}$$

$$\begin{pmatrix} 0 & 1 & 1 & 0 & 0 & 0 \\ 1 & 0 & 0 & 1 & 0 & 0 \\ 1 & 0 & 0 & 1 & 0 & 0 \\ 0 & 1 & 1 & 0 & 0 & 0 \\ 0 & 0 & 0 & 0 & 0 & 1 \\ 0 & 0 & 0 & 0 & 1 & 0 \end{pmatrix}$$

✪ (a)   (b)

✪**2.6.**   What can you say about the sum of the numbers in any row or column of an adjacency matrix?

✪**2.7.**   The following diagrams illustrate a graph with three different labelings. Find the adjacency matrix in each case, and explain the connections between these three matrices.

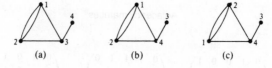

(a)   (b)   (c)

2.8.   Write down the incidence matrices of the following graphs:

✪ (a)   (b)

✪**2.9.**   Draw the graph whose incidence matrix is

$$\begin{pmatrix} 1 & 1 & 1 & 1 & 0 & 0 & 0 & 0 \\ 1 & 1 & 0 & 0 & 1 & 1 & 0 & 0 \\ 0 & 0 & 0 & 0 & 0 & 0 & 0 & 0 \\ 0 & 0 & 0 & 1 & 0 & 1 & 1 & 1 \\ 0 & 0 & 1 & 0 & 1 & 0 & 1 & 1 \end{pmatrix}$$

2.10. What can you say about the sum of the numbers in
   a.   any row of an incidence matrix?
   b.   any column of an incidence matrix?

2.11.[†] Consider the following graph:

Write down the adjacency matrix M of this graph, and compute the matrices M^2 and M^3. What does the entry in row i and column j of each of these matrices represent? Make a guess as to what the entries of M^k represent, and prove your result.

2.12.[†] (For those who have studied linear algebra.) The **eigenvalues** of a simple graph are defined as the eigenvalues of its adjacency matrix.
   a.   Use the results of the previous problem to prove that
        i.   the sum of the eigenvalues of G is zero;
        ii. the sum of their squares is $2m$, where m is the number of edges of G;
        iii. the sum of their cubes is $6t$, where t is the number of triangles in G.
   b.   Show that the eigenvalues of K_n are -1 ($n-1$ times), and $n-1$.
   c.   What are the eigenvalues of $K_{r,s}$?

Paths and Cycles

○2.13. Complete the statements concerning the graph shown.

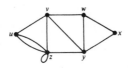

   a.   *xyzzvy* is a _____ of length _____ between _____ and _____;
   b.   *vuvzv* is a _____ of length _____ between _____ and _____;
   c.   *vw* is a _____ of length _____ between _____ and _____;
   d.   *uvwxyzu* is a _____ of length _____ between _____ and _____.

2.14. In the following graph, find

    a. a walk of length 7 between u and w;

    b. cycles of lengths 1, 2, 3, and 4;

    c. a path of maximum length.

2.15. Find all the paths between s and z in the graph

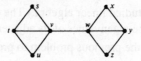

2.16. In the following graph, find

    a. a closed walk which is not a closed trail;

    b. a closed trail which is not a cycle;

    c. all the cycles of lengths 1, 2, 3, and 4.

Examples of Graphs

2.17. Draw the following graphs:

    a. K_8;   c. C_8;   e. $K_{4,4}$;   g. $\overline{K}_{1,5}$.

    b. N_8;   d. P_8;   f. $\overline{K}_{3,3}$;

○2.18. Fill in the following table:

	K_9	N_9	C_9	$K_{9,9}$	Q_5	tetra-hedron	cube	octa-hedron	dodeca-hedron	icosa-hedron	Petersen
number of vertices											
number of edges											
degree of each vertex											

2.19. Complete the following statements:

    a. the graph $K_{r,s}$ is a regular graph only when _____;

    b. the only bipartite Platonic graph is the _____;

    c. the graph $\overline{K}_{r,s}$ is the union of _____ and _____;

    d. if G is a simple graph with n vertices which is regular of degree r, then $\overline{G}$ is regular of degree _____;

    e. if G is a simple graph with n vertices and m edges, then $\overline{G}$ has _____ vertices and _____ edges.

2.20. From the set of graph cards, locate the cards that depict the graphs

    a. N_4;   e. $K_{1,5}$;   i. $\overline{C}_4$;

    b. K_5;   f. $K_{2,3}$;   j. $\overline{P}_4$.

    c. C_6;   g. the tetrahedron graph;

    d. P_5;   h. the union of K_2 and K_3;

2.21 Which of the following graph cards depict bipartite graphs?

    a. number 38;   d. number 128;   g. number 152;

    b. number 78;   e. number 129;   h. number 154.

    c. number 106;   f. number 130;

2.22 Using your graph cards, determine the number of connected bipartite graphs with five vertices.

○2.23. Show that in any bipartite graph all cycles have even length.

2.24.[†] The **complete tripartite graph** $K_{r,s,t}$ consists of three sets of vertices of sizes r, s, and t, with edges joining two vertices if and only if they lie in different sets.

    a. Draw the graphs $K_{2,2,2}$ and $K_{2,3,3}$.

    b. How many vertices and edges has $K_{r,s,t}$?

    c. What is the complement of $K_{r,s,t}$?

2.25. The **girth** of a graph is the length of its shortest cycle. Find the girths of (a) K_9; (b) $K_{5,8}$; (c) the Petersen graph; (d) the Platonic graphs; (e) the 6-cube Q_6.

2.26. The **circumference** of a graph is the length of its longest cycle. Find the circumferences of (a) K_9; (b) $K_{5,8}$; (c) the Petersen graph; (d) the dodecahedron graph; (e) the 4-cube Q_4.

2.27.[†] How many different cycles of length 5 does the Petersen graph have?

2.28. Locate the graph cards depicting the complement of each of the following graphs:

    a. the path graph P_n;

    b. the complete bipartite graph $K_{2,4}$.

2.29. How many components has each of the following graphs?
(a) N_5; (b) $K_{3,3}$; (c) $\overline{K}_{1,5}$.

◦2.30. Prove that a graph and its complement cannot both be disconnected.

2.31. A graph is called **self-complementary** if it is isomorphic to its complement.

    a. Show that C_5 is self-complementary, and find two other self-complementary graphs.

    b. Prove that a self-complementary graph has $4k$ or $4k + 1$ vertices, for some integer k.

◦2.32. There are 14 trees with six or fewer vertices. Draw them, and locate the graph cards depicting them.

2.33. There are 11 trees with seven vertices. Draw them.

◦2.34. Show that if a tree has n vertices then it has $n - 1$ edges.

2.35. Use the handshaking lemma to prove that every tree with two or more vertices has at least two vertices of degree 1.

2.36. Show that every tree is a bipartite graph.

◦2.37. Find all the spanning trees in each of the following graphs:

        (a)   (b)

2.38. Draw some (but not all!) of the 2000 spanning trees of the Petersen graph.

2.39.[†] The **line graph** $L(G)$ of a simple graph G is the graph obtained by taking the *edges* of G as vertices, and joining two of these vertices whenever the corresponding edges of G have a vertex in common. Find an expression for the number of edges of $L(G)$ in terms of the degrees of the vertices of G, and show that:

    a. if C_n is the cycle graph with n vertices, then $L(C_n)$ is isomorphic to C_n;

    b. $L(K_n)$ has $\frac{1}{2}n(n-1)$ vertices, and is regular of degree $2n - 4$;

    c. L(tetrahedron) = octahedron;

    d. the complement of $L(K_5)$ is the Petersen graph.

CHAPTER 3

APPLICATIONS OF GRAPHS

In this chapter we give brief descriptions of several areas in which graphs have been found useful. These range from chemistry and sociology to recreational mathematics and the bracing of plane frameworks. In particular, we show how the ideas of compatibility graph and interval graph can arise in several seemingly unrelated contexts, such as genetics, ecology, archaeology, and the phasing of traffic lights, and we illustrate the use of trees in areas ranging from linguistics and computing to game theory.

A full treatment of these topics is clearly impossible here. All we can hope to do is to illustrate the very wide range of topics in which graphs have been used, and leave it to you to follow up any topics which appeal to you. A list of suggestions for further reading is given at the end of the book.

3.1 CHEMISTRY

You have already seen in Chapter 1 how a chemical molecule can be represented as a graph whose vertices correspond to the atoms and whose edges correspond to the chemical bonds connecting them. For example, the molecule C_2H_5OH (ethanol) can be represented by the following graph:

In such a graph, the degree of each vertex is simply the valency of the corresponding atom—the carbon vertices have degree 4, the oxygen vertex has degree 2, and the hydrogen vertices have degree 1.

Diagrams of the above type were first used in 1864 to represent the arrangement of atoms in a molecule. They were introduced by Alexander Crum Brown (1838–1922), who explained, for the first time, the phenomenon of *isomerism*—the existence of isomers (molecules with the same chemical formula but different chemical properties). For example, the molecules *n*-butane and 2-methyl propane (formerly called butane and isobutane) both have the chemical formula C_4H_{10}; note the different ways in which the atoms are arranged inside the molecule:

n-butane   2-methyl propane

It is natural to ask whether there are any other molecules with the formula C_4H_{10}, and this leads us directly to the problem of *isomer enumeration*—the determination of the number of different molecules with a given chemical formula. The most celebrated problem of this kind is that of counting the alkanes (paraffins) C_nH_{2n+2}. For small values of *n*, we can construct a table. For clarity, we have drawn the carbon vertices as small circles and the hydrogen vertices as black blobs.

n	chemical formula	name	molecule	graph

1   CH_4 methane

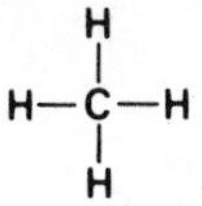

2   C_2H_6 ethane

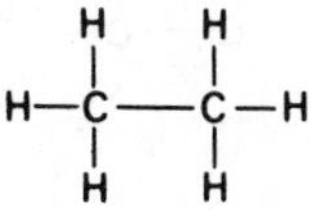

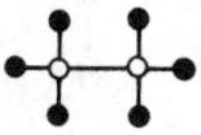

3   C_3H_8 propane

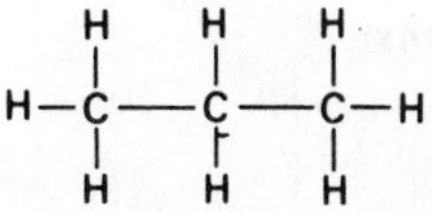

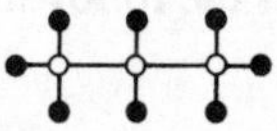

4   C_4H_{10} (a) *n*-butane

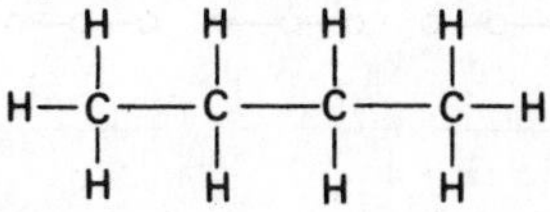

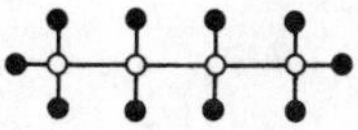

(b) 2-methyl propane

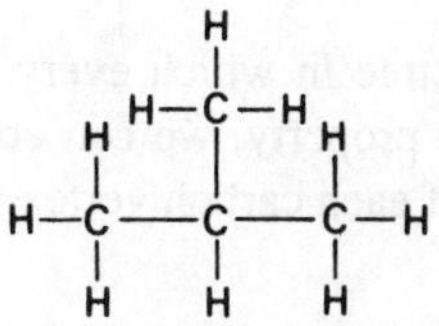

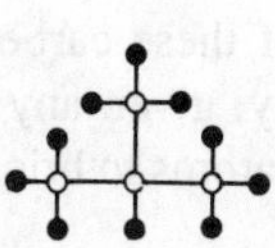

5   C_5H_{12} (a) *n*-pentane

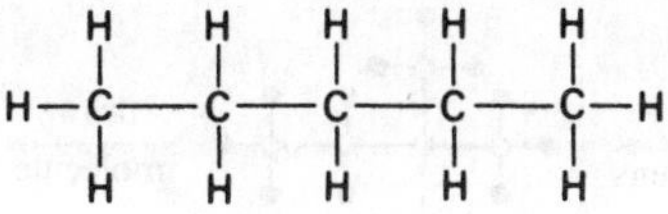

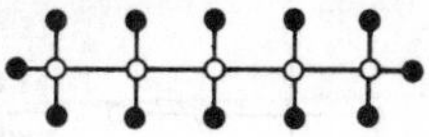

(b) 2-methyl butane

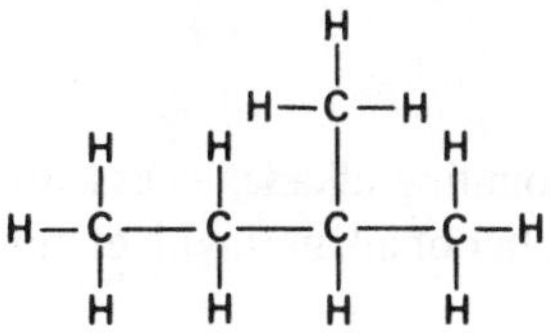

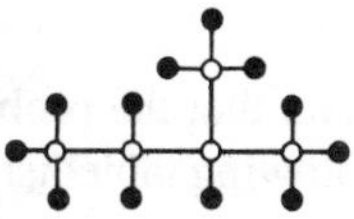

(c) 2,2-dimethyl propane

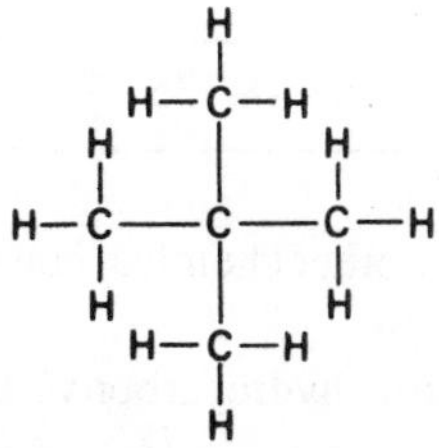

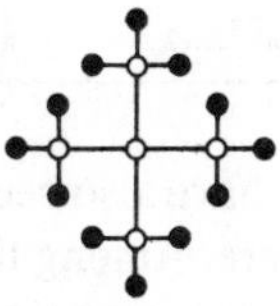

It is clear that these diagrams are going to become very complicated as n increases. We can simplify them considerably by removing the hydrogen atoms:

This leaves the following *carbon-graphs*:

Each of these carbon-graphs is a tree in which every vertex has degree 4 or less. Conversely, given any tree with this property, we can construct an alkane by adding hydrogen atoms to bring the degree of each carbon vertex up to 4, as follows:

It follows that the problem of counting alkanes is essentially a tree-counting problem. The following table lists the number of alkanes with at most 15 carbon atoms:

n	1	2	3	4	5	6	7	8	9	10	11	12	13	14	15
alkanes C_nH_{2n+2}	1	1	1	2	3	5	9	18	35	75	159	355	802	1858	4347

Graphs have also been used in many other chemical contexts which we cannot discuss in detail here. Among these are

1. the representation of "polycyclic hydrocarbons" by carbon-graphs containing cycles;

2. the use of graph-theoretical ideas to name molecules, and to represent them in a form suitable for storing in a computer—the adjacency matrix of the carbon-graph, and various modifications of it, have proved particularly useful in this area;
3. the use of graphs to represent chemical reactions, where the vertices correspond to molecules and the edges correspond to reactions involving these molecules.

Historical note Although graph-like diagrams had been used as far back as 1789 to represent chemical molecules, it was not until the 1850s that ideas about atoms and the way they combine were sufficiently well understood for meaningful diagrams to be drawn. This occurred when various chemists, among them August Kekulé and Edward Frankland, put forward ideas which led to the theory of valency. Crum Brown's diagrams were just what was needed to represent this theory and explain the nature of isomerism, and were soon accepted universally. Meanwhile, the mathematician Arthur Cayley had spent some time studying and counting trees, and in 1875 presented a paper to the British Association describing a method for calculating, in principle at least, the number of alkanes with a given number of carbon atoms. Although successful, Cayley's methods were cumbersome and impractical, and it was over 50 years before any significant new results were obtained. In the period 1927–1937 there appeared a number of important papers on isomer enumeration, culminating in the fundamental work of George Pólya (see page 17). Pólya's papers included a powerful method which can be applied to counting problems involving a degree of symmetry. In particular, Pólya's methods have been used to great effect in problems relating to the counting of graphs and molecules.

3.2 SOCIAL SCIENCES

Graphs have also been used extensively in the social sciences to represent *interpersonal relationships*. The vertices correspond to individuals in a group or society, and the edges join pairs of individuals who are related in some way—for example, x is joined to y if x likes, hates, agrees with, avoids, or communicates with y. For the time being, we shall assume that all relationships are symmetric (x likes y if and only if y likes x). Unsymmetric relationships will be discussed in Chapter 5.

Such representations have been extended to relationships between groups of individuals, and have proved useful in a number of contexts ranging from the study of kinship relationships in certain cultures to the relationships between political parties. Graphs have also been used by political scientists to study *international relations,* where the vertices correspond to nations or groups of nations, and the edges join pairs of nations which are allied, maintain diplomatic relations, agree on a particular strategy, etc.

We can analyze the possible tensions in such situations by using the concept of a **signed graph.** This is a graph with either + or − associated with each edge, indicating a positive relationship (likes, loves, agrees with, communicates with, etc.) or a negative one (dislikes, hates, disagrees with, avoids, etc). For example, in the signed graph below, Jack likes Jill but not John, Jill likes Jack and Mary but not John, Mary likes John and Jill, and John likes Mary but not Jack or Jill; note that Jack and Mary have no strong feelings about each other, and are therefore not adjacent in the graph.

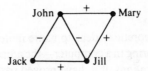

Now consider the following diagrams, which illustrate some of the situations that can occur when three people work together. Which of these situations is most likely to cause tension between John, Jack, and Jill?

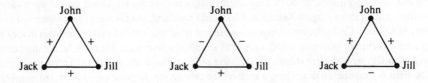

In the first case all three get on well, and there is no tension. In the second case Jack and Jill get on well and both dislike John; the result is that John works on his own, and again there is no tension. In the third case John likes both Jack and Jill and would like to work with them, but Jack and Jill dislike each other and do not wish to work together; in this case (the so-called 'eternal triangle'), a suitable working arrangement cannot be found, and there is tension. We express this by saying that the first two situations are *balanced,* whereas the third is *unbalanced.*

Using these examples as motivation, we can give a general definition of balance. We say that a signed graph is **balanced** if we can color its vertices black or white in such a way that positive edges have ends of the same color, and negative edges have a black end and a white end. You can easily check that the first two of the above diagrams can be colored in this way, whereas the third cannot. Note that this definition resembles that of a bipartite graph. You can see the connection by taking a balanced signed graph and removing all the positive edges; this leaves a bipartite graph, as indicated by the following diagram:

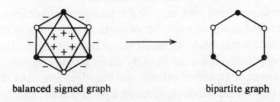

balanced signed graph   bipartite graph

We can exploit this connection between balanced signed graphs and bipartite graphs a little further. Recall from Problem 2.23 that in any bipartite graph all cycles have an even number of edges. For balanced signed graphs the corresponding result is that all cycles have an even number of negative edges, as we shall ask you to show in Problem 3.10.

3.3 TREES

The concept of a tree first arose in connection with G. Kirchhoff's work on electrical networks in the 1840s, and with Cayley's work on the enumeration of chemical molecules in the 1870s. More recently, trees have been proved to be of use in many areas, ranging from linguistics to computing. We now briefly describe some of these uses; our treatment is mainly pictorial and intuitive.

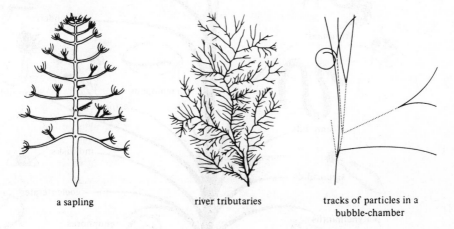

a sapling   river tributaries   tracks of particles in a
                                                          bubble-chamber

Many trees are characterized as having a *physical* structure which may be natural or man-made. Natural trees clearly include the vegetable variety with trunk, limbs, branches, and leaves. Another example of a natural tree is the drainage system of tributaries forming a river basin; this is clearly tree-like in appearance, and is frequently referred to as "dendritic". Less obvious examples arise from the tracks of particles in a bubble chamber and from the chemical structure of certain chemical molecules, such as the alkanes C_nH_{2n+2} discussed earlier. An example of the man-made variety of tree is given by an oil or gas pipeline distribution system, such as that shown

Louisiana

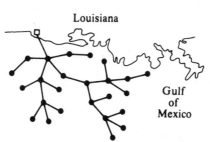

Gulf
of
Mexico

Other trees do not have a well-defined physical structure, but are conceptual in nature. A familiar example of a conceptual tree is the *tree of life*, which represents the evolutionary relationship between various animal or vegetable species. This has a pure tree form only if we disallow interbreeding of species.

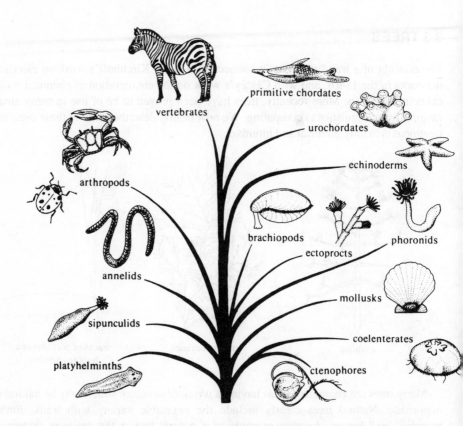

A *family tree*, depicting ancestors and descendants, is also of this type. A family tree has a pure tree form only if we forbid incestuous relationships. The following family tree shows the Saxon kings of the ninth century in England:

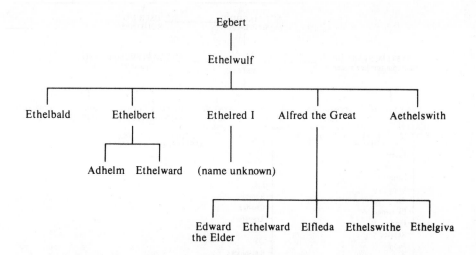

There are also many instances of man-made conceptual trees. As an example of these, we can consider any tree representing an administrative hierarchy; the following tree depicts part of the administrative structure of the British Open University:

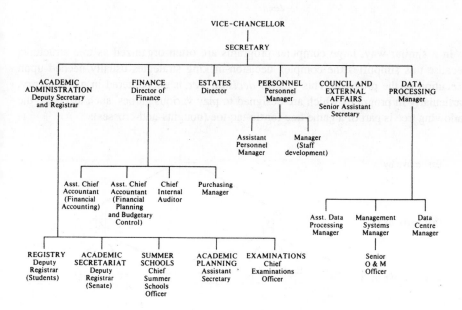

Recently, there has been considerable interest in tree structures arising in the computer sciences and in artificial intelligence. We often meet such structures when organizing data in a computer memory store or when organizing the flow of information through a system. Indeed, many computer operating systems are designed to be tree structures, since it is easier for a user to access information and files by tracing through the different levels of a tree than by searching any other type of graph. The following tree represents a PASCAL operating system:

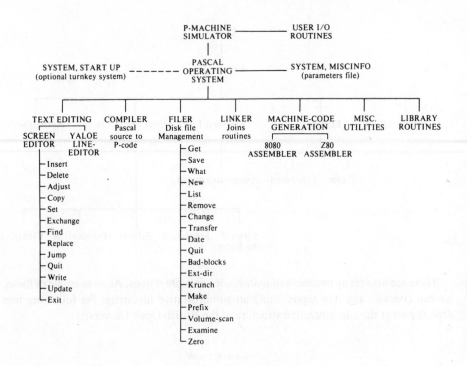

In a similar way, large computer programs are often organized as tree structures because this simplifies the complex decision-making strategies usually needed upon execution of the program. This type of *decision tree* is encountered in game theory, particularly in programs which are designed to play various games, such as chess; the following tree is part of a game tree for tic-tac-toe (noughts-and-crosses):

first move by X :

first move by O :

second move by X :

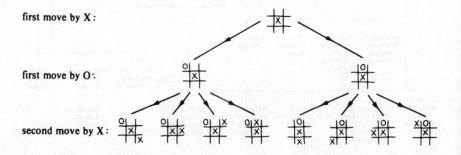

Another interesting example of a tree structure is provided by the parsing of a sentence in a natural language, such as English. The tree represents the interrelationships between the words and phrases of the sentence, and thereby shows the underlying syntactic structure:

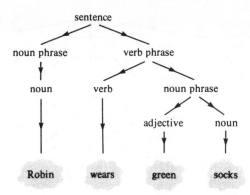

Another important type of decision tree is a *sorting tree*. These arise when we want to make a succession of choices, each dependent on the previous one. For example, consider the Dewey decimal classification system, which is often used for cataloguing books in libraries. This system starts with a crude classification of subjects into ten areas

0–099	General works	500–599	Pure sciences
100–199	Philosophy	600–699	Applied sciences
200–299	Religion	700–799	Fine arts
300–399	Social sciences	800–899	Literature
400–499	Philology	900–999	History

Each of these areas is classified into ten more specialized areas (for example, in the Pure Sciences the numbers 510–519 are allocated to Mathematics), and each of these is then classified into ten more. For example, the Mathematics class is subdivided as

510	General mathematical works	515	Analysis
511	Mathematical foundations	516	Geometry
512	Algebra	517	Unassigned
513	Arithmetic	518	
514	Topology	519	Probability

Further classification is possible with the introduction of decimal fractions. For example, Graph Theory is classified as 511.5 and Combinatorial Analysis is classified as 511.6. To represent this process, we can use a sorting tree, part of which is

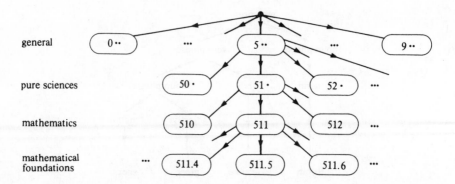

We can also use sorting trees to find the longest increasing sequence in a given list, such as 5, 11, 6, 1, 3, 9, 10, 4. In order to represent this problem as a sorting tree, we join each number to those later numbers in the sequence which exceed it. The complete sorting tree for the above list is then

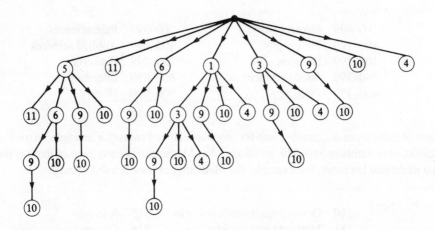

We deduce that the two longest increasing sequences are 5, 6, 9, 10 and 1, 3, 9, 10.

In the above examples of tree structures occurring naturally and in the man-made world, one particular type of tree occurs repeatedly. This is the hierarchical structure in which one vertex is singled out as the starting point, and the branches fan out from this vertex. We call such trees **rooted trees**, and refer to the starting vertex as the **root vertex**, often indicated by a small square. Because rooted trees are important and wide-spread, we need to be able to recognize them when they occur in different forms. The diagrams illustrate four equivalent ways of representing the same rooted tree.

| a rooted tree | subsets of a set | nested parentheses | sections of a report |

The first diagram has the conventional appearance of a tree. The second is a system of subsets of a set representing, say, the organization of subsystems within a complex machine system; this has the same tree structure as the first diagram, but in this case the different levels are defined by the depth of nesting. The third representation is a system of nested parentheses as used in English text, mathematical equations or the computer language LISP; again, the level is defined by the depth of nesting. The fourth representation is provided by the organization of a report such as a legal contract; these are often arranged in nested sections (subsections, paragraphs, etc.), and the level of each section is determined by indentation, and by the length of the decimal number in the heading. Books are often organized in this tree-like way (volumes, chapters, sections, paragraphs), as are dictionaries (the lexicographical ordering of words). The programming languages ALGOL and PASCAL similarly take advantage of tree arrangements with their nested block-structure.

The great advantage of all such tree structures is the ease and cheapness with which they can be altered or updated. This is particularly important in computer applications, where one can insert or delete branches (such as subroutines) without having to change the whole system. On the other hand, a major drawback of tree structures is that they are very vulnerable to faults or damage. The removal of a single vertex or the breaking of a single edge can disconnect or destroy the whole system, which can be disastrous for efficient operation of the system, although it may be useful for potential saboteurs. A striking example of this vulnerability was given by the collapse of the Inca civilization which virtually disintegrated overnight when the Spanish conquistador Pizarro captured the chief Inca, Emperor Atahuallpa, in 1532. The latter occupied the top position in a rigid hierarchical social pyramid, and his removal destroyed the top of the tree, thereby breaking the chain of command.

3.4 BRACING RECTANGULAR FRAMEWORKS

We now use the properties of bipartite graphs to solve a problem in structural engineering. Many buildings are supported by steel frameworks consisting of rectangular arrangements of girder beams and welded or riveted joints. This is particularly the case if they are designed as high-rise buildings or skyscrapers. For many purposes, however, these structures can be treated as planar (rather than spatial) structures, with pin-joints (rather than rigid welds) holding the beams together. The simplest type is a rectangle consisting of just four beams and four joints:

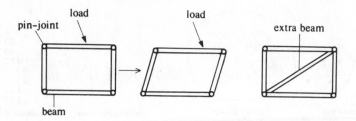

It is clear that such a structure can be deformed under sufficiently high loads into a lozenge shape, or parallelogram, so that it is inherently unstable. It must therefore be braced, and this may be done by introducing a single extra diagonal beam which can resist both tension and compression. (The diagonal beam can join either pair of diagonally opposite corners.)

In the case of a larger structure containing many rectangular cells, it is not necessary to brace every cell in order to ensure rigidity. We must therefore derive a method for determining the *minimum number* of braces required to prevent collapse, and then obtain a suitable arrangement of these. The rationale for seeking such a *minimum bracing* is that if we use more than the minimum number of braces, then we may improve the safety factors but we incur an unnecessary cost penalty.

Consider the three structures

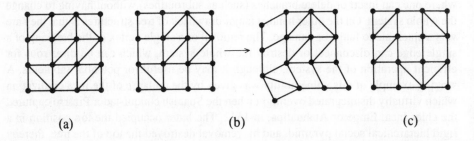

(a)   (b)   (c)

Framework (a) is rigid, but is heavily overbraced. Framework (b) is not rigid, since it can be deformed as shown. But how about framework (c)? To answer this question, we describe a simple method for determining whether any given rectangular structure is rigid, and if it is, whether any of the braces can be removed.

The method we use to determine the rigidity of a braced framework is to draw a bipartite graph in which one set of vertices corresponds to the rows of the framework, the other set of vertices corresponds to the columns of the framework, and an edge joins a row-vertex and a column-vertex whenever the cell in the corresponding row and column is braced. The bipartite graphs corresponding to frameworks (a), (b), and (c) are

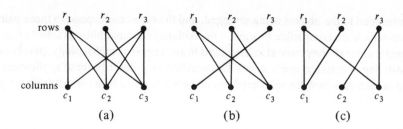

(a) (b) (c)

If you look at these bipartite graphs, you can easily see that the rigid framework (a) gives rise to a connected graph, whereas the non-rigid framework (b) gives rise to a disconnected graph. These are instances of the following general rule, which shows that framework (c) is also rigid since it corresponds to a connected bipartite graph:

rigid bracings correspond to connected bipartite graphs
non-rigid bracings correspond to disconnected bipartite graphs

To see why these results hold, note that each brace in a framework forces the corresponding row and column to remain perpendicular to each other. Thus, in the graph of framework (a), the path $r_1c_2r_2c_3r_3c_1$ connecting all six vertices shows that row 1 is perpendicular to column 2, column 2 is perpendicular to row 2, row 2 is perpendicular to column 3, and so on. Thus every row is perpendicular to every column, and the framework cannot be distorted. However, in the graph of framework (b), there is no path connecting either of the vertices r_3 and c_1 to any of the vertices r_1, r_2, c_2, or c_3, and so row 3 and column 1 need not remain perpendicular to rows 1 and 2 or columns 2 and 3, and the framework can be distorted as shown above.

We can also use the bipartite graph representation to determine which braces in a braced framework can be removed so as to yield a minimum bracing. In the graph of framework (c) there are no cycles, and so the removal of any edge disconnects the graph. Thus the removal of any brace yields a non-rigid framework, and the given bracing of framework (c) is therefore a minimum bracing. However, in the graph of framework (a) there are several cycles, and therefore several braces that we can remove without affecting the rigidity of the framework. For example, $r_1c_1r_3c_3r_1$ is a cycle, and so we can remove the brace in any one of the cells r_1c_1, r_1c_3, r_3c_1, r_3c_3 without affecting the rigidity. In fact, in this example we can remove up to three suitably chosen braces (such as r_1c_1, r_1c_3, and r_3c_3) and still have a rigid framework; at each stage we simply select any cycle in the bipartite graph and remove any one of its edges.

It follows from the above discussion that a minimum bracing corresponds to a connected bipartite graph containing no cycles—that is, a spanning tree:

minimum bracings correspond to spanning trees

3.5 COMPATIBILITY AND INTERVAL GRAPHS

Compatibility graphs have been used extensively in problems involving the arrangement of data into a particular (e.g., chronological) order. In such graphs, the vertices correspond to the objects being arranged, and the edges correspond to those pairs of objects which are compatible in some way. Although compatibility graphs first arose in a genetic context, they have also been used in such areas as archaeology, psychology, and the dating of classical manuscripts. Our aim here is to describe these applications, showing in each case how the relevant data can be represented by a compatibility graph.

Phasing Traffic Lights

Our first application of compatibility graphs is to the phasing of traffic lights. To see what is involved, consider the following road intersection:

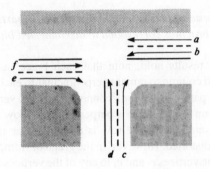

Some of the traffic streams at this junction are *compatible,* in that they can move at the same time without dangerous consequences. For example, stream *a* is compatible with streams *b*, *c*, *e*, and *f*, but not with stream *d*, whereas stream *f* is compatible with streams *a* and *e*, but not with streams *b*, *c*, and *d*. We can represent such compatibilities by a **compatibility graph** in which the vertices represent the traffic streams, and the edges join those pairs of vertices which correspond to compatible streams. The compatibility graph of the above intersection is

Suppose now that a traffic engineer wishes to control the traffic at this intersection by means of traffic lights. How can the lights be phased in such a way that incompatible streams of traffic do not occur simultaneously?

If the traffic lights operate on a 60-second cycle (say), then one solution is to let each stream through the lights for 10 seconds. We can represent this solution diagrammatically using the *clock diagram*

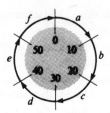

where we indicate the moving of each stream by an arc of the circle. This particular arrangement is unsatisfactory, however, since each stream of traffic is stationary for most of the time. We want a solution which takes account of the fact that compatible streams of traffic can proceed simultaneously, since this reduces the total amount of 'waiting time'. One possible arrangement is given by our next clock diagram in which there are three compatible streams of traffic proceeding at any time—namely,

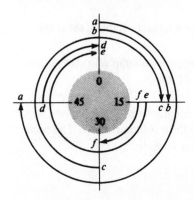

0–15 seconds: streams a, b, and c proceed

15–30 seconds: streams a, e, and f proceed

30–45 seconds: streams a, c, and e proceed

45–60 seconds: streams c, d, and e proceed

This means that, in each period of 60 seconds, streams a, c, and e can proceed for 45 seconds, and streams b, d, and f can proceed for 15 seconds. This gives a total 'waiting time' of $(3 \times 15) + (3 \times 45) = 180$ seconds—a 40 percent reduction on the original waiting time of $(6 \times 50) = 300$ seconds.

Another solution, giving rise to the same total waiting time of 180 seconds, is given in the third clock diagram. In this solution there are still three compatible streams of traffic proceeding at any time—namely,

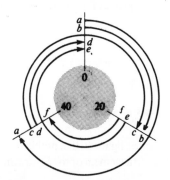

0–20 seconds: streams a, b, and c proceed

20–40 seconds: streams a, e, and f proceed

40–60 seconds: streams c, d, and e proceed

In each period of 60 seconds, streams a, c, and e can proceed for 40 seconds, and streams b, d, and f can proceed for 20 seconds.

Which of the two solutions is preferable will usually depend on other factors, such as the likely amount of traffic in each stream, or the need to give each stream a minimum time of (say) 20 seconds. Our concern here is to obtain a number of efficient solutions which can then be examined to see whether they satisfy these other requirements.

We can find these solutions by looking at the compatibility graph. Since our aim is to get the maximum number of traffic streams flowing at the same time, we want to find subgraphs of the compatibility graph which reflect this requirement. In particular, we are interested in *complete subgraphs,* since these correspond to streams which are mutually compatible. Examples of such complete subgraphs are the triangles formed from the vertices *abc,* or *aef,* or *ace,* or *cde.* Note that these are precisely the traffic streams appearing in the above solutions. This idea applies more generally, and leads to the general guidelines:

(1)   draw the compatibility graph;

(2)   for each vertex of the compatibility graph, find a largest complete subgraph containing it;

(3)   divide the time available by the number of complete subgraphs in step (2), and allocate a complete subgraph to each period of time.

In the above examples, step (2) gives the complete subgraphs *abc, aef,* and *cde,* which together contain all six vertices, and give rise to the third solution above. The second solution arises if we include the complete subgraph *ace* as well.

Assigning Radio Frequencies

The above ideas have also been applied to problems involving the assignment of radio frequencies to particular localities. Consider, for example, a mobile radio system such as that used by the police. Each police car maintains contact by means of a two-way radio which uses one channel from a preassigned band of frequencies allocated to the locality. Unless we can ensure that the frequency bands in neighboring localities do not overlap, we shall get interference. How can the frequencies be allocated?

We can represent this problem by a compatibility graph in which the vertices correspond to the localities and the edges correspond to pairs of non-neighboring localities, as illustrated by

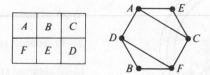

The problem is now very similar to that of the phasing of traffic lights. In that problem we had a certain allocation of time (60 seconds), and we found an arrangement of traffic streams

which allows the traffic to move for a good proportion of the time. We expressed this solution by means of circular arcs on a clock diagram. In the frequency assignment problem we are allocated a range of allowable frequencies (say, 99–101 MHz), and we want to find an arrangement of frequencies which gives each locality a reasonably wide frequency band.

We solve this problem by drawing the compatibility graph and looking for a set of complete subgraphs containing each vertex. We then assign a frequency band to each of these complete subgraphs, and represent these bands, not by arcs on a circle, but by open intervals on a line. (An open interval is an interval without its endpoints.) For example, the above compatibility graph gives rise to the complete subgraphs *ACE* and *BDF*. We can then assign the subgraph *ACE* the frequency band 99–100 MHz and the subgraph *BDF* the frequency band 100–101 MHz, giving the frequency allocation

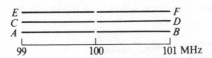

Interval Graphs

You have just seen how the solution of the frequency allocation problem can be depicted in terms of open intervals on a line, with compatible frequency allocations corresponding to overlapping intervals. We can extend this idea by associating a graph with any set of open intervals. To see what is involved, consider the intervals

$$(0,3), (2,7), (-1,1), (2,3), (1,4), (6,8),$$

which may be depicted as

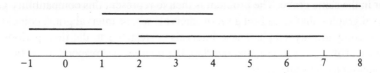

We associate a graph with these intervals by taking the intervals as vertices, and joining two of these vertices by an edge whenever the corresponding intervals have at least one point in common. For example, the intervals $(0,3)$ and $(1,4)$ have a point in common, as do the intervals $(2,7)$ and $(6,8)$, and so the corresponding vertices are joined in each case. Since the intervals $(-1,1)$ and $(1,4)$ are open intervals, they do not have a point in common, and so the corresponding vertices are not joined. The resulting graph is

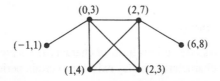

Any graph which can be formed from a set of intervals in this way is called an **interval graph**. Note that *every interval graph is a compatibility graph,* but *not every compatibility graph is an interval graph.* This is because non-overlapping intervals can sometimes give rise to adjacent vertices in a compatibility graph, whereas in an interval graph non-overlapping intervals always give rise to non-adjacent vertices.

Archaeology

At the end of the last century archaeologists were interested in the various types of pottery and other artifacts that had been found in several graves in predynastic Egypt (c. 4000–2500 BC). In particular, Sir Flinders Petrie used the data from nine hundred graves in the cemeteries of Naqada, Ballas, Abadiyeh, and Hu in an attempt to arrange the graves chronologically and assign a time period to each artifact found in them. This process is usually known as *sequence dating* or *seriation.*

In dating the graves they assumed that if two different artifacts occur together in the same grave, then their time periods must have overlapped. They also assumed, since the number of graves was large, that if the time periods of two artifacts overlapped, then the artifacts should appear together in some of the graves.

One of the most promising approaches to seriation problems in archaeology has been the representation of such data as a compatibility graph in which the vertices correspond to the artifacts, and the edges correspond to those pairs of artifacts which have appeared together in the same grave. The problem is then to represent this compatibility graph as an interval graph—that is, to find a set of intervals whose interval graph coincides with the given compatibility graph. These intervals correspond to the time periods during which each artifact was in use, and overlapping intervals correspond to artifacts which occur together in the same grave.

Unfortunately, the problem is not as simple as this in practice. For example, we might find several different arrangements of intervals which lead to the same compatibility graph, and we may not be able to choose the correct interval graph unless other information is available. In spite of this drawback, however, the interval graph approach has had some spectacular successes, and has led to the solution of many seriation problems, including the chronological ordering of bronze-age material in Central Europe, arrow-heads in a Paleo–Indian site in Wyoming, and Greek inscriptions at Histria in Rumania.

Developmental Psychology

Suppose that we wish to study various traits or characteristics present in children as they grow up. Each of these characteristics may exist for a certain period of time and then disappear, and the problem is to construct a time scale in which the various characteristics appear in chronological order. We can investigate this problem by studying the various characteristics present in a number of children and observing when two different characteristics are present in the same child. The situation is now the same as in our archaeological example, except that the word *artifact* is replaced by *characteristic,* and the word *grave* is replaced by *child.* By looking at the various ways in which our compatibility graph can be represented as an interval graph, we may be able to put the various characteristics in chronological order, thereby solving our problem.

Classical Studies

Another example of the use of seriation has arisen in the chronological ordering of various Greek and Latin literary works. Among other works, those of Plato have been studied extensively from this point of view, and the problem of determining the likely order of these works has been subjected to much mathematical analysis.

Among the most promising approaches to this problem has been the idea of analyzing change in an author's style by studying his use of prose rhythm. In the case of Plato, attention has concentrated on the *clausulae* (ends of sentences), since the clausula is rhythmically the most important part of the sentence. Each clausula was taken to consist of the last five syllables, each of which can be short or long, and the frequencies of the 2^5 (=32) possible combinations of these symbols were calculated for each of Plato's works. We can represent these data in the form of a graph by noting the appearance of each of the clausulae in the works under investigation, and drawing the corresponding compatibility graph. As before, we may then be able to determine the most likely chronological order by looking at the various ways in which the resulting graph can be represented as an interval graph.

Similar techniques have been used to investigate the authorship of a disputed piece of writing. In particular, the New Testament epistles and Shakespeare's plays have been subjected to this form of analysis.

Genetics

For some time, geneticists have regarded the chromosome as a linear arrangement of genes, and it is natural to ask whether the fine structure inside the gene is also arranged in a linear manner. (This problem is called *Benzer's problem.*) Unfortunately, this fine structure is too detailed to be observed directly, and so one has to study changes in the structure of the gene, known as *mutations.*

In analyzing the genetic structure of a particular bacterial virus called *phage T4,* Seymour Benzer considered the mutations which result when part of the gene is missing. In particular, he studied mutations in which the missing segments overlap, and expressed his results in the form of an *overlap matrix,* part of which is shown in figure (a). This 19×19 matrix is the adjacency matrix of the compatibility graph in figure (b), in which the vertices correspond to mutations, and the edges correspond to pairs of mutations whose missing segments overlap. In these terms, Benzer's problem is that of determining whether the matrix in figure (a) represents the overlapping of a suitably chosen collection of intervals, or (equivalently) of determining whether the compatibility graph in figure

(b) is an interval graph. In figure (c) we see that this is indeed the case—there *are* intervals which give rise to this adjacency matrix and compatibility graph.

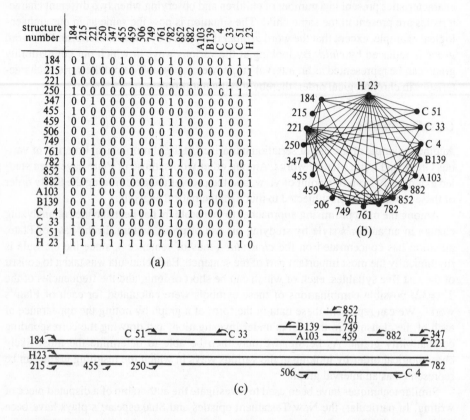

(a)

(b)

(c)

Note that, although the representation of this data as an interval graph does not *prove* that the fine structure inside the gene is arranged linearly, it certainly provides support for such a hypothesis. In fact, Benzer extended his analysis to no fewer than 145 mutations and showed that, even with this number of rows, the resulting matrix can still be represented by an interval graph. By this means he was able to show that, for this virus at least, the evidence for a linear arrangement is overwhelming.

Ecology

Snakes eat frogs, and birds eat spiders; birds and spiders both eat insects; frogs eat snails, spiders, and insects. Given any such tangle of interrelationships between predator and prey, how does an ecologist sort out the overall predatory behavior of the various species under investigation?

When studying relationships between animals and plants and their environment, ecologists use a graph with 'directed edges' known as a *food web*. The vertices correspond to the species under investigation, and there is a directed edge from a species *A* to a species *B* whenever *A* preys on *B*. As an example of a food web, consider the following diagram which represents the predatory habits of organisms in a Canadian willow forest.

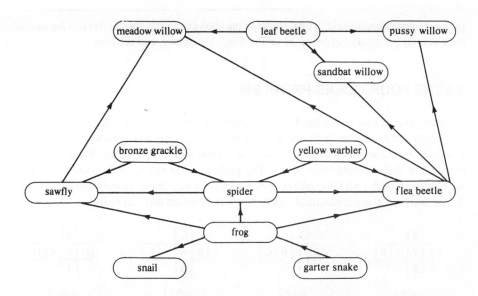

In untangling such food webs, ecologists introduce a graph that tells them which species compete for food. This graph is known as the *niche overlap graph,* or *competition graph,* and its edges join pairs of species which share a common prey. For example, in the above food web the bronze grackle and the yellow warbler both eat spiders, and so must be adjacent in the niche overlap graph

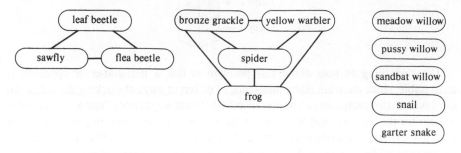

Most niche overlap graphs which arise in practice are interval graphs. For example, the above niche overlap graph can be represented by the set of intervals

					frog	
					flea beetle	spider
					leaf beetle	yellow warbler
meadow willow	pussy willow	sandbat willow	snail	garter snake	sawfly	bronze grackle

Such a representation has ecological significance in that overlapping intervals tend to correspond to species which react in the same way to particular environmental factors such as temperature, humidity or altitude. In the above example, the beetles and the sawfly have similar predatory behavior, as do the birds, the spider, and the frog.

3.6 THE FOUR-CUBES PROBLEM

An intriguing puzzle which has been marketed under the name of *Instant Insanity* concerns four cubes whose faces are colored red, blue, green and yellow (or sometimes white), in such a way that each cube has at least one face of each color. These cubes are depicted in flattened-out form below. The problem is *to pile up these cubes on top of each other in such a way that all four colors appear on each side of the resulting 'stack'*. As we shall see, there is essentially only one way in which this can be done.

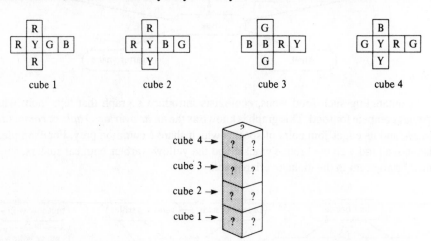

The first thing to note about this problem is that a trial-and-error approach is inadvisable, since there are many thousands of different ways of stacking the cubes. To see this, note that each cube can be placed in 24 different ways (since there are six possible choices for the top face, and the cube can then be rotated so as to bring any of the four sides to the front), and so the total number of possible stacks is $24^4 = 331776$. This number can be reduced by a factor of 4 if we regard two stacks as the same when we rotate one of them to get the other, but this still leaves us with $24^4/4 = 82944$ essentially different stacks. So we need a systematic approach which minimizes the amount of guesswork involved. The second thing to note is that if one face of a cube appears on one side of the stack, then the opposite face of the cube must appear on the opposite side of the stack. It follows from this that our concern is with opposite pairs of faces, and that we must decide for each cube which two of the three opposite pairs are the ones which appear on the sides of the stack.

In order to solve this problem, we represent each cube by a graph which tells us which pairs of colors appear on opposite faces. More precisely, we represent each cube by a graph with four vertices (corresponding to the colors red, blue, green, and yellow) in which two vertices are adjacent if and only if the cube in question has the corresponding colors on opposite faces. For example, in cube 1, blue and yellow appear on opposite faces, and so the vertices B and Y are joined in the corresponding graph. The four graphs we get for the above set of cubes are given below; underneath we have superimposed them to give a new graph G.

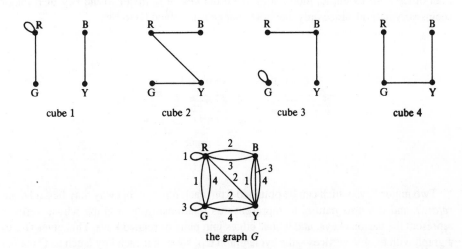

cube 1   cube 2   cube 3   cube 4

the graph G

A solution for the four-cubes problem is obtained by considering the two subgraphs of G pictured below. The subgraph H_1 tells us which pair of colors appears on the front and back faces of each cube, and the subgraph H_2 tells us which pair of colors appears on the left-hand and right-hand faces of each cube. The solution can then be read off from these subgraphs, as illustrated.

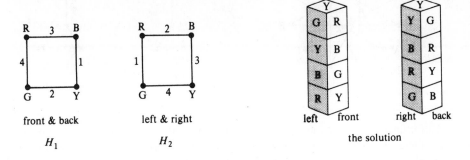

front & back   left & right   left front   right back

H_1 H_2 the solution

Why did we choose these particular subgraphs H_1 and H_2? Could we have obtained any other solutions by choosing different subgraphs? It is easy to see that H_1 and H_2 satisfy three properties:

    a.   Each contains exactly one edge from each cube;

    b.   Each is regular of degree 2;

    c.   They have no edges in common.

We leave it to you to explain why these three properties are relevant to the four-cubes problem (see Problem 3.32).

3.7 MUSIC

In a piece of music, certain changes of key (*modulations*) tend to sound more natural than others. For example, modulating from the key of C major to the key of F major seems very natural, since only one note change is involved (B to B♭):

Two major keys which can be obtained from each other in this way may be said to be *related,* and it seems natural to represent this relationship by a graph whose vertices represent the various keys, and whose edges join pairs of related keys. This gives rise to a graph with twelve vertices—the cycle graph C_{12}. Note that each key (such as C major) is joined to its *dominant* (G major) and *subdominant* (F major). We are here assuming 'equal temperament' so that $C^{\sharp} = D^{\flat}$, $E^{\sharp} = F$, and so on.

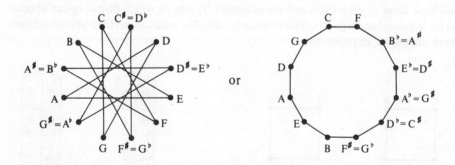

Unfortunately, we run into difficulties when we try to extend this idea to minor keys, since there are many key changes that sound very natural, but involve several note changes. In this case it is usual to say that each key has *five* closely related keys—its dominant and subdominant, as before, and also their relative minor keys. For example, the key of C major is closely related to G major and F major, and to their relative minors, A minor, E minor, and D minor. Joining up those closely related keys leads to the following attractive graph, which has 24 vertices and is regular of degree 5. For convenience, we have indicated the minor keys by lower case letters—for example, c♯ means C sharp minor.

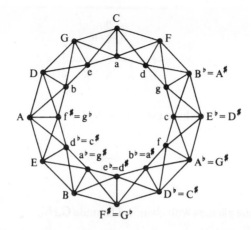

Although a knowledge of this graph may not add significantly to your enjoyment of a piece of music, it is nevertheless useful for representing and analyzing successions of key changes. This is because any modulation can be regarded as a combination of the basic key changes indicated in the above graph. For example, the modulation C$^{\sharp}$minor to G major can be split up into three constituent basic key changes (C$^{\sharp}$minor to F$^{\sharp}$minor, F$^{\sharp}$minor to B minor, and B minor to G major), and is represented in the graph by a path of length 3. In fact, any modulation corresponds to a path in the graph, and we can use the length of the shortest path between any two given keys as an indication of the 'remoteness' of the two keys involved. For example, the modulation C major to F$^{\sharp}$major (path of length 6) is more remote than D$^{\sharp}$major to A$^{\flat}$ minor (path of length 4), which in turn is more remote than B$^{\flat}$ major to C minor (path of length 1). As a general rule, the longer the path in the graph, the stranger the key change will sound.

The 24-vertex graph above is only one of several graphs which have arisen in a musical context. In fact, graph-like diagrams have been used by several composers, ranging from the baroque era (Bach's 'harmonic circle') to the recent pioneering work of Milton Babbitt, Andrzej Panufnik, and others whose compositions are based either wholly or in part on combinatorial considerations.

We conclude by noting without comment that when Igor Stravinsky was asked how he would describe his music pictorially, he replied

this is *my* music: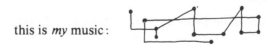

PROBLEMS

Chemistry

☉3.1. Draw the carbon graph of the molecule

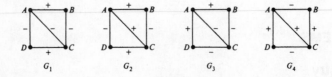

3.2. Draw the molecule whose carbon graph is

○3.3. Draw all the alkanes with chemical formula C_6H_{14}.

○3.4. a. Calculate the number of vertices and edges in the graph of the molecule C_nH_{2n+2}.

   b. Any connected graph in which

$$\text{(the number of vertices)} - \text{(the number of edges)} = 1$$

is necessarily a tree (see Chapter 10). Use this fact to show that the graph of any alkane C_nH_{2n+2} is a tree.

3.5. a. There are two different molecules with chemical formula C_3H_7OH. Draw the graphs representing these molecules, and verify that each is a tree.

   b. Use the method of Problem 3.4(b) to show that the graph of any alcohol $C_nH_{2n+1}OH$ is necessarily a tree.

3.6. By calculating the difference between the number of vertices and the number of edges in each case, determine whether the graph corresponding to each of the molecules is a tree:

(a) $C_7H_{15}OH$;   (b) $C_7H_{14}O_2$;   (c) $C_5H_{11}OH$;   (d) $C_6H_{12}O_6$.

Social Sciences

○3.7. Decide which of the following signed graphs are balanced, and find the corresponding bipartite graph in each case:

3.8. John likes Joan, Jean, and Jane, but dislikes both Joe and Jill; Jill likes Joe who dislikes Joan, Jean, and Jane; Joan, Jean, and Jane like each other, but each dislikes Jill. Draw the signed graph representing these relationships, and determine whether or not this signed graph is balanced.

3.9. Determine whether the signed graph representing each of the following sets of relationships is balanced. (You may assume that all relationships are symmetric—that is, x likes y if and only if y likes x.)

   a. Alan likes Chris and Edward, but dislikes Bob and David; Bob likes David but dislikes Chris; David dislikes Chris and Edward.

   b. Amy likes Beth and Doreen, but dislikes Edna; Beth dislikes Cathy, Doreen and Edna; Doreen dislikes Cathy and Edna.

   c. John likes Len and Mike, but dislikes Keith; Mike dislikes Ian and Keith; Len dislikes Ian, Keith, and Mike.

   d. Margaret likes Ida and Liz, but dislikes Jenny and Karen; Karen dislikes Ida and Liz; Jenny likes Karen but dislikes Liz.

⊕3.10. a. Show that in any balanced signed graph every cycle has an even number of negative edges. (Note that 0 is an even number.)

   b. Verify this result for the balanced signed graphs in Problem 3.7.

Trees

⊕3.11. Use a tree structure to parse the sentence *Good students read books*.

3.12. The ambiguous sentences *Help rape victims* and *Council rents rocket* appeared as newspaper headlines, and can each be interpreted in two ways. Draw two tree structures for each sentence.

3.13. Explain how a sorting tree might be used to represent the sorting of mail according to zip code.

3.14. Use a sorting tree to find all the increasing sequences of maximum length in the following list:

$$21, 23, 9, 20, 17, 6, 26, 14.$$

⊕3.15. Use a sorting tree to find all the decreasing sequences of maximum length in the following list:

$$5, 11, 6, 1, 3, 9, 10, 4.$$

3.16. The diagram on page 59 shows four equivalent ways of representing a rooted tree. Illustrate this equivalence by explicitly labeling the vertices, subsets, parentheses, and sections.

☉3.17. Write down the corresponding subsets of a set and the corresponding nested parentheses for the following rooted tree:

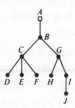

3.18. The following diagram represents a binary tree in which there are exactly two edges coming down from each intermediate vertex. Show that the number of levels of such a tree is at most $\frac{1}{2}(n+1)$, where n is the number of vertices.

3.19.[†] Suppose that you are given eight coins, seven of which are of equal weight, and the eighth is heavier or lighter than the rest. You are provided with an equal-arm balance for comparing coins, but you may use it only *three times*. Construct a suitable binary tree which will help you to identify the odd coin and to determine whether it is heavier or lighter than the rest.

Bracing Rectangular Frameworks

☉3.20. By constructing the corresponding bipartite graphs, determine whether the following braced frameworks are rigid. Is either of them a minimum bracing?

(a)   (b)

3.21. a. Check that the following is a minimum bracing:

b. Construct another minimum bracing of a 3×5 rectangular framework.

3.22. Determine whether each of the following bracings is
  a. a rigid bracing;
  b. a minimum bracing.

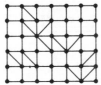 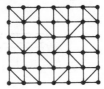

3.23. Show that
  a. if we permute the rows (or columns) of any rigid bracing, then we obtain another rigid bracing;
  b. if we permute the rows (or columns) of any minimum bracing, then we obtain another minimum bracing.

○3.24. How many cells are braced in a minimum bracing of an $r \times s$ rectangular framework?

Compatibility and Interval Graphs

3.25. Consider the following intersection, in which traffic can proceed only in the directions indicated (for example, stream g cannot turn left or right):

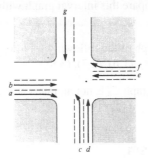

In solving the phasing-of-traffic-lights problem, we find a set of complete subgraphs of the compatibility graph G containing (between them) every vertex of G. Is each of the following such a set of subgraphs of G?

  (a) $\{abe, cdg, ef\}$;   (b) $\{abef, acd, fg\}$.

3.26. Consider the following intersection involving a one-way street:

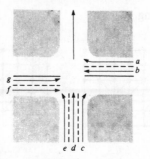

a. Draw the compatibility graph G.

b. Find a set of complete subgraphs containing each vertex of G.

c. Use the result of b. to find a suitable traffic light sequence, and calculate the total waiting time involved, assuming a 60-second cycle.

3.27. Suppose that in the radio frequency allocation problem (on page 64) localities A and E and localities B and F are also required to have non-overlapping frequency bands.

a. Draw the new compatibility graph G.

b. Find a set of complete subgraphs containing each vertex of G.

c. Use the result of b. to find a suitable frequency allocation, and illustrate your answer by means of intervals on a line.

3.28. Draw the interval graph associated with the following set of intervals: A = (99,99.5), B = (100,100.5), C = (99,100), D = (100,101), E = (99.5,100), F = (100.5,101). Compare this interval graph with the compatibility graph in Problem 3.27.

3.29. Draw the interval graph of the following set of open intervals: (1,2), (3,4), (5,6), (7,8), (1,6), (2,7), (3,8).

3.30.[†] Show that the cycle graph C_4 is not an interval graph.

The Four-Cubes Problem

3.31. Verify that the subgraphs H_1 and H_2 used in our solution of the four-cubes problem (on page 71) satisfy the following three properties:

a. each contains exactly one edge from each cube;

b. each is regular of degree 2;

c. they have no edges in common.

Explain why these three properties are relevant to the problem.

○3.32. Show that our solution to the four-cubes problem is the only one possible by showing that H_1 and H_2 are the only pair of subgraphs of G which satisfy properties a., b., and c. in Problem 3.31.

[*Hint*: first try looking for subgraphs which satisfy a., b., and c., and contain the loop at R. Then repeat the process with the loop at G and the edge joining R and Y. After you have eliminated these edges, the rest is easy.]

3.33. Decide whether the four-cubes problem with the following set of cubes has a solution:

3.34.[†] Show that there is no solution of the four-cubes problem with the following cubes:

Music

○3.35. Which of the following key changes is the least 'remote'?

a. A^b minor to $G^{\sharp}$ major;   c. A major to $D^{\sharp}$ minor;

b. D minor to B^b minor;   d. $G^{\sharp}$ minor to D^b major.

3.36. Which of the following key changes is the least 'remote'?

a. D major to E^b minor;   c. $F^{\sharp}$ minor to $F^{\sharp}$ major;

b. $A^{\sharp}$ minor to F major;   d. $D^{\sharp}$ major to $C^{\sharp}$ minor.

CHAPTER 4

WHAT IS A DIGRAPH?

4.1 INTRODUCTION

Up to now our concern has been almost exclusively with graphs, and we have seen how graphs can be used to depict a variety of situations in which various objects (represented by vertices) are related to each other in some way (these interrelations being represented by edges). In particular, we have seen how graphs can be used to represent route maps, chemical molecules, architectural floor plans, electrical networks, and so on. All these situations have one important common feature—the graphs tell us which pairs of vertices are joined, but do not imply any dominance of one vertex over another.

An exception was the ecological food web on page 69, which represented the predatory behavior between species, and which can be drawn as

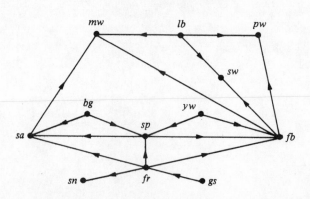

Such an object is called a *directed graph,* usually abbreviated to *digraph.* The points are called *vertices,* and the 'directed lines' or 'arrows' are called *arcs.* As with graphs, the terminology is not completely standard; for example, some authors allow the word *graph* to mean what we have called a *digraph*—that is, they allow graphs to have directed edges.

4.2 THE DEFINITION OF A DIGRAPH

DEFINITIONS.   *A* **digraph** D *consists of a set of elements, called* **vertices,** *and a list of ordered pairs of these elements, called* **arcs.** *The set of vertices is called the* **vertex-set** *of* D, *denoted by* **V(D),** *and the list of arcs is called the* **arc-list** *of* D, *denoted by* **A(D).** *If* v *and* w *are vertices of* D, *then an arc of the form* vw *is said to be* **directed from** v **to** w, *or to* **join** v **to** w.

DEFINITION.   *Let* D *be a digraph. The* **underlying graph** *of* D *is the graph obtained by replacing each arc of* D *by the corresponding (undirected) edge.*

In forming the underlying graph, we simply 'remove the arrows' from the arcs; for example,

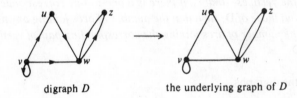

digraph *D*   the underlying graph of *D*

Just as for graphs, it is useful at this stage to introduce some further terminology. In particular, we can extend the concepts of multiple edges, loops, and simple graphs to digraphs.

DEFINITIONS.   *Two or more arcs joining the same pair of vertices in the same direction are called* **multiple arcs,** *and an arc joining a vertex to itself is called a* **loop.** *A digraph with no loops or multiple arcs is called a* **simple digraph.**

We can also define a concept analogous to that of a subgraph of a graph.

DEFINITION. *Let* D *be a digraph with vertex-set* V(D) *and arc-list* A(D). *A* **subdigraph** *of* D *is a digraph all of whose vertices belong to* V(D) *and all of whose arcs belong to* A(D).

For example, if *D* is the digraph shown above, where

$$V(D) = \{u,v,w,z\} \quad \text{and} \quad A(D) \text{ is } (uw,vu,vv,vw,wz,wz).$$

then the following digraphs are all subdigraphs of *D*:

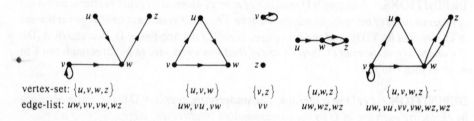

vertex-set: $\{u,v,w,z\}$ $\{u,v,w\}$ $\{v,z\}$ $\{u,w,z\}$ $\{u,v,w,z\}$

edge-list: uw,vv,vw,wz uw,vu,vw vv uw,wz,wz uw,vu,vv,vw,wz,wz

Next, we can extend the concept of isomorphism to digraphs, as follows:

DEFINITION. *Two digraphs* C *and* D *are* **isomorphic** *if* D *can be obtained from* C *by relabeling the vertices—that is, if there is a one-to-one correspondence between the vertices of* C *and those of* D, *such that the number of arcs joining any pair of vertices in* C *is equal to the number of arcs joining the corresponding pair of vertices (in the same direction) in* D.

For example, the digraphs

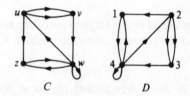

C   *D*

are isomorphic, as you can see by considering the one-to-one correspondence

$$
\begin{array}{ccccc}
C: & u & v & w & z \\
 & \updownarrow & \updownarrow & \updownarrow & \updownarrow \\
D: & 2 & 3 & 4 & 1
\end{array}
$$

Note that
    the two arcs *uv* in *C* correspond to the two arcs 23 in *D*;
    the arc *wz* in *C* corresponds to the arc 41 in *D*;
    the loop at *w* in *C* corresponds to the loop at 4 in *D*;
and so on.

As with graphs, when checking whether or not two digraphs are isomorphic, we can ignore the actual symbols used to label the vertices, since the vertices can be relabeled as necessary. In view of this, we often drop the labels altogether when they are not relevant to the problem at hand, and say (for example) that the following unlabeled digraphs are isomorphic:

We can summarize the above as follows:

Labeled Digraphs

These labeled digraphs are the same.   These labeled digraphs are not the same, but are isomorphic.

Unlabeled Digraphs

These unlabeled digraphs are isomorphic.

As you probably noted, the beginning of this chapter is very similar to parts of Chapter 1, and you will find that the similarity between graph and digraph concepts continues throughout the chapter. Most of the terms in this chapter are analogs of those given in

Chapters 1 and 2 and, in view of this, you may like to try to define digraph analogs of some of the following yourself before they are given:

    a. *v* and *w* are *adjacent* vertices;

    b. the edge *e* is *incident* with *v*;

    c. the *degree* of *v*;

    d. the *handshaking lemma*;

    e. the *adjacency and incidence matrices* of *G*;

    f. a *path* of length *k*;

    g. a *connected graph*;

    h. a *cycle*.

4.3 ADJACENCY AND INCIDENCE

We start by defining the digraph analogs of *adjacency* and *incidence*. These are similar to the corresponding definitions for graphs, except that we need to take account of the directions of the arcs.

DEFINITIONS. *Let* v *and* w *be vertices of a digraph. If* v *and* w *are joined by an arc* e, *then* v *and* w *are said to be* **adjacent**. *If the arc* e *is directed from* v *to* w, *then the arc* e *is said to be* **incident from *v* and incident to *w*.**

v and *w* are *adjacent*,
e is *incident from v*,
and *incident to w*.

Using these terms, we can give the digraph analogs of the degree of a vertex in a graph.

DEFINITIONS. *Let* D *be a digraph and let* v *be a vertex of* D. *The* **out-degree** *of* v *is the number of arcs incident from* v, *and is denoted by* **outdeg** *v*. *Similarly, the* **in-degree** *of* v *is the number of arcs incident to* v *and is denoted by* **indeg** *v*. *The* **out-degree sequence** *of* D *is the sequence obtained by listing the out-degrees in non-decreasing order, and the* **in-degree sequence** *of* D *is defined analogously.*

(Note that, if the digraph contains loops, then each loop contributes 1 to both the out-degree and the in-degree of the corresponding vertex.)

For example, the digraph below has the following out-degrees and in-degrees:

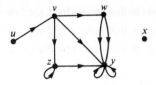

outdeg u = 1, outdeg v = 3, outdeg w = 2, outdeg x = 0, outdeg y = 2, outdeg z = 2,

indeg u = 0, indeg v = 1, indeg w = 1, indeg x = 0, indeg y = 6, indeg z = 2,

and the out-degree and in-degree sequences are (0,1,2,2,2,3) and (0,0,1,1,2,6), respectively.

We observe that for the above digraph the sum of the out-degrees is 10 and the sum of the in-degrees is 10. We also observe that this digraph has 10 arcs. In other words, the sum of the out-degrees and the sum of the in-degrees are each equal to the number of arcs. This leads to the following analog of the handshaking lemma, called the *handshaking di-lemma*(!):

THE HANDSHAKING DI-LEMMA.   *In any digraph, the sum of all the out-degrees and the sum of all the in-degrees are each equal to the number of arcs.*

Proof   Since each arc has two ends, it must contribute exactly 1 to the sum of the out-degrees and exactly 1 to the sum of the in-degrees. The result follows immediately. ☐

In Chapter 2 you saw two ways of representing a graph—as an *adjacency matrix* and as an *incidence matrix*. These representations both have digraph analogs which are frequently used when storing large digraphs in a computer. For simplicity, *we restrict our attention to digraphs without loops.*

The Adjacency Matrix

When defining the adjacency matrix of a digraph, we have to take into account the fact that each arc is *directed*. The following example shows how we deal with this.

$$
\begin{array}{cccc}
\text{col.} & \text{col.} & \text{col.} & \text{col.} \\
1 & 2 & 3 & 4 \\
\downarrow & \downarrow & \downarrow & \downarrow
\end{array}
$$

$$
\begin{array}{l}
\text{row 1} \rightarrow \\
\text{row 2} \rightarrow \\
\text{row 3} \rightarrow \\
\text{row 4} \rightarrow
\end{array}
\begin{pmatrix}
0 & 1 & 0 & 1 \\
0 & 0 & 0 & 2 \\
0 & 1 & 0 & 0 \\
0 & 0 & 1 & 0
\end{pmatrix}
$$

On the left-hand side we have a digraph with *four vertices,* and on the right-hand side we have a 4 × 4 *matrix.* The numbers appearing in the matrix refer to the number of arcs joining the corresponding vertices in the digraph. For example, vertices 1 and 2 are joined (in that order) by **1** arc, so **1** appears in row 1 column 2

vertices 2 and 4 are joined (in that order) by **2** arcs, so **2** appears in row 2 column 4

vertices 4 and 1 are joined (in that order) by **0** arcs, so **0** appears in row 4 column 1

We can generalize this idea as follows:

DEFINITION. *Let* D *be a digraph without loops, with* n *vertices labeled* 1,2,3, ..., n. *The* **adjacency matrix** *M(D) is the* n × n *matrix in which the entry in row* i *and column* j *is the number of arcs from vertex* i *to vertex* j.

Note that the adjacency matrix depends on the particular way in which the vertices are labeled, and that we obtain one adjacency matrix from another by interchanging a number of rows and the corresponding columns.

The Incidence Matrix

Whereas the adjacency matrix of a digraph involves the adjacency of vertices, the incidence matrix involves the incidence of vertices and arcs. Since an arc can be either incident *from* a vertex or incident *to* a vertex, we have to take account of this when defining the matrix. To see what is involved, consider the following example; we have circled the labels of the vertices to distinguish them from the labels of the arcs:

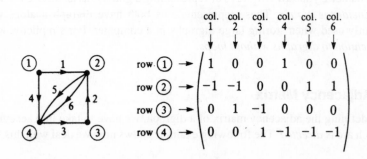

$$
\begin{array}{c}
\text{row } ① \rightarrow \\
\text{row } ② \rightarrow \\
\text{row } ③ \rightarrow \\
\text{row } ④ \rightarrow
\end{array}
\begin{pmatrix}
1 & 0 & 0 & 1 & 0 & 0 \\
-1 & -1 & 0 & 0 & 1 & 1 \\
0 & 1 & -1 & 0 & 0 & 0 \\
0 & 0 & 1 & -1 & -1 & -1
\end{pmatrix}
$$

On the left we have a digraph with *four vertices* and *six arcs,* and on the right we have a 4 × 6 *matrix.* Each of the numbers appearing in the matrix is either 1, −1, or 0, depending on whether or not the corresponding arc is incident from, or to, the corresponding vertex. For example,

arc 4 is incident *from* vertex ①,   so **1** appears in row 1 column 4

arc 5 is incident *to* vertex ④,   so **−1** appears in row 4 column 5

arc 4 is not incident with vertex ②, so **0** appears in row 2 column 4

We can generalize this idea, as follows:

DEFINITION. *Let* D *be a digraph without loops, with* n *vertices labeled* ①,②,③, …,Ⓝ *and* m *arcs labeled* 1,2,3, …, m. *The* **incidence matrix** *I(D) is the* n × m *matrix in which the entry in row* ① *and column* j *is*

     1, *if arc* j *is incident from vertex* ①
   −1, *if arc* j *is incident to vertex* ①
     0, *otherwise*

Note that the incidence matrix depends on the particular way in which the vertices and arcs are labeled, and we obtain one incidence matrix from another by interchanging rows (corresponding to relabeling the vertices) and columns (corresponding to relabeling the arcs).

4.4 PATHS AND CYCLES

Just as you can 'get from one vertex of a graph to another' by tracing the edges of a walk, trail, or path, so you can 'get from one vertex of a digraph to another' by tracing the arcs of a 'directed' walk, trail, or path. This means that you have to follow the directions of the arcs as you go, just as if you were driving around a one-way system in a town.

     We can make this idea precise, as follows.

DEFINITIONS. *A* **walk of length** *k in a digraph* D *is a succession of* k *arcs of* D *of the form*

$$uv, \; vw, \; wx, \; \ldots, \; yz.$$

We denote this walk by uvwx … yz, *and refer to it as a* **walk from** *u* **to** *z*. *If all the arcs (but not necessarily all the vertices) of a walk are different, then the walk is called a* **trail**. *If, in addition, all the vertices are different, then the trail is called a* **path**.

In the following diagram, *vwxyvwyzzu* is a *walk of length* 9 from *v* to *u*, which includes the arc *vw* twice, and the vertices *v,w,y*, and *z* twice. The walk *uvwyvz* is a *trail* which is not a path (since the vertex *v* occurs twice), whereas the walk *vwxyz* has no repeated vertices, and is therefore a *path*.

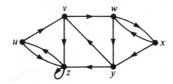

The terms *closed walk, closed trail,* and *cycle* can also be defined for digraphs.

DEFINITIONS.   *A* **closed walk** *in a digraph* D *is a succession of arcs of* D *of the form*

$$uv, \ vw, \ wx, \ \ldots, \ yz, \ zu.$$

If all of these arcs are different, then the walk is called a **closed trail**. *If, in addition, the vertices* u,v,w,x, . . . ,y, z *are all different, then the trail is called a* **cycle**.

In the above digraph, the closed walk *uvwyvzu* is a *closed trail* which is not a cycle (since the vertex *v* occurs twice), whereas the closed trails *zz, wxw, vwxyv,* and *uvwxyzu* are all *cycles*. Note that in describing closed walks we can allow any vertex to be the starting vertex. For example, the *triangle vwyv* can equally well be described by the letters *wyvw* or *yvwy*.

As with graphs, we can use the concept of a path to tell us whether or not a digraph is connected. Recall that a graph is connected if it is 'in one piece', and this means that there is a path between any given pair of vertices. For digraphs *these two ideas are not the same,* and this leads to two different definitions of the word *connected*.

DEFINITIONS.   *A digraph* D *is* **connected** *if its underlying graph is a connected graph, and* **disconnected** *otherwise. It is* **strongly connected** *if there is a path in* D *from any vertex to any other*.

The difference between these types of digraph is illustrated below:

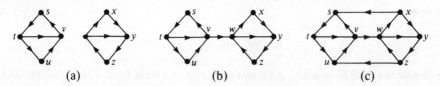

(a)   (b)   (c)

Digraph (a) is *disconnected* since its underlying graph is a disconnected graph, whereas digraph (b) is *connected but not strongly connected* since there is no path from *w* to *v*. Digraph (c) is *strongly connected* since there are paths joining all pairs of vertices.

Alternatively, you can think of driving around a one-way system in a town. If the town is strongly connected then you can drive from any part of the town to any other, following the directions of the one-way streets as you go, whereas if the town is merely connected then you can still drive from any part of the town to any other, but you may have to ignore the directions of the one-way streets! It follows that *every strongly connected digraph is connected,* but *not every connected digraph is strongly connected*.

In the following diagram (a) we see that the edges of the complete graph K_5 can be 'directed' in such a way that the resulting digraph is strongly connected. On the other hand, it is impossible to 'direct' the edges of the graph in diagram (b) in such a way that the resulting graph is strongly connected, since the 'bridge' must be directed one way or the other.

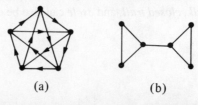

(a)   (b)

Now imagine that the graph in diagram (b) represents a system of two-way streets that we wish to make one-way. We clearly have a problem, since no matter how we do it, there must be some part of the town that is inaccessible from another part of town. This leads to the following definition.

DEFINITION. *A graph* G *is* **orientable** *if it is the underlying graph of a strongly connected digraph—that is, if it is possible to 'direct' the edges of* G *in such a way that the resulting digraph is strongly connected.*

We have seen above that *if a graph contains a 'bridge', then it cannot be orientable.* The following theorem establishes the converse result, but first we define a bridge.

DEFINITION. *An edge in a connected graph is a* **bridge** *if its removal leaves a disconnected graph.*

THEOREM 4.1. *A connected graph* G *is orientable if and only if it has no bridges.*

Proof We have already observed that an orientable graph cannot contain a bridge. To prove the converse, we suppose that *G* is a connected graph with no bridges. We must show that it is possible to direct the edges of *G* in such a way that the resulting digraph is strongly connected.

Since there are no bridges, each edge must be contained in some cycle (see Problem 4.24). We begin by taking any cycle C_1 of *G*, and direct its edges so as to give a 'directed cycle'. We can then get from any vertex of C_1 to any other vertex of C_1 by following the direction of the arcs.

Next we take any edge (not in C_1) that is incident to a vertex of C_1. This edge is contained in some cycle C_2 of *G*, and we direct the edges of C_2 cyclically, except for any edges of C_1 that have already been directed. We can now get from any vertex of C_1 or C_2 to any other vertex of C_1 or C_2 by following the direction of the arcs. Since *G* is connected, we can continue in this way until all the edges of *G* have been directed. The result is a strongly connected digraph. ☐

PROBLEMS

The Definition of a Digraph

○4.1.   Write down the vertex-set and arc-list of each of the following digraphs:

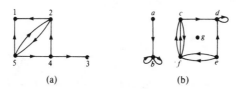

(a)   (b)

○4.2. Which of the following digraphs are subdigraphs of digraph (a) in Problem 4.1?

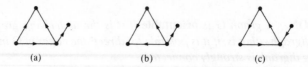

(a)   (b)   (c)

4.3. Let D be the digraph

Which of the following are subdigraphs of D?

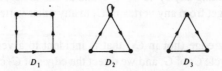

D_1 D_2 D_3

○4.4. Of the following four digraphs, which two are the same, which one is isomorphic to these two, and which is not isomorphic to any of the others?

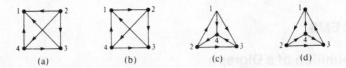

(a)   (b)   (c)   (d)

4.5. Which two of the following digraphs are isomorphic?

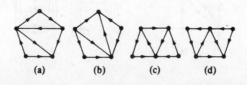

(a)   (b)   (c)   (d)

4.6. Which two of the following digraphs are isomorphic?

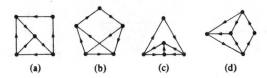

(a)   (b)   (c)   (d)

4.7. Draw two non-isomorphic non-simple digraphs with four vertices and six arcs.

4.8. There are 16 simple digraphs (up to isomorphism) with three vertices. Draw them.

Adjacency and Incidence

4.9. Consider the following digraph:

Classify each of the following statements as TRUE or FALSE:

a. c is incident to u;

b. d is incident from x;

c. a is incident to e;

d. g is incident from x.

☉4.10. Consider the following digraph D:

Classify each of the following statements as TRUE or FALSE:

a. u and z are adjacent;   d. f is incident from v;

b. v and z are adjacent;   e. a is incident to u;

c. b is incident from z;   f. e is incident to z.

○4.11. Write down the out-degree and in-degree sequences of each of the following digraphs:

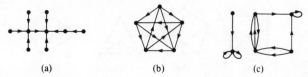

(a)   (b)   (c)

○4.12. Verify the handshaking di-lemma for each of the digraphs in Problem 4.11.

4.13. Verify the handshaking di-lemma for each of the following digraphs:

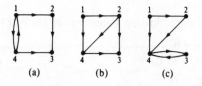

(a)   **(b)**

4.14. Match up each of the following digraphs with its arc-list, adjacency matrix and incidence matrix:

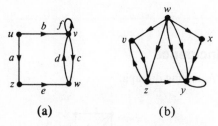

(a)   (b)   (c)

Arc-Lists

$$L_1:\ 12, 14, 43, 24, 34$$
$$L_2:\ 12, 14, 43, 24, 23$$
$$L_3:\ 12, 14, 43, 41, 23$$

Adjacency Matrices

$$\begin{pmatrix} 0 & 1 & 0 & 1 \\ 0 & 0 & 1 & 0 \\ 0 & 0 & 0 & 0 \\ 1 & 0 & 1 & 0 \end{pmatrix} \quad \begin{pmatrix} 0 & 1 & 0 & 1 \\ 0 & 0 & 0 & 1 \\ 0 & 0 & 0 & 1 \\ 0 & 0 & 1 & 0 \end{pmatrix} \quad \begin{pmatrix} 0 & 1 & 0 & 1 \\ 0 & 0 & 1 & 1 \\ 0 & 0 & 0 & 0 \\ 0 & 0 & 1 & 0 \end{pmatrix}$$

Incidence Matrices

$$\begin{pmatrix} 1 & 1 & 0 & 0 & 0 \\ -1 & 0 & 0 & 1 & 1 \\ 0 & 0 & -1 & 0 & -1 \\ 0 & -1 & 1 & -1 & 0 \end{pmatrix} \quad \begin{pmatrix} 1 & 1 & 0 & 0 & 0 \\ -1 & 0 & 0 & 1 & 0 \\ 0 & 0 & -1 & 0 & 1 \\ 0 & -1 & 1 & -1 & -1 \end{pmatrix} \quad \begin{pmatrix} 1 & 1 & 0 & -1 & 0 \\ -1 & 0 & 0 & 0 & 1 \\ 0 & 0 & -1 & 0 & -1 \\ 0 & -1 & 1 & 1 & 0 \end{pmatrix}$$

4.15. Write down the adjacency matrices of the following digraphs:

(a)   (b)   (c)

○4.16. Draw the digraph whose adjacency matrix is

$$
\begin{pmatrix}
0 & 1 & 0 & 0 & 1 \\
1 & 0 & 0 & 1 & 0 \\
0 & 0 & 0 & 0 & 0 \\
1 & 0 & 0 & 0 & 0 \\
0 & 1 & 0 & 2 & 0
\end{pmatrix}
$$

○4.17. What can you say about the sum of the numbers in
 a. any row of an adjacency matrix?
 b. any column of an adjacency matrix?

4.18. Write down the incidence matrix of each of the following digraphs:

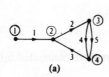 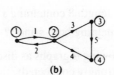 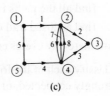

(a)   (b)   (c)

○4.19. Draw the digraph whose incidence matrix is

$$
\begin{pmatrix}
1 & -1 & 1 & -1 & 0 & 0 & 0 & 0 \\
-1 & 1 & 0 & 0 & -1 & 1 & 0 & 0 \\
0 & 0 & 0 & 0 & 0 & 0 & 0 & 0 \\
0 & 0 & 0 & 1 & 0 & -1 & -1 & -1 \\
0 & 0 & -1 & 0 & 1 & 0 & 1 & 1
\end{pmatrix}
$$

4.20. What can you say about the number of 1's and −1's in
 a. any row of an incidence matrix?
 b. any column of an incidence matrix?

Paths and Cycles

4.21.   In the following digraph, (if possible)

    a.   find a walk of length 7 from u to w;

    b.   find cycles of length 1, 2, 3, and 4;

    c.   find a path of maximum length.

✪4.22.   In the following digraph,

    a.   find all the paths from s to z;

    b.   find all the paths from z to s;

    c.   find a closed trail of length 8 containing s and z.

Are there any cycles containing both s and z?

✪4.23.   Classify each of the following digraphs as disconnected, connected but not strongly connected, or strongly connected:

      (a)   (b)   (c)   (d)

4.24.   Prove that

    a.   each edge of a tree is a bridge;

    b.   in a graph without bridges, each edge is contained in a cycle.

4.25.   Show that the Petersen graph is orientable, by directing its edges in such a way that the resulting digraph is strongly connected.

4.26.   Beginning with a triangle, use the method of proof of Theorem 4.1 to direct the edges of the complete graph K_5 so that the resulting digraph is strongly connected.

4.27.[†] A **tournament** is a digraph whose underlying graph is a complete graph.

    a. Draw the tournaments with 2, 3, and 4 vertices, and write down their out-degree sequences.

    b. Show that no tournament can contain more than one source (vertex of in-degree 0) or more than one sink (vertex of out-degree 0).

CHAPTER 5

APPLICATIONS OF DIGRAPHS

In Chapter 3 we described several areas in which graphs have been found useful. We now carry out a similar procedure for digraphs. Other important applications of digraphs include the calculation of a maximum flow in a capacitated network, and the calculation of currents and voltage in an electrical network. These topics are discussed in full in the companion volume on *Networks*.

5.1 SIGNED DIGRAPHS

In Chapter 3 we described the use of graphs to represent symmetric relationships (*x* likes *y* if and only if *y* likes *x*). If the relationships are not all symmetric (*x* likes *y*, but *y* dislikes *x*), we use a **signed digraph.** This is a digraph with either + or − associated with each arc, indicating a positive relationship (likes, supports, threatens, etc.) or a negative one (dislikes, is junior to, is afraid of, etc.). For example, in the signed graph below, John and Jack like each other, Mary likes Jill but Jill dislikes Mary, John dislikes Jill but we have no information about Jill's feelings for John, and so on. Note that a negative arc from *x* to *y* (Jill dislikes Mary) is *not* the same as a positive arc from *y* to *x* (Mary likes Jill).

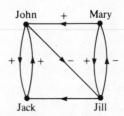

Many of the problems of modern society involve extremely complex systems made up of a number of variables which are constantly changing and interacting. In many of these problems we need to be able to predict the future development of the system when the amount of available information is minimal. For such situations, signed digraphs have often proved to be the most convenient form of mathematical model available, and their use has frequently led to precise and valid conclusions. In particular, they have success-fully been applied to problems of waste disposal, energy planning, research funding, environmental contamination, allocation of medical resources, and so on. Although our discussion here will necessarily be somewhat simplified, the ideas we introduce are equally valid for more complex examples.

Solid Waste Disposal

The signed digraph below is a simplified version of one used to describe the relation-ships among the variables in the solid waste disposal problem of a city. The arc from w to b is marked *positive* since an increase in waste leads to an increase in bacteria, whereas the arc from s to d is marked *negative* since an improvement in sanitation facil-ities leads to a decrease in the number of diseases. There is no arc from d to w since an increase in the number of diseases has little (if any) direct effect on the amount of waste.

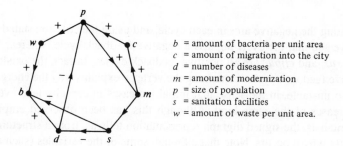

b = amount of bacteria per unit area
c = amount of migration into the city
d = number of diseases
m = amount of modernization
p = size of population
s = sanitation facilities
w = amount of waste per unit area.

Of particular interest in this digraph are the cycles. Note that an increase in population (p) results in an increase in waste (w), that, in turn, produces an increase in bacteria (b) and disease (d), that then reduces the population (p). A cycle of this kind, in which an increase in one of the variables (p) ultimately gives rise to a decrease in the same variable, is called a **negative feedback cycle.** On the other hand, an increase in population (p) increases the pressure towards modernization (m), leading to an improvement in sanita-tion facilities (s), a decrease in the number of diseases (d) and hence a further increase in population (p). A cycle of this kind, in which an increase in one of the variables (p) ultimately gives rise to a further increase in the same variable, is called a **positive feedback cycle.** Negative and positive feedback cycles are sometimes referred to as *deviation-counteracting* and *deviation-amplifying cycles,* respectively.

It is easy to see whether a given cycle is a positive or negative feedback cycle, since *every positive feedback cycle has an even number of negative arcs,* whereas *every negative feedback cycle has an odd number of negative arcs.* The reason for this is that whenever a deviation (increase or decrease) is counteracted in a positive feedback cycle, then the counteraction is itself counteracted by the next negative arc. In a negative feedback cycle, the last of these counteractions is never counteracted.

Electrical Energy Demand

The signed digraph below gives a simplified representation of the consequences of changes in energy use. The arc from p to u is marked *positive* since an increase in population in a given area is likely to increase the amount of energy used, whereas the arc from u to r is marked *negative* since the more energy we use, the less we tend to pay per unit. There is no arc from j to r since an increase in the number of available jobs has little (if any) direct effect on the cost of electricity.

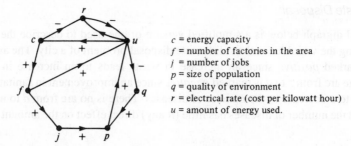

c = energy capacity
f = number of factories in the area
j = number of jobs
p = size of population
q = quality of environment
r = electrical rate (cost per kilowatt hour)
u = amount of energy used.

By counting the negative arcs in each cycle, and using the criterion stated in the last example, we see that the cycle *uqpu* is a negative feedback cycle, whereas the cycles *cruc, cfuc, rur,* and *cfjpuc* are all positive feedback cycles. In fact, the existence of all these positive feedback cycles containing the vertex c explains why the energy capacity system is so unstable, in the sense that initial increases in capacity lead eventually to further increases of the same kind. Although this has been observed empirically by environmentalists, the signed digraph representation tells us, from a structural point of view, exactly why it occurs. Note that although some of the variables (such as 'quality of environment') may be difficult or impossible to measure, this makes no difference to the conclusions we can draw. Even with such a simple model as this, we can make some remarkably accurate predictions.

5.2 FINITE STATE MACHINES

Digraphs can also be used to represent machines. Our particular concern here is with *finite state machines* (sometimes called *finite automata, digital systems,* or *discrete systems*), since their operation can be described completely in terms of digraphs. However, you should not be misled by the apparent simplicity of the representation, or of the examples we choose to illustrate it, since everything we do here applies equally well to a simple on–off switch for an electric light or to the enormous complexity of a modern digital computer. Moreover, although the machines considered here may not be the most general type, they can be made to approximate many of the processes that can be done by other finite physical systems.

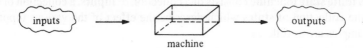

In its simplest form, a machine can be regarded as a 'black box' with input and output channels. Whenever we put something into the machine, the machine acts on it in some way and produces an output. For example,

a combine harvester is a machine whose inputs are the corn stalks in the field, and whose outputs are the resulting bales;

a coding machine is a machine whose inputs are the words to be encoded, and whose outputs are the encoded words;

the gas pedal of a car may be considered as a machine where the input pressure applied by the foot results in an increase of speed.

Note that we study the effectiveness of machines like this by comparing their inputs and outputs, and we do not need to know what goes on inside the black box. Just as we can drive a car without understanding how the transmission system works, and we can digest food without understanding how our digestive system works, so we can study machines simply by looking at what goes in and what comes out.

This applies well when we consider finite state machines. As their name suggests, finite state machines are machines that can assume any one of a finite number of 'states' at each moment of time. Applying an input to such a machine causes the state to change and produce a resulting output. Note that the word *state* can be understood in its everyday usage. For example, we often talk about being in a happy or unhappy state of mind; if we now apply an input (such as a piece of good or bad news), this can produce a change of state, as the following diagram shows:

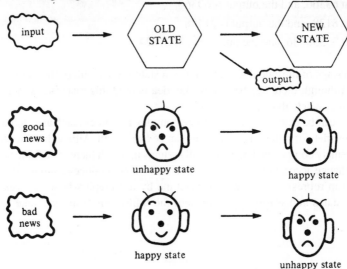

Thus a **finite state machine** consists of a collection of **inputs,** a collection of **outputs,** and a finite collection of **states** which describe the effect of the various input signals. Some examples are as follows:

An electric light cord Consider an electric light operated by a cord. If we pull the cord several times, the light goes on and off repeatedly, and we may regard the light switch as a machine whose inputs are pulls on the cord, whose states are *on* and *off,* and whose outputs are a lit and an unlit bulb.

input	old state	new state	output
pull the cord	off	on	
	on	off	

An extension of this example is a switching network whose input is an on–off setting of a number of two-way switches, and whose output is the corresponding pattern of an array of lights.

An adding machine Consider an adding machine that adds numbers up to a hundred million (say). We perform additions in the usual way, introducing the numbers one at a time and observing the results. For example, to add 63360, 8128, and 33550336, we simply

input 63360, and the output is 63360;

input 8128, and the output is 71488;

input 33550336, and the output is 33621824.

At each stage of the calculation, the current state is the result of the calculation up to that point. Although there are 10^8 states, the idea behind this machine is identical to that of the on–off switch above.

These can be extended to much more complex machines (such as a digital computer) in which a variety of different calculations can be carried out. Although the resulting machines are extremely complicated, they are still systems in which there are a finite number of states which change according to different inputs and which produce resulting outputs.

We can represent a finite state machine by a digraph whose vertices represent the various states and whose arcs represent the transitions from one state to another. For example, the two-way switch above can be represented by a digraph with two vertices, *on* and *off*, and two arcs representing the pulling of the cord:

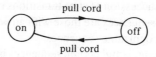

If we have two switches *A* and *B* and the inputs consist of switching either or both of the switches, then the resulting digraph is as follows:

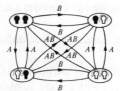

Another example is the *two-moment delay machine,* represented by the following digraph. It has four states, denoted by 00, 01, 10, and 11, and two possible inputs (0 and 1). If we start in state 00 and apply an input of 0 we stay in the same state; if, on the other hand, we apply an input of 1, then we move to state 01.

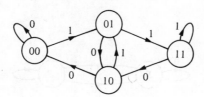

If, now, we start in *any* state (10, say) and apply inputs of 1 and 1, then we end up in state 11, as you can easily check. Similarly, if we start in any state and apply inputs of 0 and 1, then we end up in state 01. In every case the state we end in after two inputs tells us what the two inputs were, and we get the same answer whatever state we started in. Thus a two-moment delay machine always 'remembers' the two previous inputs.

Another type of machine is the *parity machine* below which can recognize whether the total number of 1's which have been input up to a given time is even or odd. You can verify this by starting at *even* and trying various sequences of inputs, such as 00, 110, 0101, 011010, or 011010011. Any sequence containing an even number of 1's must end up in state *even*, whereas any sequence containing an odd number of 1's must end up in state *odd*.

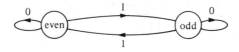

If we now insist that every succession of state transitions must start and end at *even*, then the only allowable sequences are those with an even number of 1's and we say that, with this choice of initial and final states, the machine *recognizes* only these sequences. Similarly, if we insist that every succession of state transitions must start at *even* and finish at *odd*, then the only allowable sequences are those with an odd number of 1's and we now say that these are the only recognizable sequences.

This idea of a machine 'recognizing' certain sequences is important when we consider the relationships between machines and languages. Although the word *language* can refer to a natural language like English or French, it often refers to an artificial one such as a computer language. For our purposes, a **language** is any collection of *words* made up from a given *alphabet* such as (*a*,*b*,*c*,...) or (0,1,...). For example, we can take our alphabet to be the two letters *a* and *b,* and we can consider a language with just five words

$$b,\ aba,\ aabaa,\ aabbaa,\ aababaabba,$$

or we can take our alphabet to consist of the numbers 0 and 1, and we can consider a language whose words are sequences with an odd number of 1's.

For a language like this to be useful, we need to be able to construct machines which recognize all of their words but no other combination of symbols. We do this by calling one state the **starting state** S and another state the **finishing state** F, and calling a word **recognizable** if we can start at S, input the letters of the word one at a time, and end at F. The recognizable words are simply the sequence of inputs which give the output F.

Example 1

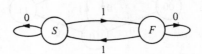

Alphabet: 0,1.

Here the only words that are recognizable are those with an odd number of 1's, since it is only for these words that we can start at S and finish at F.

Example 2

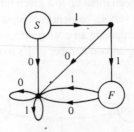

Alphabet: 0,1

Here the only way of getting from S to F is by means of the inputs 1 and 1. It follows that this machine recognizes the word 11 and no other word.

Example 3

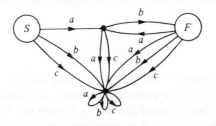

Alphabet: *a,b,c.*

Here we can get from S to F by means of the sequences *ab, abab, ababab,* ..., and by no other sequences. It follows that this machine recognizes these words and no others.

We conclude with a couple of remarks. First, as we stated at the beginning of this section, you should not be misled by the apparent simplicity of the examples included here. Although our examples involved only a few states, the underlying ideas remain essentially the same for machines with many millions of states, such as a computer or the human brain. Second, the main use of digraphs above is to provide a convenient diagrammatic way of showing what is happening. However, at a more advanced level, we can use results about digraphs in general to deduce results about finite state machines, and it is here that the main advantages of using digraphs are recognized.

5.3 SIGNAL-FLOW GRAPHS

The circuit shown in the following diagram uses an amplifier with a voltage gain of A_v.

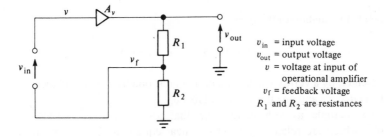

v_{in} = input voltage
v_{out} = output voltage
v = voltage at input of operational amplifier
v_f = feedback voltage
R_1 and R_2 are resistances

The voltages are related by the following equations:

$$v = v_{in} + v_f, \quad v_f = kv_{out}, \quad v_{out} = A_v v.$$

Here $k = R_2/(R_1 + R_2)$ is the fraction of the output voltage fed back to the input. By eliminating v and v_f from these equations, we can express the output voltage v_{out} in terms of the input voltage v_{in}:

$$v_{out} = \frac{A_v}{1-kA_v} v_{in}.$$

We now give an alternative method for obtaining such an expression. This method has been of widespread use in control engineering, and involves a digraph called a **signal-flow graph**. Although *signal-flow digraph* might be a better name, the one given here is the standard terminology; it is sometimes abbreviated to *flowgraph*. The term *signal-flow* derives from the observation that such a diagram resembles a signal transmission network, with 'signals' ($1, A_v$, etc.) traveling along the arcs.

In our example the signal-flow graph has four vertices, corresponding to the variables v_{in}, v_{out}, v_f, and v, and may be drawn as

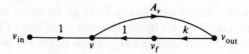

Note the connection between the labels on the arcs and the above equations. The vertex v has two incoming arcs, one from v_{in} with label 1, and one from v_f with label 1; this expresses the equation

$$v = 1v_{in} + 1v_f.$$

Similarly, the vertex v_f has one incoming arc from v_{out} with label k; this expresses the equation

$$v_f = kv_{out}.$$

In general, an equation of the form

$$x = a_1 x_1 + a_2 x_2 + \ldots + a_k x_k$$

is represented by a vertex x with k incoming arcs, one from x_1 with label a_1, one from x_2 with label $a_2, \ldots$, and one from x_k with label a_k.

In this example, as with many others that arise in practice, we have a number of variables which are related by a set of linear equations. By solving these equations directly, we can find the relationship between any given pair of variables. However, it is sometimes easier to solve the equations by constructing a signal-flow graph and reducing it (using procedures which we describe below) to a digraph consisting of two vertices joined by an arc. The required relationship can then be read directly from the digraph. For example, the reduced digraph arising from the above example is

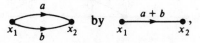

and this gives rise to the relationship stated above.

The reduction procedures we apply to the digraph correspond to operations on the original equations. Some of the most useful of these operations are

1. *eliminating multiple arcs*: we can replace

since if $x_2 = ax_1 + bx_1$, then $x_2 = (a + b) x_1$;

2. *eliminating vertices in a path*: we can replace

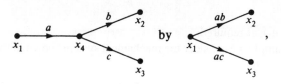

since if $x_3 = ax_1$ and $x_2 = bx_3$, then $x_2 = (ab)x_1$;

3. *eliminating the stem of a 'Y'*: we can replace

since if $x_4 = ax_1$, $x_2 = bx_4$, and $x_3 = cx_4$, then $x_2 = (ab)x_1$ and $x_3 = (ac)x_1$;

4. *eliminating a loop*: we can replace

since if $x_2 = ax_1 + bx_2$, then $x_2 = ax_1/(1 - b)$;

5. *eliminating cycles of length 2*: we can replace

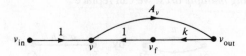

since if $x_3 = ax_1 + cx_2$ and $x_2 = bx_3$, then $x_2 = abx_1/(1 - bc)$.

To see how these procedures can be applied in practice, let us consider two examples. The first of these is the amplifier circuit discussed earlier.

We start with the signal-flow graph

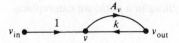

Applying reduction 2 to the path $v_{out}v_fv$, we eliminate vertex v_f:

Applying reduction 5, we eliminate the cycle of length 2:

So $v_{out} = A_v v_{in} /(1 - k A_v)$, as required.

For our second example we consider the mechanical system shown in the diagram

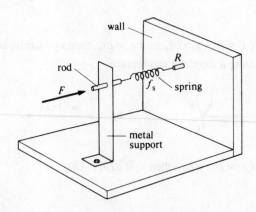

The rod can move horizontally under the influence of an external force F. When the rod moves, it bends the springy metal support which exerts a force f_m, and also compresses the spring which exerts a force f_s. The spring is attached to the wall which exerts a reaction R. The forces are related by

$$f_s = R, \quad F = f_s + f_m, \quad x_s = (1/a)f_s, \quad f_m = bx_m, \quad x_m = x_s,$$

where x_s is the decrease in the length of the spring, x_m is the distance moved by the rod, and a and b are constants. We wish to find the relationship between the force F and the reaction R. To do this we first draw the signal-flow graph

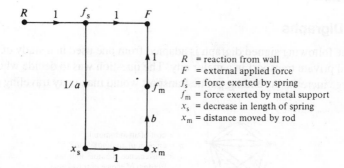

R = reaction from wall
F = external applied force
f_s = force exerted by spring
f_m = force exerted by metal support
x_s = decrease in length of spring
x_m = distance moved by rod

Next we apply reduction 2 to the path $f_s\, x_s\, x_m f_m\, F$ to eliminate the vertices f_m, x_m, and x_s:

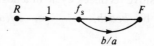

[We wrote the third equation in the form $x_s = (1/a)f_s$, rather than $f_s = ax_s$, so that we could apply this reduction. With practice you should be able to write the equations in such a way that they can easily be reduced.]

Applying reduction 1, we eliminate the multiple arcs

Applying reduction 2, we eliminate the vertex f_s:

$$R \quad 1+b/a \quad F$$

The relationship is, therefore, $F = (1 + b/a)R$.

PROBLEMS

Signed Digraphs

⊘5.1. The following signed digraph is adapted from one used in a study of public and private transport in a major city. The question was to decide whether a large increase in funding public transport would make city traveling easier.

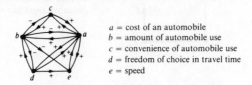

a = cost of an automobile
b = amount of automobile use
c = convenience of automobile use
d = freedom of choice in travel time
e = speed

By counting the number of negative arcs, determine whether each of the following cycles is a positive feedback cycle or a negative feedback cycle:

a. *abca*,   b. *beacb*,   c. *adea*.

5.2. The following signed digraph is adapted from one used to study world food production:

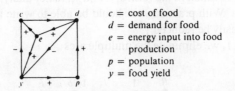

c = cost of food
d = demand for food
e = energy input into food
   production
p = population
y = food yield

List as many positive and negative feedback cycles as you can.

○5.3. The following signed digraph was prepared for a study by the Organization for Economic Co-operation and Development into the support that governments should provide for the funding of research projects in science and technology.

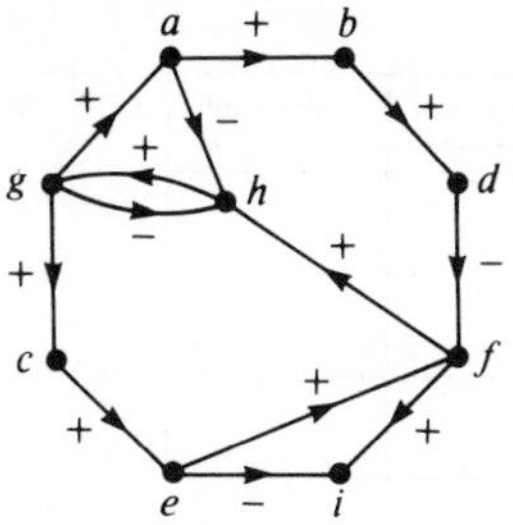

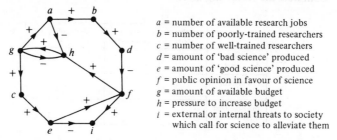

a = number of available research jobs
b = number of poorly-trained researchers
c = number of well-trained researchers
d = amount of 'bad science' produced
e = amount of 'good science' produced
f = public opinion in favour of science
g = amount of available budget
h = pressure to increase budget
i = external or internal threats to society which call for science to alleviate them

List as many positive and negative feedback cycles as you can.

5.4. The following signed digraph shows the effects of contaminating a lake by two nutrients, nitrate (N) and phosphate (P). The lake contains two forms of algae—green algae (g) which uses both nitrate and phosphate, and blue-green algae (b) which uses phosphate but releases more nitrate. In addition, green algae is sensitive to a toxin which is released by blue-green algae.

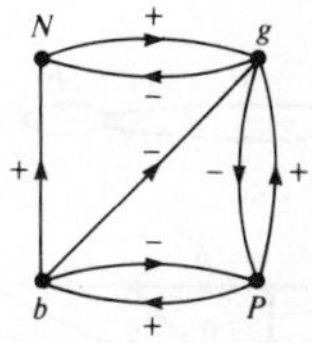

List as many positive and negative feedback cycles as you can.

Finite State Machines

5.5. Give three more examples of finite state machines. In each case describe the inputs, the states, and the outputs.

5.6. The following diagram illustrates a three-moment delay machine that 'remembers' the three previous inputs. Verify that it works by starting at any state and applying

a. inputs of 1, 0, and 1 (the result should always be state 101);
b. inputs of 0, 1, and 0 (the result should always be state 010).

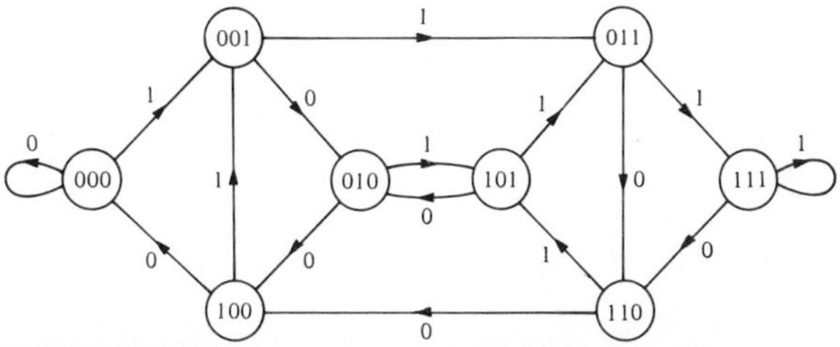

☺5.7.   a.   Construct the digraph of a one-moment delay machine with two states which 'remembers' the previous input.

b.   Complete the following table:

	number of states	out-degree of each vertex	in-degree of each vertex
one-moment delay machine			
two-moment delay machine			
three-moment delay machine			

and guess the corresponding results for an n-moment machine.

5.8.[†]   Draw a parity machine which can recognize whether the total number of 0's which have been input up to a given time is even or odd. Test whether your machine is correct by applying it to the sequences 00, 110, 0101, 011010, 011010011.

5.9.[†]   What words are recognized by each of the following machines?

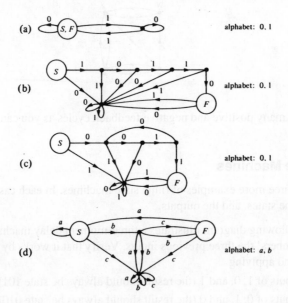

Signal-Flow Graphs

○5.10.   A complex control system gives rise to the following signal-flow graph:

Reduce this signal-flow graph to one consisting of a single arc from x_1 to x_5.

5.11.   a.   By writing down the equations relating x_1, x_2, x_3, and x_4, show that in any signal-flow graph we can replace

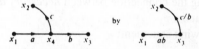

b.   The following signal-flow graph arose in the analysis of a control system in a complex chemical plant. Use the above reduction, together with those in this chapter, to eliminate the cycles. Hence find x_5 in terms of x_1.

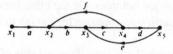

5.12.   a.   By writing down the equations relating x_1, x_2, x_3, and x_4, show that in any signal-flow graph we can replace

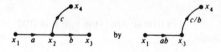

b.   The following signal-flow graph also arose in the analysis of a control system in a complex chemical plant. Use the above reduction, together with those in this chapter, to eliminate the cycles. Hence find x_5 in terms of x_1.

APPENDIX

PROOFS

To establish the truth of a mathematical statement, we need to provide a convincing argument, or *proof*. Our aim here is to explain what such a proof entails, and to describe some methods of proof.

Necessary and Sufficient Conditions

We start by explaining the connection between *necessary and sufficient conditions* and *if and only if* statements.

Consider the following statement:

if G is a tree, then G is a bipartite graph.   (Problem 2.36)

This is a true statement, and we say that being a tree is a *sufficient condition* for being a bipartite graph. However, it is not a *necessary condition*, since there are many bipartite graphs (such as $K_{3,3}$) which are not trees. On the other hand, having cycles only of even length is a *necessary and sufficient condition* for a graph to be bipartite, and we can write

G is a bipartite graph if and only if every cycle of G has even length.
(The *only if* part of this is Problem 2.23.)

Thus, in order to prove a result of the form

a is true IF AND ONLY IF b is true

we must prove two separate statements:

1. *a is true IF b is true*—that is, we must prove that IF b is true, THEN a is true.   } Here, *b is true* is SUFFICIENT to ensure that *a is true*.

2. *a is true ONLY IF b is true*—that is, we must prove that IF a is true, THEN b is true.   } Here, *b is true* is NECESSARY for us to have *a is true*.

The statement

if a is true, then b is true

is called the *converse* of the statement

if b is true, then a is true.

For example:

if G is a bipartite graph, then every cycle of G has even length

is a true statement whose converse is also *true*, whereas

if G is a tree, then G is a bipartite graph

is a true statement whose converse is *false*.

METHODS OF PROOF

To prove a result *false*, it is enough to produce a single counter-example—for example, $K_{3,3}$ is a counter-example to the false statement

if G is a bipartite graph, then G is a tree.

However, to prove a result *true*, we must produce a general argument which covers all possibilities. The three types of proof which appear most in this book are *direct proofs*, *indirect proofs* (proofs by contradiction), and *proofs by mathematical induction*. We look at each of these in turn.

Direct Proofs

In a direct proof (the most common type of proof), we start with the information we are given and proceed by a succession of logical steps to the result required. An example of such a proof is the proof we gave for consequence 3 of the handshaking lemma (Solution 1.14).

CONSEQUENCE 3. *If* G *is a graph which has n vertices and is regular of degree* r, *then* G *has exactly* $\frac{1}{2}$nr *edges.*

Proof Since G has n vertices each of degree r, the sum of all the vertex-degrees is nr. By the handshaking lemma, the number of edges is half this sum—that is, $\frac{1}{2}nr$. □

(We use the symbol □ to denote the end of a proof.)

Indirect Proofs

These proofs are often called *proofs by contradiction*, or *proofs by the method of 'reductio ad absurdum'*. In order to prove a statement of the form

if a is true, then b is true,

we prove that

if a is true and b is false, then a must also be false,

thereby obtaining a contradiction. An example of such a proof is the proof we gave for consequence 2 of the handshaking lemma (Solution 1.14):

CONSEQUENCE 2. *In any graph, the number of vertices of odd degree is even.*

Proof For any graph, the handshaking lemma holds, so that the sum of all the vertex-degrees is even (consequence 1). If the number of vertices of odd degree were odd, then the sum of all the vertex-degrees would be an odd number, giving the required contradiction. So the number of vertices of odd degree must be even. $\Box$

Proofs By Mathematical Induction

Suppose that we wish to prove a result concerning graphs with a given number of vertices—for example,

the complete graph K_n has exactly $\frac{1}{2}n(n-1)$ edges or,

every tree with n vertices has exactly $n-1$ edges.

One approach to proving results of this kind is to show that
  a. the result holds for graphs with one vertex;
  b. for each integer n, if the result holds for graphs with less than n vertices, then it must also hold for graphs with exactly n vertices.

We can thus deduce successively that, by b.,

since it holds for graphs with less than two vertices, it must hold for graphs with two vertices;
since it holds for graphs with less than three vertices, it must hold for graphs with three vertices;
since it holds for graphs with less than four vertices, it must hold for graphs with four vertices;
and so on.

We can thus deduce that the result must hold for graphs with any given number of vertices.
    This method is sometimes called the **method of strong induction.** We illustrate it by proving the two results above.

THEOREM 1. *The complete graph* K_n *has exactly* $\frac{1}{2}n(n-1)$ *edges.*

Proof The result holds when $n = 1$, since K_1 has 0 edges and $\frac{1}{2} \times 1 \times 0 = 0$.

Now assume that the result holds for complete graphs with less than n vertices—that is, that K_k has $\frac{1}{2}k(k-1)$ edges whenever $k < n$. We must deduce that K_n has $\frac{1}{2}n(n-1)$ edges.

To do this, we remove any vertex v of K_n, together with its $n - 1$ incident edges. The remaining graph is the complete graph K_{n-1} which, by our assumption, has $\frac{1}{2}(n-1)(n-2)$ edges. Reinstating v gives, for K_n, a total of

$$\tfrac{1}{2}(n-1)(n-2) + (n-1) = \{\tfrac{1}{2}(n-2) + 1\}(n-1) = \tfrac{1}{2}n(n-1)$$

edges. Thus b. holds, and the result is therefore true for all n. ☐

THEOREM 2. *Every tree with* n *vertices has exactly* n − 1 *edges.*

Proof The result holds when $n = 1$, since the only tree with one vertex is K_1, which has no edges. Now assume that the result holds for trees with less than n vertices—that is, that every tree with k vertices has $k - 1$ edges whenever $k < n$. We must deduce that every tree T with n vertices has $n - 1$ edges.

To do this, remove any edge e of T. Since T has no cycles, this gives two trees, with k_1 and k_2 vertices, say, where $k_1 + k_2 = n$. By our assumption, these trees have $k_1 - 1$ and $k_2 - 1$ edges, respectively. Reinstating e gives, for T, a total of

$$(k_1 - 1) + (k_2 - 1) + 1 = k_1 + k_2 - 1 = n - 1$$

edges. Thus b. holds, and the result is therefore true for all n. ☐

A similar approach can be used when we wish to prove a result concerning graphs with a given number of edges. For example, we can adapt the proof of Theorem 2 to show that every tree with m edges has $m + 1$ vertices; in such proofs, we usually replace a. by: *the result holds for graphs with no edges.* Another example of an induction proof involving edges, rather than vertices, is as follows.

THEOREM 3. *If* G *is a graph in which every vertex has even degree, then* G *can be split into disjoint cycles—that is, no two cycles have any edges in common.*

Proof The result clearly holds when the number of edges is zero. Now assume that the result holds for graphs with less than m edges—that is, that any graph with k edges in which every vertex has even degree can be split into disjoint cycles whenever $k < m$. We must deduce the corresponding result for graphs with m edges.

So let G be a graph with m edges in which every vertex has even degree, and let $v_0, \ldots, v_t$ be the vertices of a path P of greatest length G. Since v_t has even degree, it is joined to some vertex v other than v_{t-1}. Since P is a path of greatest length, v must be one of the vertices $v_0, \ldots, v_{t-2}$ — say $v = v_i$. Then $v_i, v_{i+1}, \ldots, v_t, v_i$ are the vertices of a cycle C in G. Removing the edges of C from G yields a graph G_1 with fewer than m edges, in which every vertex still has even degree. By our assumption, the edges of G_1 can be split into disjoint cycles; together with C, these give the corresponding cycles for G, as required. ☐

In Part II, we shall see both types of induction proofs: those involving induction on the number of vertices, and those involving induction on the number of edges.

PART II

INTRODUCTION

In this part of the book we consider a number of problems, such as the following:

The Königsberg Bridges Problem In the eighteenth century, the medieval city of Königsberg in Eastern Prussia contained a central island called Kneiphof, around which the river Pregel flowed before dividing into two. The four parts of the city were interconnected by seven bridges, as shown in the following diagram. It is said that the citizens of Königsberg entertained themselves by trying to find a route crossing each bridge exactly once, and returning to the starting point. Can this be done?

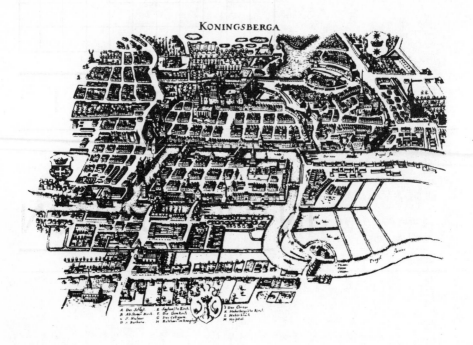

The Shortest Path Problem   A traveler wishes to drive from Los Angeles to New York in the shortest possible time. The following map gives the time (in hours) taken to drive between particular pairs of cities. Given this information, which route should the traveler take?

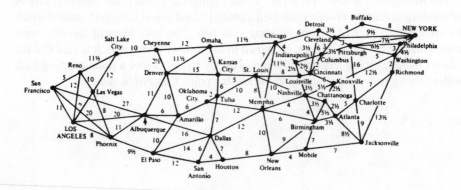

The Traveling Salesman Problem   A salesman wishes to visit a number of cities and return to the starting point, in such a way that each city is visited exactly once, and the total distance covered is as short as possible. Given the various distances between the cities, what route should be chosen?

The Printed Circuits Problem

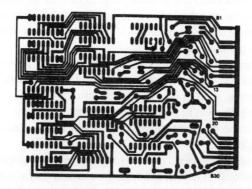

In printed circuits, electronic components are constructed by means of conducting strips printed directly onto a flat board of insulating material. Such printed connectors may not cross, since this would lead to undesirable electrical contact at crossing points. Circuits in which large numbers of crossings are unavoidable may be printed on several boards which are then sandwiched together with suitable interconnections. Each board consists of a printed circuit without crossings. What is the smallest number of such layers for a given circuit?

The Map-Coloring Problem   Consider the following map of the United States of America (excluding Alaska and Hawaii):

It is very common for maps of this kind to be colored in such a way that neighboring states are colored differently. This enables us to distinguish easily between the various states, and to locate the state boundaries. What is the minimum number of colors needed to color the entire map?

Problems of this kind are partly graph-theoretical in nature, since they all involve systems which are interconnected in some way. In fact, as we show in this part of the book, the first three can be modeled as problems involving paths or cycles in a graph, and the last two involve the decomposition of the set of vertices or edges of a graph into disjoint subsets of a particular type.

For some problems, such as the shortest path problem, our answer will take the form of an algorithm—that is, a finite step-by-step procedure for obtaining the solution in a routine way. For others, such as the Königsberg bridges problem, our answer is in the form of a theorem which gives necessary and sufficient conditions for a solution to exist. However, even for these problems, there are sometimes algorithms for finding explicit solutions when they exist.

We start Part II with two chapters on Eulerian and Hamiltonian graphs and digraphs. They are somewhat recreational in nature, although the material they contain has been used in several practical problems. The basic idea is to find a closed trail that passes through every edge or vertex of a given graph exactly once. In particular, we consider such problems as the Königsberg bridges problem, the knight's tour problem on a chessboard, and the tracing of mazes, as well as problems in telecommunications and coding theory.

In Chapter 8, on path algorithms, we describe an algorithm for solving the shortest path problem. We also describe an algorithm for finding the longest path in a given digraph, and briefly relate this algorithm to the problem of scheduling a number of interdependent activities, such as those involved in a complex building project. In Chapter 9 a discussion of connectivity is presented, in which we investigate the extent to which a given graph or digraph is connected. Such considerations are important when designing telecommunication networks or road systems.

In Chapter 10 we discuss trees and their applications in various areas. In particular, we introduce methods for searching trees, and we illustrate the use of a tree algorithm in finding a lower bound for the solution of the traveling salesman problem.

In Chapter 11 we study planar graphs and develop techniques for attacking such problems as the printed circuits problem. Chapters 12 and 13 give a detailed discussion of the coloring of graphs and maps, with particular reference to the map-coloring problem described above. In Chapter 14 we interrelate these topics by formulating them as decomposition problems which involve splitting the vertices or edges of a graph into subsets with certain specified properties. Finally, in Chapter 15, we point out and discuss some common themes running through the book.

The problems we discuss in Part II vary considerably in terms of how much work has been done on them, and how much is known about their solution. Some have elegant theoretical solutions but lack efficient algorithms. Others have good algorithms which work in practice, but lack complete theoretical solutions. For some problems, such as that of determining whether a given graph is planar, there exists a complete theoretical solution together with a number of efficient algorithms. Finally, there is the map-coloring problem which has a theoretical solution which is so complicated that it originally took 1200 hours of computer time to find it!

CHAPTER 6

EULERIAN GRAPHS
AND DIGRAPHS

6.1 INTRODUCTION

This chapter and the next are somewhat recreational in nature, although the material they contain has been used in several practical problems. In particular, we consider two types of problem.

The Explorer's Problem   An explorer wishes to explore all the routes between a number of cities. Can a tour be found which traverses each route only once?

The Traveler's Problem   A traveler wishes to visit a number of cities. Can a tour be found which visits each city only once?

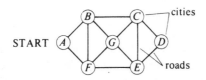

To appreciate the difference between these two problems, consider the above road map. The explorer wishes to find a tour which starts at A, goes along each road exactly once, and ends back at A. Examples of such a tour are

$$ABCDEFBGCEGFA \quad \text{and} \quad AFGCDEGBCEFBA.$$

The traveler wishes to find a tour which starts at A, goes to each city exactly once, and ends back at A. Examples of such a tour are

$$ABCDEGFA \quad \text{and} \quad AFEDCGBA.$$

Note that the explorer travels along each road just once but may visit a particular city several times, whereas the traveler visits each city just once but may omit several of the roads on the way.

Let us now regard this road map as a graph whose vertices correspond to the cities and whose edges correspond to the roads. The explorer's problem is then the problem of *finding a closed trail which includes every edge of the graph,* whereas the traveler's problem is that of *finding a cycle which includes every vertex of the graph.*

With this in mind, we make the following definitions—the reason for these names will appear later. You can easily remember which of these definitions is which, since *E*ulerian graphs involve *E*dges.

DEFINITIONS. *A connected graph* G *is* **Eulerian** *if there is a closed trail which includes every edge of* G; *such a trail is called an* **Eulerian trail**.

A connected graph G *is* **Hamiltonian** *if there is a cycle which includes every vertex of* G; *such a cycle is called a* **Hamiltonian cycle**.

For example, consider the four graphs

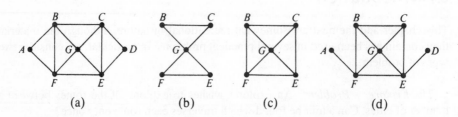

(a)   (b)   (c)   (d)

Graph (a) is both Eulerian and Hamiltonian, as we saw above;

Graph (b) is Eulerian, but not Hamiltonian; an Eulerian trail is $BCGFEGB$;

Graph (c) is Hamiltonian, but not Eulerian; a Hamiltonian cycle is $BCGEFB$;

Graph (d) is neither Eulerian nor Hamiltonian.

We now consider these two types of graph in turn. In this chapter, we give a *necessary and sufficient* condition for a connected graph to be Eulerian, and we show the connections between Eulerian graphs and snow-clearing the roads in a city, escaping from a maze, and a problem in telecommunications. In the next chapter, we give *sufficient* conditions for a connected graph to be Hamiltonian, and show the connections between Hamiltonian graphs and a chess problem, the theory of codes, and product testing. Because of the importance of Eulerian and Hamiltonian graphs in the development of graph theory, much of the material in these chapters is presented from a historical point of view.

6.2 EULERIAN GRAPHS

The four parts (A, B, C, and D) of the city of Königsberg were interconnected by seven bridges (a, b, c, d, e, f, and g) as shown in the following diagram:

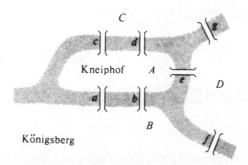

Try as they might, the citizens of Königsberg could find no route crossing each bridge exactly once and returning to the starting point, and they began to believe the task impossible. However, it was not until Leonhard Euler (1707–1783) investigated the problem that it was *proved* to be impossible. (Euler was one of the most prolific mathematicians of all time, and made substantial contributions to a number of different areas.)

Euler's proof appeared in his 1736 paper *Solutio problematis ad geometriam situs pertinentis,* which was mentioned in Chapter 2. Although this paper was not written in the language of graphs, the ideas in it are essentially graph-theoretical in nature, and it can fairly be described as the earliest paper on the subject. The portion of this paper which relates directly to the solution of the Königsberg bridges problem is given in an Appendix to this chapter.

We can express the Königsberg bridges problem in terms of a graph by taking the four land areas as vertices and the seven bridges as edges joining the corresponding pairs of vertices. This gives the graph shown below. The problem of *finding a route crossing each bridge exactly once* corresponds exactly to that of *finding an Eulerian trail in this graph.* As we shall see, no such Eulerian trail exists. It follows that there is no route of the desired kind crossing the seven bridges of Königsberg.

Euler also considered the corresponding problem of finding a route crossing all the bridges in a more general arrangement of bridges and land areas. This led him to present a rule which tells us when such a route is possible, and hence when the corresponding graph is Eulerian.

Consider the following diagram, adapted from Euler's paper:

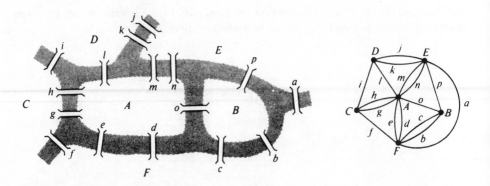

By drawing the corresponding graph and finding an Eulerian trail in it, we can obtain a route which crosses each of the sixteen bridges exactly once and returns to the starting point. For example, we can start at E and cross the bridges in the order

$$a\,b\,c\,d\,e\,f\,g\,h\,i\,j\,k\,l\,m\,n\,o\,p.$$

It is clear that finding a route which crosses each bridge just once (that is, finding an Eulerian trail in the graph) is possible if and only if the following condition is satisfied:

whenever you cross into a part of the city, you must be able to leave it by another bridge.

This means that whenever you go into any vertex, you must be able to leave it by another edge. It follows that each time you pass through a vertex you contribute exactly 2 to the degree of that vertex. (This is also true of the first and last edges, which contribute 2 to the degree of the starting vertex.) So, in an Eulerian graph, each vertex-degree must be a sum of 2's—that is, an even number.

degree 6

The rule that Euler presented (in different terminology) is:

to test whether a given connected graph is Eulerian, look at the degrees of the vertices: if they are all even, then the graph is Eulerian; if not, then the graph is not Eulerian.

In short, check whether or not all the vertex-degrees are even. Thus, the condition *all the vertex-degrees of* G *are even* is necessary and sufficient to ensure that G is *Eulerian*. We now justify this rule.

THEOREM 6.1. *Let G be a connected graph. Then G is Eulerian if and only if every vertex of G has even degree.*

Proof   There are two parts to the proof:

1. If G is Eulerian, then every vertex of G has even degree;
2. If every vertex of G has even degree, then G is Eulerian.

Part 1 shows that the condition is *necessary;* part 2 shows that it is *sufficient.*

1. If G has an Eulerian trail, then we can travel along that trail, using each edge once, and return to our starting point. Whenever we pass through a vertex of G, there is a contribution of 2 towards the degree of that vertex—including the initial vertex, since we end there. Since each edge of G is used just once, the degree of each vertex is the sum of a number of 2's—that is, an even number.
2. Suppose that every vertex of G has even degree. We must show that we can find an Eulerian trail in G. First, we note that G contains a cycle C, by the proof of Theorem 3 in the Appendix on Proofs.

We now use mathematical induction on m, the number of edges in G. For $m = 0$, the only connected graph in which every vertex has even degree is the complete graph K_1, which is clearly Eulerian. So assume that the statement in part 2 is true for any connected graph with fewer than m edges, and consider a graph G with m edges. Delete the edges of the cycle C from G. The resulting graph H then has fewer than m edges and every vertex in H has even degree. Although H may not be connected, each component of H is connected and has only vertices of even degree. Therefore, by the induction hypothesis, each component of H is Eulerian.

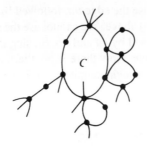

We can now find an Eulerian trail for G as follows. We start at any vertex v on the cycle C and traverse the edges of C until we come to one of the components of H. We then take the Eulerian trail for this component, eventually returning to the cycle C. We continue along C in this fashion, taking Eulerian trails of the components of H as we come to them, and eventually return to the starting vertex v having traversed each edge of G exactly once—that is, we have obtained an Eulerian trail. ☐

The disadvantage of the above proof is that it is not constructive, in the sense that it does not show us how to construct an Eulerian trail in a given graph. One way of constructing an Eulerian trail is to use the following algorithm, or step-by-step procedure, which we state without proof. Recall (from Chapter 4) that a **bridge** in a connected graph is an edge whose removal disconnects the graph.

FLEURY'S ALGORITHM.   *If G is an Eulerian graph, then the following steps can always be carried out, and produce an Eulerian trail in G:*

STEP 1   Choose a starting vertex *u*.

STEP 2   At each stage, traverse any available edge, choosing a bridge only if there is no alternative.

STEP 3   After traversing each edge, erase it (erasing any vertices of degree 0 which result), and then choose another available edge.

STEP 4   STOP when there are no more edges.

This algorithm is very easy to apply. At each stage, we choose a bridge *only as a last resort*—this qualification is clearly essential, since once we have traversed a bridge, we cannot return to the part of the graph we have just left.

We illustrate the use of Fleury's algorithm by applying it to the following graph (a):

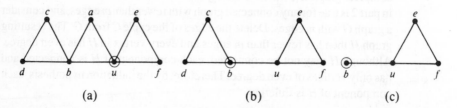

(a)   (b)   (c)

Starting at *u*, we may choose the edge *ua*, followed by *ab*. Erasing these edges (and the vertex *a*) gives us graph (b) above. We cannot use the edge *bu* since it is a bridge, so we choose the edge *bc*, followed by *cd* and *db*. Erasing these edges (and the vertices *c* and *d*) gives us graph (c) above. Now there is no alternative—we have to traverse the bridge *bu*. Traversing the cycle *uefu* completes the Eulerian trail. The trail is therefore *uabcdbuefu*.

6.3 EULERIAN-TYPE PROBLEMS

There are several simple modifications of the above ideas which are worth mentioning. These range from puzzles of a recreational nature to a study of snow-clearing routes in a major city.

Edge-traceable graphs

Suppose that the citizens of Königsberg were still interested in crossing each of the seven bridges exactly once, but were content to start and finish their walk at different places. Would the walk be possible under these less restrictive conditions?

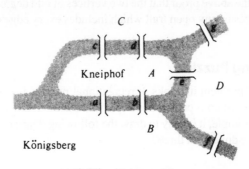

A little experimentation with the diagram above will convince you that, even with this modification to the conditions, such a walk is not possible. This leads us to define an **open trail** to be a trail whose ends do not coincide.

DEFINITION. *A connected graph* G *is* **edge-traceable** *if there is an open trail which includes every edge of* G.

Using Theorem 6.1, we can easily give a necessary and sufficient condition for a graph to be edge-traceable.

THEOREM 6.2. *Let* G *be a connected graph. Then* G *is edge-traceable if and only if* G *has exactly two vertices of odd degree.*

Proof Let G be an edge-traceable graph, and let v and w be the starting and finishing vertices of the open trail. If we add an edge e joining the vertices v and w, we get an Eulerian graph in which, by Theorem 6.1, every vertex must have even degree. If we now recover G by removing the edge e, we see that v and w are the only vertices of odd degree.

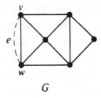

G

Now suppose that G has exactly two vertices v and w of odd degree. If we add an edge e joining the vertices v and w, we get a connected graph in which every vertex has even degree. By Theorem 6.1, this graph must be Eulerian, and so must possess an Eulerian trail. Removal of the edge e from this trail produces an open trail which includes every edge of G, so G is edge-traceable. □

It follows from the above proof that the two vertices of odd degree must be the starting and finishing vertices of any open trail which includes every edge of G.

Diagram-Tracing Puzzles

A common type of problem in books of recreational puzzles is that of drawing a given diagram in as few continuous penstrokes as possible, without covering any part of the diagram twice. For example, it is easy to draw the following diagram with four continuous strokes, but can it be done with three?

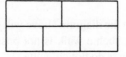

In 1809, L. Poinsot showed that diagrams consisting of n interconnected points can be drawn in one continuous stroke if n is odd, but not if n is even:

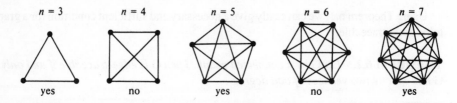

In the terminology of graph theory, this amounts to saying that the complete graph K_n is Eulerian only for odd values of n, as follows from Theorem 6.1. What is remarkable about Poinsot's account of the subject is that he gave an ingenious construction for finding an Eulerian trail when n is odd—no mean feat, as you would see if you tried to describe a method for constructing an Eulerian trail in (say) K_{99}.

In 1847, J. B. Listing wrote an important treatise entitled *Vorstudien zur Topologie (Introductory Studies in Topology)*, which included a discussion of diagram-tracing puzzles. In particular, he observed that the diagram in the puzzle posed above has eight vertices of odd degree, and so cannot possibly be drawn with fewer than four continuous strokes. He also remarked that the following diagram can be drawn in one continuous stroke, starting at one end and ending at the other, since these are the only points which correspond to vertices of odd degree:

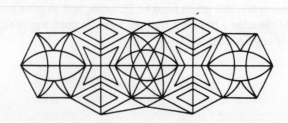

Dominoes

We have already seen that the complete graph K_7 is Eulerian, since each of its vertices has degree 6. If the vertices are labeled 0, 1, 2, 3, 4, 5, and 6, then an Eulerian trail is obtained by tracing the edges in the following order:

01,12,23,34,45,56,60,02,24,46,61,13,35,50,03,36,62,25,51,14,40.

We can regard each of these edges as a domino—for example, the edge 24 corresponds to the domino

It follows that the above Eulerian trail corresponds to an arrangement of all the dominoes of a normal set (other than the doubles 0–0, 1–1, ..., 6–6) in a continuous sequence. Once this basic sequence is found, we can then insert the doubles at appropriate places, thereby showing that a complete game of dominoes is possible. The following ring of dominoes corresponds to the above Eulerian trail:

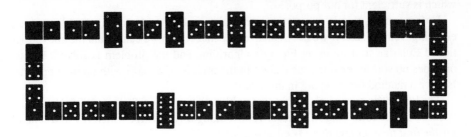

Mazes and Labyrinths

At the end of the nineteenth century much attention was devoted to the problem of escaping from a maze. We can explain what is involved, and show how it relates to Eulerian graphs, by choosing a particular maze, such as the one at Hampton Court.

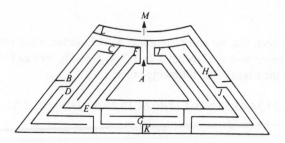

If we have access to a map of the maze, we can represent it by a graph which indicates the available choices at each junction. For example, in the Hampton Court maze, we have two choices at the point *B*—to go to *C* or to *D*—and we obtain

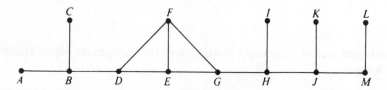

We can get from the center of the maze (A) to the exit (M) by following the path *ABDEGHJM*, and ignoring all other passages.

Let us now look for a path which starts at the center and ends at the exit of an arbitrary maze. In fact, we shall be less specific and ask simply for a walk which contains every edge of the corresponding graph, since such a walk must pass through the center and exit at some stage. Provided that the graph is connected, we can always find such a walk. To see this, simply replace each edge by a pair of multiple edges; the result is a new graph in which every vertex has even degree, and so this graph has an Eulerian trail. It follows that in the original graph there is always a walk which contains each edge exactly twice, which is sufficient for our purposes.

Unfortunately, this is an *existence* argument, and provides no method for actually escaping from a maze. If we have a map of the maze, then we can obtain the above-mentioned Eulerian trail by using Fleury's algorithm, and the problem is solved. But this provides no solace for someone caught in the middle of a maze with no map provided. Is there a method for escaping in this case?

The best maze-tracing algorithm was published by Gaston Tarry in 1895. His method is based on the following rule: *never return along any passage which led to a junction for the first time, unless there is no alternative.*

By tracing through the maze, following this rule at each junction, we can escape from any connected maze passing at most twice (once in each direction) along each passage. The only difficulty is in recognizing which of the passages leading to a junction was the one which led there for the first time. Fortunately, Tarry also gave some rules for doing this:

    a.   *When traversing a passage for the first time, leave two markers at the entrance, and one or three markers at the exit, depending on whether the junction has been visited previously or not.*

b. *When entering a passage with a single marker, leave a second marker in the same place.*

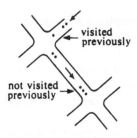

Using these rules, we can immediately recognize whether or not a given passage has been previously traversed, as follows:

No marker: the passage has not been traversed in either direction, so may be used;

One marker: the passage has been traversed *into* the junction, so may now be used *out of* it;

Two markers: the passage has already been traversed out of that junction, so may not be used again in that direction;

Three markers: this was the first passage traversed into the junction, so may not be taken unless there are no passages with 0 or 1 markers.

By applying Tarry's rules, we can escape from the center of a maze without traversing any passage more than twice (once in each direction).

The Chinese Postman Problem

An important problem which has appeared in various guises is the so-called *Chinese postman problem*. (The word *Chinese* refers to the problem, not the postman! The problem was formulated in 1962 by Meigu Guan.) It may be stated as follows:

The Chinese Postman Problem   A postman wishes to deliver mail along all the streets in his area, and then return to the post office. How can the route be planned so as to cover the smallest total distance?

If the map of the postman's area happens to correspond to an Eulerian graph, then there is no difficulty with this problem—the postman simply chooses an Eulerian trail (using Fleury's algorithm, if necessary), and such a trail will involve the smallest total distance. What usually happens in practice, of course, is that the postman needs to visit some parts of the route more than once, and wants to minimize the amount of retracing. We may assume that we know the length of each part of the route.

Similar problems have arisen in other contexts. For example, there was a major study of snow-clearing routes in Zurich some years ago. Since snow-clearing equipment is expensive to operate, it was necessary to arrange a route which involved reclearing streets as little as possible. Other cities have initiated similar investigations into the sweeping or cleaning of streets.

We can reformulate the Chinese postman problem in terms of *weighted graphs*, defined as follows:

DEFINITION.   *A* **weighted graph** *is a graph to each edge of which has been assigned a positive number, called its* **weight.**

Using this definition, the Chinese postman problem becomes: *find a closed walk of minimum total weight which includes every edge at least once.*

This problem has been solved in general, using a method which combines features of Fleury's algorithm and the shortest path algorithm (discussed in Chapter 8). We can get an idea of what is involved, by considering the particular case of a graph with just two vertices v and w of odd degree, such as graph (a):

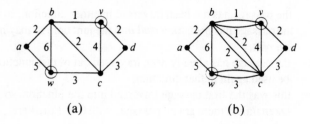

(a)   (b)

The path of minimum weight from v to w is easily seen to be *vbcw*, with total weight $1 + 2 + 3 = 6$. If we 'double up' each of the edges in the path, we get the Eulerian graph (b) above. The required closed walk of minimum total weight is then obtained by taking an Eulerian trail in this graph, such as *abvdcvbcbwcwa*. Note that the only edges which need to be retraced are the edges of the path *vbcw*.

For graphs with more than two vertices of odd degree, we can adapt this method, linking such vertices with shortest paths. Unfortunately, the details of this procedure are too complicated to be included here.

Eulerian Digraphs

Up to now our discussion has been concerned with the problem of finding a trail which includes every edge of a *graph* exactly once, and it is natural to consider the corresponding problem for digraphs. This immediately leads to the following definitions.

DEFINITIONS.   *A connected digraph D is* **Eulerian** *if there is a closed trail which includes every arc of D; such a trail is called an* **Eulerian trail** *in D. A connected digraph D is* **arc-traceable** *if there is an open trail which includes every arc of D.*

For example, consider the digraphs

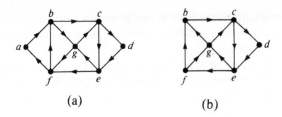

(a)   (b)

Digraph (a) is Eulerian: an Eulerian trail is *abcdefbgcegfa*;
digraph (b) is arc-traceable: a suitable open trail is *fgcdegbcefb*.

Most of the earlier discussion of Eulerian graphs can be adapted very easily to Eulerian digraphs. In particular, there are natural analogs of Theorems 6.1 and 6.2:

THEOREM 6.3. *Let* D *be a connected digraph. Then*

1. D *is Eulerian if and only if the out-degree of each vertex equals the in-degree*;
2. D *is arc-traceable if and only if there are two vertices* x *and* y *of* D *such that*

$$\text{outdeg } x - \text{indeg } x = 1, \text{ indeg } y - \text{outdeg } y = 1$$

and indeg v = outdeg v *for all vertices* v *other than* x *or* y.

The proof of this theorem is very similar to the proofs of Theorems 6.1 and 6.2, and is left to you to supply if you wish. In the sufficiency parts of the proof, the essential idea is to show that *D* contains a (directed) cycle, and then use induction, as in the proof of Theorem 6.1.

The Rotating Drum Problem

We conclude our brief discussion of Eulerian digraphs with a problem which arises in telecommunications—the so-called *rotating drum problem* or *teleprinter's problem*.

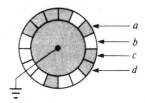

The surface of a rotating drum is divided into 16 parts, as shown on the left. We can represent the position of the drum by means of four binary digits *a, b, c,* and *d,* as indicated on the right. In this diagram, the shaded areas represent conducting materials and the unshaded areas represent non-conducting materials. Depending on the position of the drum, the terminals represented by *a, b, c,* and *d* will either be grounded or be insulated from the earth—for example, in the above diagram, the grounded terminals are *a, c,* and *d.*

In order that the 16 positions of the drum may be represented uniquely by the signals

a, b, c, and d, the conducting areas must be placed in such a way that all possible patterns of four consecutive conducting and non-conducting positions occur. Can this be done and, if so, how can it be arranged?

A solution is given in the right-hand diagram above. The position shown corresponds to the binary number 1011, where 1 corresponds to a shaded (conducting) area, and 0 corresponds to an unshaded (non-conducting) area. Rotating the drum counterclockwise successively gives us the following binary numbers:

$$0110, 1100, 1001, 0010, 0100, 1000, 0000, 0001,$$

$$0011, 0111, 1111, 1110, 1101, 1010, 0101, 1011.$$

These four-bit numbers are all different, and represent all 16 positions of the drum. But how did we obtain this solution, and are there any other solutions?

In order to answer these questions, we construct a digraph: there are eight vertices, corresponding to the three-bit binary words

$$000, 001, 010, 011, 100, 101, 110, 111;$$

there are arcs from each vertex abc to the vertices $bc0$ and $bc1$. This gives us the digraph

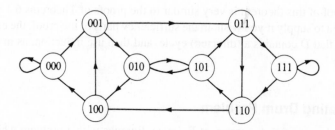

This digraph is clearly Eulerian, since the in-degree and out-degree of each vertex are equal to 2. Any Eulerian trail can then be used to give a solution of the rotating drum problem. For example, if we take the Eulerian trail

$$101 \to 011 \to 110 \to 100 \to 001 \to 010 \to 100 \to 000 \to$$
$$000 \to 001 \to 011 \to 111 \to 111 \to 110 \to 101 \to 010 \to 101,$$

we can 'compress' consecutive terms cumulatively (for example, $011 \to 110$ compresses to 0110) to give the sequence

$$1\,0\,1\,1\,0\,0\,1\,0\,0\,0\,0\,1\,1\,1\,1\,0\,\ldots.$$

This gives the circular arrangement shown in the diagram.

Using a similar argument, we can answer the corresponding question for rotating drums with 32, 64, ... divisions.

PROBLEMS

Eulerian Graphs

○6.1. Decide which of the following graphs are Eulerian or Hamiltonian, or both, and write down an Eulerian trail or Hamiltonian cycle where possible.

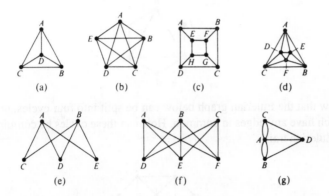

(a)   (b)   (c)   (d)

(e)   (f)   (g)

6.2. Give an example with at most six vertices of each of the following:

a. a Hamiltonian graph which is not Eulerian;

b. an Eulerian graph which is not Hamiltonian.

○6.3. It was reported in 1875 by L. Saalschütz that an extra bridge had been built in Königsberg, joining the land areas B and C:

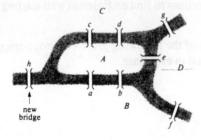

Is the walk now possible?

6.4. Show how the citizens of Königsberg could have built *two* new bridges in such a way that they could have taken their tour and returned to their starting point.

○6.5. Which of the following graphs are Eulerian?

a. the complete graphs K_n;

b. the complete bipartite graphs $K_{r,s}$;

c. the cycle graphs C_n;

d. the five Platonic graphs;

e. the cube graphs Q_n;

f. the Petersen graph.

6.6. Using the graph cards in Chapter 1, determine which graphs with six vertices are Eulerian.

6.7. Show how the Eulerian graph below can be split into cycles, no two of which have any edges in common. (There are five possible solutions.) How can these cycles be recombined to form an Eulerian trail?

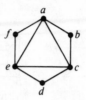

☉6.8. Show that the Eulerian graph below can be split into four cycles, no two of which have any edges in common. How can these cycles be combined to form an Eulerian trail?

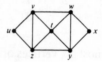

Eulerian-type Problems

☉6.9. Use Fleury's algorithm to find an Eulerian trail starting with *uvz* in the graph of Problem 6.8.

☉6.10. Determine which of the following graphs are edge-traceable, and give a corresponding open trail in each case.

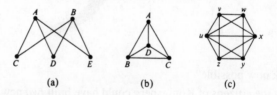

(a)   (b)   (c)

6.11. Decide whether each of the following graphs is Eulerian, edge-traceable, or neither.

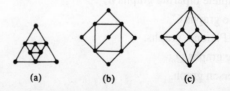

(a)   (b)   (c)

○6.12. Theorems 6.1 and 6.2 tell us about the properties of graphs with zero or two vertices of odd degree. What can you say about graphs with exactly one vertex of odd degree?

6.13. How many continuous penstrokes are required to draw the following diagrams without covering any part twice?

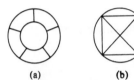

    (a)   (b)   (c)   (d)

6.14.† Show how Listing's diagram (on page 128) can be drawn in one continuous stroke.

○6.15. Show that, if a graph G has $2k$ vertices of odd degree, then the smallest number of continuous penstrokes needed to cover all the edges of G is k.
(*Hint*: Add k edges to G in a suitable manner.)

6.16. By finding an Eulerian trail in K_5, arrange a set of 15 dominoes (from 0–0 to 4–4) in a ring.

6.17. Draw the graph corresponding to the following maze, and use it to find a way into the center (*) and out again.

○6.18. If you were tracing the Hampton Court maze (page 130) using Tarry's algorithm, and you followed the walk

$$ABCBDEFDFGHIHJM,$$

how many markers would you put down at each stage?

○6.19. Solve the Chinese postman problem for the following graph:

6.20. Solve the Chinese postman problem for the following graph:

6.21. Solve the Chinese postman problem for the following graphs:

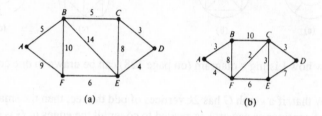

(a)   (b)

Eulerian Digraphs

☼6.22. Determine which of the following digraphs are Eulerian or arc-traceable, and give a suitable trail in each case.

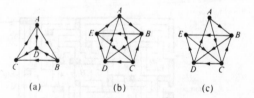

(a)   (b)   (c)

6.23. Determine whether the following digraph is Eulerian or arc-traceable, and give a suitable trail.

6.24. Consider the rotating drum problem for a drum with eight positions. Choose one of the following digraphs to solve this problem, and find two sequences which give rise to suitable circular arrangements.

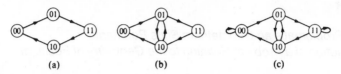

(a)   (b)   (c)

6.25.† Solve the rotating drum problem for a drum with 32 divisions.

APPENDIX TO CHAPTER 6

L. Euler

Solutio Problematis ad Geometriam Situs Pertinentis
(The Solution of a Problem Relating to the Geometry of Position)

Commentarii Academiae Scientiarum Imperialis Petropolitanae **8***(1736)*,
128–140.

1.   In addition to that branch of geometry which is concerned with magnitudes,
and which has always received the greatest attention, there is another branch,
previously almost unknown, which Leibniz first mentioned, calling it the *geometry of position*. This branch is concerned only with the determination of position and its properties; it does not involve measurements, nor calculations
made with them. It has not yet been satisfactorily determined what kind of
problems are relevant to this geometry of position, or what methods should be
used in solving them. Hence, when a problem was recently mentioned, which
seemed geometrical but was so constructed that it did not require the measure-
ment of distances, nor did calculation help at all, I had no doubt that it was concerned with the geometry of position—especially as its solution involved only
position, and no calculation was of any use. I have therefore decided to give
here the method which I have found for solving this kind of problem, as an example of the geometry of position.

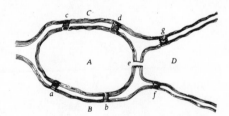

2.   The problem, which I am told is widely known, is as follows: in Königsberg in
Prussia, there is an island *A*, called *the Kneiphof*; the river which surrounds it
is divided into two branches, as can be seen in the figure, and these branches
are crossed by seven bridges *a, b, c, d, e, f,* and *g*. Concerning these bridges, it
was asked whether anyone could arrange a route in such a way that he would
cross each bridge once and only once. I was told that some people asserted that
this was impossible, while others were in doubt; but nobody would actually as-
sert that it could be done. From this, I have formulated the general problem:
whatever be the arrangement and division of the river into branches, and however many bridges there be, can one find out whether or not it is possible to
cross each bridge exactly once?

3.   As far as the problem of the seven bridges of Königsberg is concerned, it can be solved by making an exhaustive list of all possible routes, and then finding whether or not any route satisfies the conditions of the problem. Because of the number of possibilities, this method of solution would be too difficult and laborious, and in other problems with more bridges it would be impossible. Moreover, if this method is followed to its conclusion, many irrelevant routes will be found, which is the reason for the difficulty of this method. Hence I rejected it and looked for another method concerned only with the problem of whether or not the specified route could be found; I considered that such a method would be much simpler.

4.   My whole method relies on the particularly convenient way in which the crossing of a bridge can be represented. For this I use the capital letters A, B, C, D for each of the land areas separated by the river. If a traveler goes from A to B over bridge a or b, I write this as AB—where the first letter refers to the area the traveler is leaving, and the second refers to the area he arrives at after crossing the bridge. Thus if the traveler leaves B and crosses into D over bridge f, this crossing is represented by BD, and the two crossings AB and BD combined I shall denote by the three letters ABD, where the middle letter B refers both to the area which is entered in the first crossing and to the one which is left in the second crossing.

5.   Similarly, if the traveler goes on from D to C over the bridge g, I shall represent these three successive crossings by the four letters $ABDC$, which should be taken to mean that the traveler, starting in A, crosses to B, goes on to D, and finally arrives in C. Since each land area is separated from every other by a branch of the river, the traveler must have crossed three bridges. Similarly, the successive crossing of four bridges would be represented by five letters, and in general, however many bridges the traveler crosses, his journey is denoted by a number of letters one greater than the number of bridges. Thus the crossing of seven bridges requires eight letters to represent it.

6.   In this method of representation, I take no account of the bridges by which the crossing is made, but if the crossing from one area to another can be made by several bridges, then any bridge can be used, so long as the required area is reached. It follows that if a journey across the seven bridges can be arranged in such a way that each bridge is crossed once, but none twice, then the route can be represented by eight letters which are arranged so that the letters A and B are next to each other twice, since there are two bridges, a and b, connecting the areas A and B; similarly, A and C must be adjacent twice in the series of eight letters, and the pairs A and D, B, and D, and C and D must occur together once each.

7.   The problem is therefore reduced to finding a sequence of eight letters, formed from the four letters A, B, C, and D, in which the various pairs of letters occur the required number of times. Before I turn to the problem of finding such a sequence, it would be useful to find out whether or not it is even possible to arrange the letters in this way, for if it were possible to show that there is no such arrangement, then any work directed towards finding it would be wasted.

I have therefore tried to find a rule which will be useful in this case, and in others, for determining whether or not such an arrangement can exist.

8.   In order to try to find such a rule, I consider a single area A, into which there lead any number of bridges a, b, c, d, etc. Let us take first the single bridge a which leads into A: if a traveler crosses this bridge, he must either have been in A before crossing, or have come into A after crossing, so that in either case the letter A will occur once in the representation described above. If three bridges ($a, b,$ and c, say) lead to A, and if the traveler crosses all three, then in the representation of his journey the letter A will occur twice, whether he starts his journey from A or not. Similarly, if five bridges lead to A, the representation of a journey across all of them would have three occurrences of the letter A. And in general, if the number of bridges is any odd number, and if it is increased by one, then the number of occurrences of A is half of the result.

9.   In the case of the Königsberg bridges, therefore, there must be three occurrences of the letter A in the representation of the route, since five bridges (a, b, c, d, e) lead to the area A. Next, since three bridges lead to B, the letter B must occur twice; similarly, D must occur twice, and C also. So in a series of eight letters, representing the crossing of seven bridges, the letter A must occur three times, and the letters $B, C,$ and D twice each—but this cannot happen in a sequence of eight letters. It follows that such a journey cannot be undertaken across the seven bridges of Königsberg.

(Reprinted, with permission, from N.L. Biggs, E.K. Lloyd, and R.J. Wilson, *Graph Theory 1736–1936*, Oxford University Press, Oxford, England, 1976.)

CHAPTER 7

HAMILTONIAN GRAPHS
AND DIGRAPHS

7.1 INTRODUCTION

We now turn our attention to Hamiltonian graphs—graphs in which there is a cycle passing through every vertex. The name *Hamiltonian* derives from a game invented by Sir William Rowan Hamilton (1805–1865), one of the leading mathematicians of his time. He was a child prodigy, became Astronomer Royal of Ireland at 22, and was knighted at 30. He did brilliant work in geometrical optics, dynamics, and algebra.

Hamilton's Icosian Game and the Knight's Tour Problem

One of the most significant of Hamilton's discoveries was the existence of algebraic systems in which the commutative law for multiplication ($xy = yx$) does not hold. His *algebra of quaternions,* or *Icosian calculus* (as he called it), can be expressed in terms of Hamiltonian cycles on the regular dodecahedron

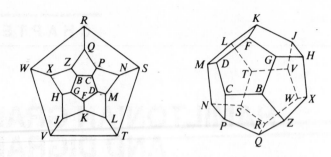

He also turned the problem into a game, the *Icosian game,* in which the player has to find Hamiltonian cycles starting with five given initial letters. For example, given the initial letters *BCPNM,* the player can complete a Hamiltonian cycle in exactly two possible ways:

$$BCPNMDFKLTSRQZXWVJHGB \quad \text{and} \quad BCPNMDFGHXWVJKLTSRQZB.$$

The game was marketed in 1859, accompanied by a printed leaflet of instructions. It also appeared in a solid dodecahedron form under the title *A Voyage Round the World,* with the vertices representing places—Brussels, Canton, Delhi, ..., Zanzibar. Hamilton sold the idea of the Icosian game to a wholesale dealer of games and puzzles for £25, but it turned out to be a bad bargain—for the dealer.

The name *Hamiltonian cycle* can be regarded as a misnomer, since Hamilton was not the first to look for cycles which pass through every vertex of a graph. An earlier example of a problem which can be expressed in terms of Hamiltonian cycles is the celebrated *knight's tour problem.* (A knight moves two squares in one direction and one square in a perpendicular direction, as illustrated below.)

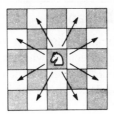

Knight's Tour Problem   Can a knight visit each square of a chessboard by a sequence of knight's moves, and finish on the same square as it began?

In order to see the connection between this problem and that of finding Hamiltonian cycles in a graph, consider the simplified problem of finding a knight's tour on a 4 × 4 chessboard. We can represent the board as a graph in which each vertex corresponds to a square, and edges correspond to those pairs of squares connected by a knight's move. The following diagram shows a 4 × 4 chessboard and its associated graph.

In fact, there is no knight's tour on a 4 × 4 chessboard, as you will see if you experiment a bit. There is also no knight's tour on a chessboard with an odd number of squares (such as a 5 × 5 chessboard), as you will see in Problem 7.12. However, for some other chessboards, a knight's tour is possible.

A solution of the knight's tour problem appeared in a paper in 1759 by Euler. In this paper Euler described a systematic approach to solving the problem, and another systematic treatment was given 12 years later by A.–T. Vandermonde. The following diagram illustrates a knight's tour on an ordinary 8 × 8 chessboard, thus answering the original knight's tour problem in the affirmative.

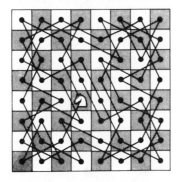

50	11	24	63	14	37	26	35
23	62	51	12	25	34	15	38
10	49	64	21	40	13	36	27
61	22	9	52	33	28	39	16
48	7	60	1	20	41	54	29
59	4	45	8	53	32	17	42
6	47	2	57	44	19	30	55
3	58	5	46	31	56	43	18

This solution is particularly interesting, because if we write the order of the moves, as in the right-hand diagram, we get a *magic square* in which the numbers in each row or column have the same total, 260.

Hamiltonian Graphs and Digraphs

At first sight, the problem of deciding whether or not a given graph is Hamiltonian seems very similar to the problem of deciding whether or not it is Eulerian, and we might expect there to be a simple necessary and sufficient condition for a graph to be Hamiltonian, analogous to that of Theorem 6.1 for Eulerian graphs. However, no such condition is known, and the search for necessary or sufficient conditions for a graph to be Hamiltonian is a major area of study in graph theory today.

Faced with this situation, the best we can do is to look for various types of graphs which are Hamiltonian. For example, it is clear that the cycle graph C_n is Hamiltonian for all values of n. Note also that K_n is Hamiltonian if $n \geq 3$; if the vertices are denoted by $1, 2, \ldots, n$, then a Hamiltonian cycle is $123 \ldots n1$.

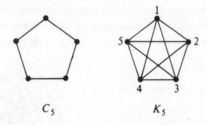

$$C_5 \qquad\qquad K_5$$

If we take a Hamiltonian graph and add more edges to it, then the result will still be a Hamiltonian graph, since we can take the same Hamiltonian cycle as before. It follows that graphs with many edges are more likely to be Hamiltonian than graphs with fewer edges. We can make this idea precise in various ways. Two of the most important of these are the following sufficient conditions of G. A. Dirac and O. Ore, published in 1952 and 1960, respectively.

THEOREM 7.1 (DIRAC'S THEOREM). *Let G be a simple graph with* n *vertices, where* n $\geq$ 3. *If deg* v $\geq \frac{1}{2}$n *for each vertex* v, *then G is Hamiltonian.*

THEOREM 7.2 (ORE'S THEOREM). *Let G be a simple graph with* n *vertices, where* n $\geq$ 3. *If*

$$\deg v + \deg w \geq n,$$

for each pair of non-adjacent vertices v *and* w, *then G is Hamiltonian.*

We illustrate the use of these theorems by considering the graphs

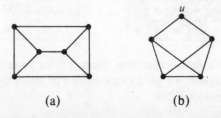

(a)   (b)

For graph (a), $n = 6$ and deg $v = 3$ for each vertex v, so this graph is Hamiltonian by Dirac's theorem.

For graph (b), $n = 5$ but deg $u = 2$, so Dirac's theorem does not apply. However, deg $v +$ deg $w \geq 5$ for all pairs of non-adjacent vertices v and w (in fact, for all pairs of vertices v and w), so this graph is Hamiltonian by Ore's theorem.

Note that if deg $v \geq \frac{1}{2}n$ for each vertex v, then deg $v +$ deg $w \geq n$ for each pair of vertices v and w. It follows that Dirac's theorem can be deduced from Ore's theorem, so we prove only Ore's theorem.

Proof of Ore's Theorem   We give a proof by contradiction. Suppose that there exists a *non-Hamiltonian* graph G in which deg $v +$ deg $w \geq n$ for each pair of non-adjacent vertices v and w. We may assume, by adding more edges to G if necessary, that G is 'only just' non-Hamiltonian, in the sense that the addition of any more edges would make it Hamiltonian. This means that there must be a path $v_1v_2v_3 \ldots v_n$ which includes every vertex, but for which the vertices v_1 and v_n are not adjacent, as shown in the following diagram (note that adding the edge v_nv_1 creates a Hamiltonian cycle):

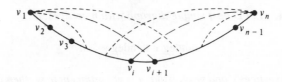

Since v_1 and v_n are not adjacent, we must have

$$\deg v_1 + \deg v_n \geq n;$$

that is,

$$\deg v_n \geq n - \deg v_1.$$

It follows that if deg $v_1 = r$, then *there are at most* r *vertices not adjacent to* v_n*, including the vertex* v_n *itself.*

Now consider the vertices adjacent to v_1, and let S be the set of vertices preceding each of these vertices in the path; for example, if v_1 is joined to v_k, then v_{k-1} is a vertex in S. Then S *contains* r *vertices, and* v_n *is not one of them.*

It follows from the two italicized statements that S must contain a vertex v_i adjacent to v_n, and so there must be edges joining v_1 and v_{i+1}, and v_i and v_n, as shown in the above diagram. But we can now write down a Hamiltonian cycle in G—namely,

$$v_1v_2\ldots v_{i-1}v_iv_nv_{n-1}\ldots v_{i+1}v_1,$$

contradicting the assumption that G is non-Hamiltonian. This contradiction establishes the theorem. $\square$

Just as for Eulerian graphs, there are several variations of the above ideas and results. For example, *vertex-traceable graphs* are graphs which possess a path, but not a cycle, passing through each vertex exactly once; such a path is usually called a *Hamiltonian path*. We can also define Hamiltonian digraphs:

DEFINITIONS.   *A connected digraph* D *is* **Hamiltonian** *if there is a (directed) cycle which includes every vertex of* D. *Such a cycle is called a* **Hamiltonian cycle** *in* D.

There are digraph analogs of both Dirac's theorem and Ore's theorem, but these are considerably harder to prove than their counterparts for graphs. We state two of these without proof.

THEOREM 7.3.   *Let* D *be a simple digraph with* n *vertices. If*

$$\text{outdeg } v \geq \tfrac{1}{2}n \ \text{ and } \ \text{indeg } v \geq \tfrac{1}{2}n$$

for every vertex v *of* D, *then* D *is Hamiltonian.*

THEOREM 7.4.   *Let* D *be a simple digraph with* n *vertices. If*

$$\text{outdeg } v + \text{indeg } w \geq n$$

for every pair of vertices v *and* w *such that* v *is not adjacent to* w, *then* D *is Hamiltonian.*

7.2 HAMILTONIAN-TYPE PROBLEMS

We conclude this chapter by describing some connections between Hamiltonian graphs and digraphs and problems in coding theory, optimization, and tournaments.

Gray Codes

The communication of information from one person or place to another has a long history, and the development of suitable techniques to accomplish it satisfactorily has often been colored by intrigues (mainly of a political or military nature). For reasons of privacy or security there have arisen, over the years, various codes and ciphers whose main purpose was to prevent the information getting into the wrong hands. However, in recent times, with the rapid growth of information-processing industries, codes have come to be widely used for representing information. This is largely due to the introduction of *digital techniques,* so that even an analog signal (one that varies continuously, such as a sound wave) is now usually chopped up into discrete slices and represented in digital form. As a result of this trend, the notion of a code has come to have a more specific meaning and now refers to a finite system of distinct symbols which is used to process or transmit digital information over a communication channel.

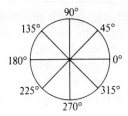

Suppose that we wish to represent the angular position (in multiples of 45°) of a shaft which is rotating continuously. By using three brushes on a commutator, we can convert the angle through which the shaft has rotated into a three-bit binary word, as follows:

0°–45°	45°–90°	90°–135°	135°–180°	180°–225°	225°–270°	270°–315°	315°–360°
000	001	011	010	110	111	101	100

If we take these binary words as codewords, we obtain a code known as a **Gray code.** As the shaft rotates, the codeword changes by only one bit at a time. Because of the construction of the equipment, multiple-bit changes (such as 110 to 101, or 111 to 000) may not be possible simultaneously, and it is partly for this reason that Gray codes have found such widespread use.

Gray codes can be found by tracing Hamiltonian cycles on the graph of the n-cube Q_n. For example, the above code, and the code

$$000 \rightarrow 100 \rightarrow 110 \rightarrow 010 \rightarrow 011 \rightarrow 111 \rightarrow 101 \rightarrow 001 \ (\rightarrow 000),$$

both correspond to Hamiltonian cycles in the 3-cube, shown below.

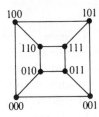

Similarly, we can find a Gray code consisting of four-bit binary words by tracing a Hamiltonian cycle in the 4-cube, shown on page 38. An example of such a code is

$$0000 \rightarrow 0001 \rightarrow 0011 \rightarrow 0010 \rightarrow 0110 \rightarrow 0111 \rightarrow 0101 \rightarrow 0100 \rightarrow$$

$$1100 \rightarrow 1101 \rightarrow 1111 \rightarrow 1110 \rightarrow 1010 \rightarrow 1011 \rightarrow 1001 \rightarrow 1000 \ (\rightarrow 0000).$$

The Traveling Salesman Problem

A traveling salesman wishes to visit a number of cities and return to the starting point, in such a way that each city is visited exactly once, and the total distance covered is as short as possible. Given the various distances between the cities, what route should be chosen?

In principle, we can solve this problem by looking at all possible routes and choosing the one which involves the least total distance. For example, if there are five cities A, B, C, D, and E, and if the connections between them are as shown below, then a traveling salesman at A should visit the cities in the order $ACBDEA$ (or in reverse order $AEDBCA$), covering a total distance of 14.

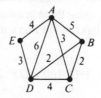

Unfortunately, as soon as we increase the number of cities, we run into difficulties, since there is no known algorithm which provides a simple and efficient solution for the problem. Although there are several ad hoc procedures which can be used to give approximate solutions, a full solution effectively involves looking at all possible routes and choosing the shortest. This is feasible if there are ten cities, since the number of possible routes is then at most 362880, and a computer sorting through these at the rate of one million per second will find the best route in about 0.36 seconds. On the other hand, if there are 20 cities, then the number of possible routes is about 1.22×10^{17}, and a computer sorting through them at the same rate would take almost 4000 years!

The traveling salesman problem is an important one in practice, since it can appear in a number of different guises. An example is the *job-sequencing problem,* which can be stated as follows.

The Job-Sequencing Problem   A number of independent jobs are to be carried out on a single machine. These jobs are complicated, and the machine must be set up for each new job after the previous one is completed. The machine is initially set up for one of the jobs, and it must be reset for that job when the other jobs are completed. If the set-up costs (involving labor and material) depend on the job just completed and the job about to be started, how can we order the jobs so that the total set-up cost is minimized?

The link between the two problems may be seen by considering the problems graphically. In the *traveling salesman problem* we draw a weighted complete graph in which the vertices correspond to the cities visited, the edges correspond to the routes joining them, and the weights correspond to the distances between pairs of cities. In the *job-sequencing problem* we draw a weighted complete graph in which the vertices correspond to the jobs, the edges link these jobs, and the weights correspond to the set-up costs associated with pairs of jobs. In each case, our aim is to find a cycle of minimum total weight which passes through every vertex—in other words, a minimum-weight Hamiltonian cycle. The traveling salesman problem may therefore be restated in graphical terms as follows.

The Traveling Salesman Problem   Given a weighted complete graph, find a minimum-weight Hamiltonian cycle in it.

Note that the formulation of the traveling salesman problem assumes that the corresponding graph is Hamiltonian—in fact, the problem can be reformulated as that of finding a minimum-length Hamiltonian cycle in the graph. If the weights of the edges refer, not to the distances between the cities, but to the time or cost involved in traveling between them, then a solution of the traveling salesman problem gives a minimum-time or minimum-cost cycle.

It is interesting to contrast this problem with the Chinese postman problem, which can be thought of as its Eulerian analog. In the case of the *Chinese postman problem*, there is no difficulty if the corresponding graph is Eulerian—we simply find an Eulerian trail by Fleury's algorithm, and any such trail must be a solution to the problem. Even if the graph is not Eulerian, there is a standard algorithm which can be used to find a minimum-weight closed walk. In the case of the *traveling salesman problem*, the graph is assumed to be Hamiltonian from the start, but there may be several different Hamiltonian cycles with different total weights. In view of this, we need an algorithm for deciding which Hamiltonian cycle is the shortest, but no good algorithm is known. Unless the number of cities is small, the best we can do is to obtain approximate solutions. For example, it is possible to obtain upper and lower bounds for the shortest total distance. A method for doing this is discussed in Chapter 10.

Ranking in Tournaments

A **tournament** is a digraph whose underlying graph is a complete graph—for example, the following diagram shows some of the tournaments with three or four vertices:

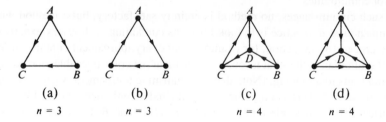

(a)   (b)   (c)   (d)

$n = 3$ $n = 3$ $n = 4$ $n = 4$

Such digraphs can be used to record the winners in a round-robin tournament, in which each player plays each of the others. For example, in tournament (a), player A beats both players B and C, and player B beats player C; whereas in tournament (d), C beats B, D, and A; B beats D and A; and A beats D.

Tournaments also arise in other contexts, such as in the *method of paired comparisons*, where we compare a number of commodities by testing them in pairs. For example, consider the following tournament, used for comparing six different types of dog food. These delicacies were tested in pairs on a number of dogs, and the preferences were recorded:

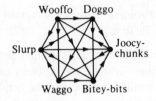

The problem now arises as to how to rank the various commodities in order of preference. For some tournaments (known as *transitive tournaments*) there is no difficulty, since we can order them in such a way that each vertex 'dominates' the others beneath it. For example, in tournaments (a) and (d) above we can rank the participants in this way, as shown below. Unfortunately, in many practical examples a direct ranking is impossible. For example, in tournaments (b) and (c) above, A beats B, B beats C, and C beats A, so it is not possible to rank these three players directly.

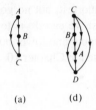

(a)   (d)

There is a similar inconsistency in the dog-food example, where *Wooffo* was preferred to *Doggo*, *Doggo* was preferred to *Joocy-chunks*, and *Joocy-chunks* was preferred to *Wooffo*. For such tournaments we must find alternative methods for ranking the participants or commodities.

In such circumstances, no method is entirely satisfactory, but a method which has been much used in practice is to look for paths containing each vertex exactly once. It can be proved (by induction, for example) that every tournament contains at least one such Hamiltonian path—that is, every tournament is vertex-traceable, and each path of this kind leads to a ranking. [Note that, in a transitive tournament, such as tournaments (a) and (d) above, there is only one such path, and so only one ranking.] For example, in tournament (c), possible rankings are A, B, D, C and B, C, A, D, whereas for the dog-food example, possible rankings are

Wooffo, Doggo, Joocy-chunks, Waggo, Slurp, Bitey-bits

and

Bitey-bits, Joocy-chunks, Wooffo, Doggo, Waggo, Slurp.

Once we have listed all the possible rankings of this kind, we must then take other considerations into account in deciding which ranking is best for our purposes.

PROBLEMS

Hamilton's Icosian Game and the Knight's Tour Problem

7.1. Use the picture of the Icosian game on page 144 to determine how many Hamiltonian cycles on the dodecahedron begin with the sequence of letters *DCPQZ*.

♂7.2. Use the picture of the Icosian game to answer the following:

    a. how many Hamiltonian cycles on the dodecahedron begin with *JVTSR*?

    b. find a path on the dodecahedron starting with *BCD*, ending with *T*, and including every vertex just once.

7.3. By drawing the corresponding graph, determine whether a knight can visit each square of the following 'chessboard' exactly once.

7.4.[†] Show that there is no knight's tour on a 4×4 chessboard, but that there is a knight's tour on a 6×6 chessboard.

Hamiltonian Graphs and Digraphs

♂7.5. Which of the following graphs are Hamiltonian?

    a. the complete graphs K_n;

    b. the complete bipartite graphs $K_{r,s}$;

    c. trees;

    d. the five Platonic graphs.

7.6. Using the graph cards in Chapter 1, determine which graphs with six vertices and nine edges are Hamiltonian.

7.7. Decide whether each of the following graphs is Hamiltonian, vertex-traceable, or neither.

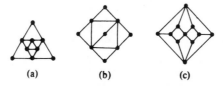

(a)   (b)   (c)

7.8.[†] Let G be the following graph:

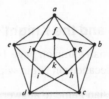

a. Prove that G has no Hamiltonian cycle which includes the edges ab, bf, and fk.

b. Find a Hamiltonian cycle containing the edges ab and bf.

7.9.[†] Let G be the following graph:

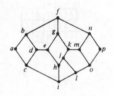

a. Prove that any Hamiltonian cycle of G must contain:
   (i) one of the paths *fbacde* and *icabde* (in either direction);
   (ii) one of the paths *kmopnf* and *kmnpol* (in either direction).

b. Deduce from part a that G contains no Hamiltonian cycles.

7.10.[†] Show that the Petersen graph is vertex-traceable, but not Hamiltonian.

7.11.[†] A mouse eats his way through a $3 \times 3 \times 3$ cube of cheese, tunneling through all 27 of the $1 \times 1 \times 1$ cubes. If the mouse starts at a corner, can he finish in the center?

⊘7.12. Prove that any bipartite graph with an odd number of vertices cannot be Hamiltonian. Use this result to show that

a. the following graph is not Hamiltonian:

b. there is no knight's tour on a 5×5 or 7×7 chessboard.

7.13. Check whether the conditions of Dirac's theorem and Ore's theorem hold for the following Hamiltonian graphs:

(a)   (b)

☯7.14. Give an example of each of the following:
   a. a Hamiltonian graph which does not satisfy the conditions of Ore's theorem;
   b. a non-Hamiltonian graph with n vertices, in which deg $v \geq \frac{1}{2}(n-1)$ for each vertex v.

☯7.15. Determine which of the following digraphs are Hamiltonian, and give a suitable cycle in each case:

(a)   (b)   (c)

7.16.[†] Prove directly that if a digraph D satisfies the condition of Theorem 7.4, then D is strongly connected.

7.17. Prove that Theorem 7.4 implies Theorem 7.3.

Hamiltonian-type Problems

7.18. Solve the traveling salesman problem for the four cities illustrated below for a salesman based in London.

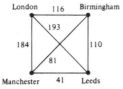

◷7.19. The King of Combinatoria decides to visit his subjects who live in the four main towns of his kingdom; his palace is at A, and the cities are at $B, C, D,$ and E. Find a route for him which involves the least possible total distance.

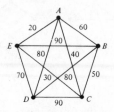

◷7.20. Describe (in general terms) how you might attempt to find the shortest route connecting the capitals of the 50 states of the United States.

7.21. Draw all tournaments (up to isomorphism) with four vertices.

7.22. How many rankings are possible in the following tournament?

7.23. A tournament D is said to be **transitive** if, whenever uv and vw are arcs of D, then uw is also an arc of D. Determine whether either of the tournaments (a) and (b) in Problem 7.15 is transitive.

7.24.[†] Prove that a tournament is transitive if and only if it contains no cycles.

CHAPTER 8

PATH ALGORITHMS

8.1 INTRODUCTION

Consider the following two problems:

1. A traveler wishes to drive from Los Angeles to New York in the shortest possible time. The following map gives the time (in hours) needed to drive between particular pairs of cities. Given this information, which route should the traveler take?

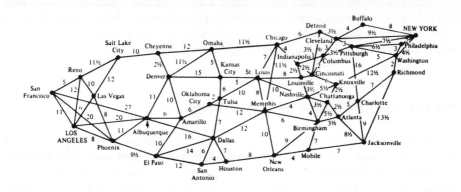

In this particular example, it is not difficult to find the solution by intelligent guesswork, but such an approach is less likely to succeed as the road network becomes more and more complicated. In this chapter we describe an algorithm which can be used to find the shortest path between any two vertices of any network.

2. The following diagram illustrates the various stages in a die-making process. The numbered vertices, called **events**, represent the various stages reached in the process. The arcs represent the various **activities** (such as *refine release* and *correct tooling*) and are labeled with numbers to indicate the number of days needed to perform each activity. The entire weighted digraph (or die-graph!) is called an **activity network** and shows which activities must be completed before others can begin. What is the minimum possible time needed to complete the process?

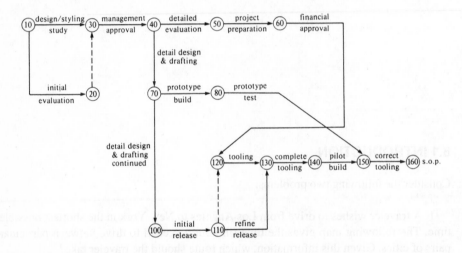

We shall describe an algorithm which can be used to find this minimum possible time and to locate which activities are 'critical' to the process and which have some 'slack'. A fuller and more comprehensive account of this topic (known as *critical path analysis*) will be found in the companion volume on *Networks*.

8.2 THE SHORTEST PATH ALGORITHM

The idea of this algorithm is to find the shortest path from vertex S to vertex T in a given network. To do this, we move across the network from left to right, calculating the shortest distance from S to each of the intermediate vertices as we go. At each stage of the algorithm, we look at all vertices reached by an arc from the current vertex and assign to each such vertex a temporary label representing the shortest distance from S to that vertex by all paths considered until now. Eventually each vertex acquires a permanent label (called its *potential,* and denoted by a square around the label) which represents the shortest distance from S to that vertex. Once T has been assigned a potential, then we have determined the shortest distance from S to T.

We illustrate the use of this algorithm by finding the shortest distance from S to T in the following network:

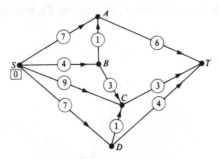

We start by assigning to S potential 0, *since the shortest distance from S to S is 0. We then look at those vertices reached by an arc from* S (that is, A, B, C, and D) *and assign to each such vertex a temporary label equal to the potential at S plus the distance from S to that vertex.* This gives the vertices A, B, C, and D temporary labels of 7, 4, 9, and 7, respectively.

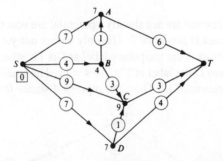

We now take the smallest label that is not a potential and mark it as a potential. In this case the relevant label is 4, at vertex B, so *we assign to* B *potential* 4. Note that this is the shortest distance from S to B, since any other path from S to B would have to go via A, C, or D, and the first stage alone of such a path would exceed 4.

Since B has just been assigned a potential, *we now look at those vertices reached directly from* B (that is, A and C). We assign to each of these vertices a temporary label equal to the potential at B plus the distance from B to that vertex, unless that vertex already has a smaller label. In this case, we assign to vertex A the new label $4 + 1 = 5$, and to vertex C the new label $4 + 3 = 7$, since these are both smaller than their previous labels.

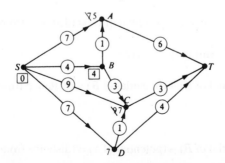

The shortest distance that is not already a potential is now 5, at *A*, so *we assign to A potential* 5; this is the shortest distance from *S* to *A*. Continuing in this way, *we now look at those vertices reached directly from* A (that is, just *T*), and assign to *T* the temporary label 5 + 6 = 11.

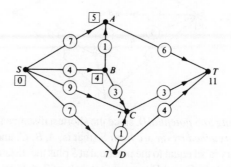

The shortest distances that are not already a potential are now the 7's at vertices *C* and *D*, so *we assign to* C *and* D *potential* 7. The only vertex not yet assigned a potential is now vertex *T*. From vertex *A* the temporary label at *T* is 11, whereas from *C* the label at *T* is 7 + 3 = 10, and from *D* the label at *T* is 7 + 4 = 11. The smallest of these numbers is 10, so *we assign to* T *potential* 10. Thus, the shortest distance from *S* to *T* is 10:

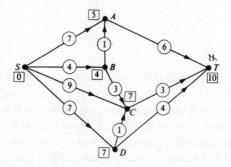

In order to find the shortest path from *S* to *T*, we work backwards from *T*, as follows. Since we have

$$\text{(potential of } T) - \text{(potential of } C) = \text{(distance from } C \text{ to } T),$$

we include the arc *CT*. Similarly, we have

$$\text{(potential of } C) - \text{(potential of } B) = \text{(distance from } B \text{ to } C)$$

and

$$\text{(potential of } B) - \text{(potential of } S) = \text{(distance from } S \text{ to } B),$$

so we include the arcs *BC* and *SB*. Thus *the shortest path from* S *to* T *is* SBCT.

We summarize the above procedure as follows.

Shortest Path Algorithm

To find the shortest path from S to T in a network:

STEP 1	Assign to vertex *S* potential 0; label each vertex *V* reached directly from *S* with the distance from *S* to *V*;
	choose the smallest of these labels, and make it the potential of the corresponding vertex or vertices.
GENERAL STEP	Consider the vertex or vertices just assigned a potential;
	for each such vertex *V*, look at each vertex *W* reached directly from *V* and assign *W* the label

$$\text{(potential of } V) + (\text{distance from } V \text{ to } W),$$

unless *W* already has a smaller label; when all such vertices *W* have been labeled, choose the smallest label in the network which is not already a potential and make it a potential at each vertex where it occurs;

repeat the GENERAL STEP with the new potential(s).

STOP	when vertex *T* has been assigned a potential; this is the shortest distance from *S* to *T*.
SHORTEST PATH(S)	Work backwards from *T*, and include an arc *VW* whenever

$$\text{(potential of } W) - (\text{potential of } V) = (\text{distance from } V \text{ to } W).$$

The Tabular Method

In applying the above algorithm, one can easily lose track of the labels at the various vertices. The following tabular method is a convenient way of recording the above calculations in the form of a table.

We label each column with a vertex of the network, and we successively label each row with the vertex or vertices that have just been assigned a potential. To complete each row, we consider the vertices reached directly from these vertices of known potential, and we assign the labels as before, bringing down any other labels not yet made into potentials. We then proceed to the next row. The table on page 162 corresponds to the above example.

Thus, the shortest distance from *S* to *T* is 10, and we can then find the shortest path (*SBCT*), as before.

vertices	S	A	B	C	D	T
S	$\boxed{0}$	7	4	9	7	...
B		5	$\boxed{4}$	7	7	...
A		$\boxed{5}$		7	7	11
C,D				$\boxed{7}$	$\boxed{7}$	10
T						$\boxed{10}$

8.3 THE LONGEST PATH ALGORITHM

We now wish to find the longest path from S to T in a network. We must assume that the network has no cycles, since otherwise we could go around a cycle as often as we please.

The algorithm we shall describe is similar to the shortest path algorithm, except that instead of looking at all vertices reached directly from a vertex of known potential, we look at all vertices that can be reached *only* from vertices of known potential. In other words, if we can reach a vertex W from a vertex whose potential we do not yet know, then we must not consider W at this stage. When assigning labels, we proceed much as before. The distance from S via a vertex V of known potential to a vertex W reached directly from V is

$$\text{(potential of } V) + \text{(distance from } V \text{ to } W),$$

so we can easily calculate all the possible distances from S to W, and the *largest* such distance will be the potential at W.

We illustrate the use of this algorithm by finding the longest path from S to T in our previous network:

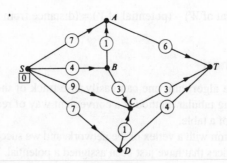

We start by assigning to S potential 0. *We then look at those vertices reached only by an arc from* S *(that is, B and D). Since the only paths from S to B and from S to D are SB and SD, they must be the longest such paths. Thus we can assign to* B *and* D *potentials 4 and 7,* respectively:

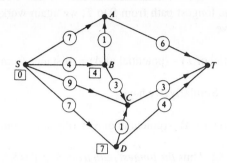

We now look at those vertices reached only from S, B, and D (that is, A and C). At vertex A, there are two possible routes—the direct route from S with distance 7, and the path via B with distance 4 + 1 = 5. The larger of these numbers is 7, so *we assign to A potential 7*. At vertex C, there are three possible routes—the direct route from S with distance 9, the path via B with distance 4 + 3 = 7, and the path via D with distance 7 + 1 = 8. The largest of these numbers is 9, so *we assign to C potential 9*.

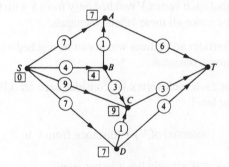

Now that we have the potentials at S, A, B, C, and D, we can consider the paths to T. There are three possible routes—the path via A with distance 7 + 6 = 13, the path via C with distance 9 + 3 = 12, and the path via D with distance 7 + 4 = 11. The largest of these numbers is 13, so *we assign to T potential 13*. Thus, the longest distance from S to T is 13:

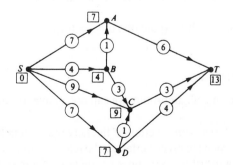

In order to find the longest path from S to T, we again work backwards from T, as follows. Since we have

$$(\text{potential of } T) - (\text{potential of } A) = (\text{distance from } A \text{ to } T),$$

we include the arc AT. Similarly, we have

$$(\text{potential of } A) - (\text{potential of } S) = (\text{distance from } S \text{ to } A),$$

so we include the arc SA. Thus *the longest path from* S *to* T *is* SAT.

We summarize the above procedure as follows:

Longest Path Algorithm

To find the longest path from S to T in a network without cycles:

STEP 1   Assign to vertex S potential 0;

label each vertex V reached only from S with the distance from S to V and make all these labels potentials.

GENERAL STEP   Consider all vertices which can be reached *only* from vertices of known potential;

for each such vertex W, consider each arc VW into W, and assign W the label

$$(\text{potential of } V) + (\text{distance from } V \text{ to } W),$$

unless W already has a larger label;

when all such arcs VW have been considered, make the label at W a potential;

repeat the GENERAL STEP with the new potentials.

STOP   when vertex T has been assigned a potential; this is the longest distance from S to T.

LONGEST PATH(S)   Work backwards from T and include an arc VW whenever

$$(\text{potential of } W) - (\text{potential of } V) = (\text{distance from } V \text{ to } W).$$

The Tabular Method

Just as with the shortest path algorithm, we can use a table to carry out the above calculations.

We label each column with a vertex of the network, and below each vertex we list those vertices from which the given vertex can be reached directly. At each stage we label the row in question with all those vertices whose potential is known. To complete each row, we consider the vertices reached *only* from these vertices of known potential, and we assign the labels as before. We then proceed to the next row. The following table corresponds to the above example:

Vertices	S · · ·	A (S,B)	B (S)	C (S,B,D)	D (S)	T (A,C,D)
S	0	· · ·	4	· · ·	7	· · ·
S, B, D		7		9		· · ·
S, B, D, A, C						13

Thus, the longest distance from S to T is 13, and we can then find the longest path (*SAT*), as before.

8.4 SCHEDULING

Suppose that we have a job to carry out (such as the building of a garage), and that this job can be divided into a number of smaller separate operations (such as laying the foundations, doing the wiring, putting on the roof, etc.). Several of these smaller operations can be performed simultaneously, whereas some will need to be completed before others can be started. It would therefore be useful if we could determine in advance which jobs should be performed at which times so that the entire job is completed in minimum time.

The algorithm which solves this problem is one you have already met—the longest path algorithm. To see why it is relevant, let us return to our earlier network, redrawn as in the activity network at the beginning of the chapter.

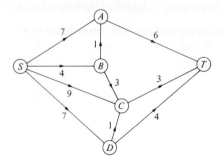

The vertex S denotes the *start* of the project, the vertex T denotes its *termination*, and the other vertices A, B, C, D represent intermediate stages, called **events**. The arcs SA, SB, . . . represent the various **activities** to be carried out, and the number next to each one represents the time (in days) needed to complete the activity. The activity network shows which activities need to precede other ones; thus, the activities SA and BA must precede the activity AT.

We have already seen that the longest path from S to T in this network is SAT, with total length 13. Since the activity SA (7 days) must precede the activity AT (6 days), these two activities will take 13 days, quite apart from the rest. It turns out that all the other activities can be fitted into a 13-day schedule, and therefore that *13 days is the required minimum time to complete the entire project*. Note also that if either of the activities *SA* and *AT* is subject to delay, then the entire project is delayed. Because of this, it is critical that the activities on the longest path *SAT* are completed on time, and the path is therefore referred to as a **critical path**.

A similar situation holds in general. Any path of maximum length from *S* to *T* is a critical path which determines the completion time of the entire project. Any delay in an activity on a critical path leads to a delay in the project. By using the longest path algorithm, as described above, we can find these critical paths and thereby determine which activities must be kept on schedule if the project is to be completed on time.

Is there any slack in the project? Although the activities on a critical path cannot be delayed, is there any flexibility in the scheduling of the other activities? In fact there is, as we now show.

Consider the activity *BC*. The longest path from *S* to *B* is *SB* with length 4, so the earliest possible starting time for the activity *BC* is after 4 days. What is the latest possible time that it can start? Since the activity *CT* takes 3 days, the activity *BC* must be completed after 10 days, so that it must start by 7 days. Thus activity *BC* can be started at any time between 4 days and 7 days, giving 3 days flexibility; we say that the **float time** of activity *BC* is 3 days.

Similarly, to find the float time of activity *DC*, we note that the earliest possible starting time is 7 days (corresponding to the path *SD*), and the latest possible starting time is 9 days (leaving 4 days to reach *T* by either of the paths *DCT* or *DT*). Thus the float time of activity *DC* is 2 days.

In general, it is not difficult to see that

> the earliest starting time for an activity XY is the length of the longest path from S to X;
> the latest starting time for an activity XY is
> (total time for the project) – (length of the longest path from X to T via XY).

Thus we obtain the following table of float times for all of the activities. Using this table, we can easily see which activities must remain on schedule and which activities can be delayed if necessary; note that the float time of any activity in the critical path is 0.

Activity	SA	SB	SC	SD	BA	BC	DC	AT	CT	DT
Earliest starting time	0	0	0	0	4	4	7	7	9	7
Latest starting time	0	2	1	2	6	7	9	7	10	9
Float time	0	2	1	2	2	3	2	0	1	2

PROBLEMS

The Shortest Path Algorithm

⊙8.1. Using the tabular method, find the shortest path from S to T in the following network:

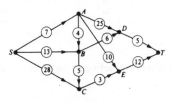

8.2. Using the tabular method, find the shortest path from S to T in the following network:

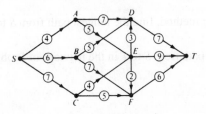

8.3.[†] Find the shortest path from S to T in the following network:

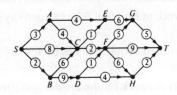

8.4. Find the shortest distance from S to each of the other vertices in the following weighted graph:

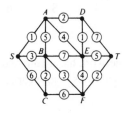

☉8.5. A company has branches in five cities A, B, C, D, and E. The fares for direct flights between these cities are as follows:

	A	B	C	D	E
A	—	50	40	25	10
B	50	—	20	90	25
C	40	20	—	10	25
D	25	90	10	—	55
E	10	25	25	55	—

What is the cost of traveling between each pair of cities by the cheapest route?

The Longest Path Algorithm

☉8.6. Using the tabular method, find the longest path from S to T in the network of Problem 8.1.

8.7. Using the tabular method, find the longest path from S to T in the network of Problem 8.2.

8.8.[†] Find the longest path from S to T in the network of Problem 8.3.

Scheduling

☉8.9. Regarding the network of Problem 8.1 as an activity network, construct a table giving the earliest and latest start times and float times of each activity.

8.10. Regarding the network of Problem 8.2 as an activity network, find the float time of each activity.

8.11.[†] Regarding the network of Problem 8.3 as an activity network, find the float time of each activity.

☉8.12. Construct an activity network for the project specified by the information given in the following table. Determine the critical path and the float time for each activity:

Activity	a	b	c	d	e	f	g	h
Duration	3	4	8	6	7	2	7	7
Predecessors	⋯	⋯	a	b	b	c,d	c,d	e,f

8.13.[†] Suppose that an activity network has a unique critical path. Show that this path consists of exactly those activities whose earliest and latest starting times coincide.

CHAPTER 9

CONNECTIVITY

In this chapter we investigate the extent to which a given graph or digraph is connected. In particular, we discuss the question: *How many edges do we need to remove from a given connected graph so that it becomes disconnected?* This, and other similar questions related to connectivity, are important ones to consider when designing telecommunications networks, road systems, and other networks—for example, in a telecommunications network it is essential that the network should be operable if some of the links between the exchanges become damaged, or are blocked by other calls.

9.1 EDGE-CONNECTIVITY

In telecommunications networks, there are usually several different paths between any given pair of subscribers (vertices). In such a situation, it is important to know how many links (edges) can be broken without preventing a call being made between two subscribers. In order to answer this and similar questions, we need to investigate connected graphs a little further.

Consider the following graphs:

 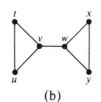  

    (a)   (b)   (c)   (d)

Graph (a) can be split up into two components by removing one of the edges *vw* or *vx*;

Graph (b) can also be disconnected by removing a single edge—edge *vw*;

Graph (c) cannot be disconnected by removing a single edge, but the removal of two edges (such as *uw* and *vw*) disconnects it;

Graph (d) can similarly be disconnected by removing two edges (*uw* and *wx*).

Recall that a **bridge** is a single edge whose removal disconnects a graph, such as *vw* or *vx* in graph (a) or *vw* in graph (b).

With these examples in mind, we define the edge-connectivity of a graph as follows.

DEFINITIONS.   *The* **edge-connectivity** $\lambda(G)$ *of a connected graph* G *is the smallest number of edges whose removal disconnects* G. *When* $\lambda(G) \geq k$, *the graph* G *is said to be* **k-edge-connected.**

Thus graphs (a) and (b) have edge-connectivity 1, and graphs (c) and (d) have edge-connectivity 2. All four graphs are 1-edge connected, and graphs (c) and (d) are 2-edge connected, but not 3-edge-connected.

If we wish to disconnect a graph by removing edges from it, we usually have a choice of edges to delete. In view of this, it seems natural to consider ways of disconnecting a graph which do not involve 'redundant edges'.

Consider the following graph:

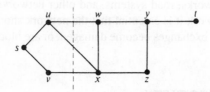

We can disconnect G by removing the three edges *uw*, *ux*, and *vx*, but we cannot disconnect it by removing just two of these edges. We can also disconnect G by removing the edges *uw*, *wx*, *xz*, and *yz*, but the edge *yz* is redundant here since we need remove only the edges *uw*, *wx*, and *xz* to disconnect G. A *cutset* is a set of edges in which no edge is redundant—such as {*uw,ux,vx*} or {*uw,wx,xz*}.

DEFINITION.   *A* **cutset** *of a connected graph* G *is a set* S *of edges with the following properties:*

    a.   *the removal of all the edges in* S *disconnects* G;

    b.   *the removal of some (but not all) of the edges in* S *does not disconnect* G.

Note that *two cutsets of a graph need not have the same number of edges.* For example, in the above graph, the sets {*uw,ux,vx*} and {*wy, xz*} are both cutsets. Note also that *the edge-connectivity* $\lambda(G)$ *of a graph* G *is simply the minimum number of edges in a cutset of* G.

9.2 VERTEX-CONNECTIVITY

We can also think of connectivity in terms of the minimum number of *vertices* which need to be removed in order to disconnect a graph. When we remove a vertex, we must also remove the edges incident to it:

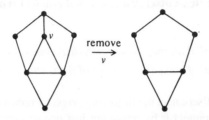

Consider again graphs (a)–(d):

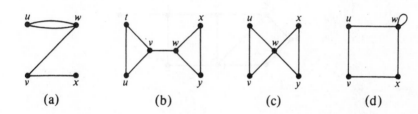

Graphs (a) and (b) can be disconnected by the removal of a single vertex (either *v* or *w*);

Graph (c) can also be disconnected by removing just one vertex (the vertex *w*);

Graph (d) cannot be disconnected by removing a single vertex, but the removal of two non-adjacent vertices (such as *v* and *w*) disconnects it.

A **cut-vertex** is a single vertex whose removal disconnects a graph, such as *v* or *w* in graph (b) or *w* in graph (c).

With these examples in mind, we define the *connectivity* (or *vertex-connectivity*) of a graph as follows. (We use the simpler terms *connectivity* and *k-connected* when there is no possibility of confusion with *edge-connectivity* and *k-edge-connected*.)

DEFINITIONS. *The* **connectivity** *(or* **vertex-connectivity**) $\kappa(G)$ *of a connected graph* G *(other than a complete graph) is the smallest number of vertices whose removal disconnects* G. *When* $\kappa(G) \geq k$, *the graph is said to be* **k-connected** *(or* **k-vertex-connected**).

Thus graphs (a), (b), and (c) have connectivity 1 and graph (d) has connectivity 2. All four graphs are 1-connected, and graph (d) is 2-connected, but not 3-connected.

The above definition breaks down if G is a complete graph, since we cannot then disconnect G by removing vertices. We therefore make the following definition:

DEFINITION.   *The* **connectivity** $\kappa(K_n)$ *of the complete graph* K_n *is* $n-1$. *When* $n-1 \geq k$, *the graph* K_n *is said to be* **k-connected**.

There is also a 'vertex analog' of the concept of a cutset. This is defined as follows.

DEFINITION.   *A* **vertex-cutset** *of a connected graph* G *is a set* S *of vertices with the following properties:*

    a.   *the removal of all the vertices in* S *disconnects* G;

    b.   *the removal of some (but not all) of the vertices in* S *does not disconnect* G.

For example, we can disconnect the following graph by removing the two vertices u and x, but we cannot disconnect it by removing just one of these vertices. It follows that $\{u, x\}$ is a vertex-cutset.

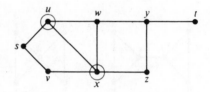

Note that *two vertex-cutsets of a graph need not necessarily have the same number of vertices.* For example, in the above graph, the sets $\{u, x\}$ and $\{y\}$ are both vertex-cutsets. Note also that *the connectivity* $\kappa(G)$ *of a graph* G *is simply the minimum number of vertices in a vertex-cutset of* G.

In the above example, you may have noted that the connectivity $\kappa(G)$ does not exceed the edge-connectivity $\lambda(G)$. This inequality holds for all connected graphs.

THEOREM 9.1.   *For any connected graph* G,

$$\kappa(G) \leq \lambda(G) \leq \delta(G),$$

where $\delta(G)$ *is the smallest vertex-degree in* G.

Proof   If v is a vertex of degree $\delta(G)$, then G can be disconnected by removing all the $\delta(G)$ edges incident with v. It follows that $\lambda(G)$, the minimum number of edges whose removal disconnects G, cannot exceed $\delta(G)$. So we get $\lambda(G) \leq \delta(G)$.

It remains to be shown that $\kappa(G) \leq \lambda(G)$. Let G be a graph with edge-connectivity λ. Then there is at least one set of λ edges whose removal disconnects G into two components G_1 and G_2, as illustrated

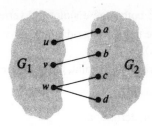

However, we can also remove these edges by removing at most λ vertices, since we have only to remove one suitably chosen end-vertex from each of these λ edges. It follows that the minimum number of vertices whose removal disconnects G cannot exceed λ—that is, $\kappa(G) \le \lambda(G)$. [In the diagram above, we can disconnect the graph by removing the end-vertices $a, b,$ and w; in this case, $\kappa(G) < \lambda(G)$, since two of the λ edges are incident with the same end-vertex w.] $\square$

Note that it is possible for both inequalities in Theorem 9.1 to be strict inequalities [that is, $\kappa(G) < \lambda(G) < \delta(G)$]. For example, in the following graph, $\kappa(G) = 1$, $\lambda(G) = 2$, and $\delta(G) = 3$:

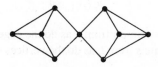

9.3 MENGER'S THEOREM FOR GRAPHS (EDGE-FORM)

Here we discuss an important result which relates the above ideas to the number of 'disjoint paths' between two vertices in a graph. This result is known as *Menger's theorem*.
    We start by defining disjoint paths in a graph.

DEFINITIONS.   *Let* G *be a connected graph, and let* s *and* t *be vertices of* G. *An* **st-path** *is a path between* s *and* t. *Two or more* st-*paths are* **edge-disjoint** *if they have no edges in common, and* **vertex-disjoint** *if they have no vertices in common (apart from* s *and* t*).*

For example, in the graph

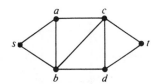

the paths *sact* and *sbdt* are both edge-disjoint and vertex-disjoint paths;

the paths *sact* and *sbct* are neither edge-disjoint nor vertex-disjoint (since they have the edge *ct* in common);

the paths *sact* and *sbcdt* are edge-disjoint, but not vertex-disjoint (since they have the vertex *c* in common).

We also need the following definitions.

DEFINITIONS. *Let G be a connected graph, and let* s *and* t *be vertices of G. We say that certain edges* **separate** s **from** t *if the removal of these edges destroys all paths between* s *and* t. *Similarly, we say that certain vertices* **separate** s **from** t *if the removal of these vertices destroys all paths between* s *and* t.

For example, in the graph

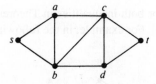

the edges *ac*, *bc*, and *bd* separate *s* from *t*, as do the edges *sa*, *ac*, *bc*, *bd*, and *dt*; the vertices *b* and *c* separate *s* from *t*, as do the vertices *a*, *b*, and *d*.

Now we show how these ideas are related to those of edge-disjoint and vertex-disjoint *st*-paths. Before doing this in general, we motivate our discussion with three examples.

Example 1:

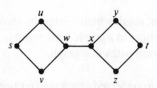

In this graph the single edge *wx* separates *s* from *t*. It follows that *there cannot be two edge-disjoint* st-*paths*, since all *st*-paths must include the edge *wx*.

Example 2:

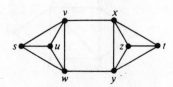

In this graph the two edges *vx* and *wy* separate *s* from *t*. It follows that *there are at most two edge-disjoint* st-*paths*, since all *st*-paths must include one of these edges.

Example 3:

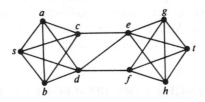

In this graph the three edges *ce*, *de*, and *df* separate *s* from *t*. It follows that *there are at most three edge-disjoint* st-*paths*, since all *st*-paths must include one of these edges.

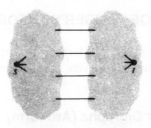

More generally, consider a set of edges separating *s* from *t* in an arbitrary connected graph. Since the removal of these edges destroys all paths between *s* and *t*, every *st*-path must include at least one of them. It follows that *the maximum number of edge-disjoint* st-*paths cannot exceed the number of edges in this set*. Since this applies to *any* set of edges separating *s* from *t*, we have

the *maximum* number of edge-disjoint *st*-paths	$\leq$	the number of edges in *any* set separating *s* from *t*.

Since this is true for *any* set of edges separating *s* from *t*, it must be true for a set with the smallest possible number of edges. So

the *maximum* number of edge-disjoint *st*-paths	$\leq$	the *minimum* number of edges separating *s* from *t*.

These two numbers are, in fact, always equal. This is the *edge-form of Menger's theorem for graphs*, which may be stated formally

MENGER'S THEOREM FOR GRAPHS (EDGE-FORM). *Let G be a connected graph, and let* s *and* t *be vertices of G. Then the maximum number of edge-disjoint* st-*paths is equal to the minimum number of edges separating* s *from* t.

It follows from Menger's theorem that, if we can find *k* edge-disjoint *st*-paths and *k* edges separating *s* from *t* (for the same value of *k*), then *k* is the *maximum* number of

edge-disjoint *st*-paths and the *minimum* number of edges separating *s* from *t*. Note that
these *k* edges separating *s* from *t* necessarily form a cutset. It follows that, when looking
for them, we need consider only cutsets whose removal disconnects *G* into two components, one containing *s* and the other containing *t*.

We can use Menger's theorem to obtain a result about edge-connectivity. Recall that
the edge-connectivity $\lambda(G)$ of a connected graph *G* is the smallest number of edges whose
removal disconnects *G*. By Menger's theorem, there are at least $\lambda(G)$ edge-disjoint paths
between any given pair of vertices. Since *G* is *k*-edge-connected if and only if $\lambda(G) \geq k$,
we can restate this result.

COROLLARY OF MENGER'S THEOREM FOR GRAPHS (EDGE-FORM). *A
connected graph* G *is* k *edge-connected if and only if any two vertices of* G *are connected
by at least* k *edge-disjoint paths.*

9.4 SOME ANALOGS OF MENGER'S THEOREM

We now present some analogs of Menger's theorem, starting with Menger's theorem for
digraphs (arc-form), and continuing with the vertex-forms for both graphs and digraphs.

Menger's Theorem for Digraphs (Arc-form)

Many of the concepts introduced earlier for graphs have analogs for digraphs. For example, the definitions that follow are almost identical to those given for graphs.

DEFINITIONS. *Let* D *be a connected digraph and let* s *and* t *be vertices of* D. *An*
st-**path** *is a path from* s *to* t. *Two or more* st-*paths are* **arc-disjoint** *if they have no arcs
in common, and* **vertex-disjoint** *if they have no vertices in common (apart from* s *and* t).

For example, in the digraph

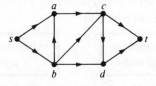

the paths *sact* and *sbdt* are both arc-disjoint and vertex-disjoint *st*-paths;

the paths *sact* and *sbct* are neither arc-disjoint nor vertex-disjoint;

the paths *sact* and *sbcdt* are arc-disjoint but not vertex-disjoint.

We also say that certain arcs **separate** *s* **from** *t* if the removal of these arcs destroys
all paths from *s* to *t*. Similarly, we say that certain vertices **separate** *s* **from** *t* if the removal
of these vertices destroys all paths from *s* to *t*. For example, in the above digraph,

the arcs *ac*, *bc*, and *bd* separate *s* from *t*, as do the arcs *sa*, *ac*, *bc*, *bd*, and *dt*; the vertices *b* and *c* separate *s* from *t*, as do the vertices *a*, *b*, and *d*.

Using this terminology, we can state Menger's theorem for digraphs:

MENGER'S THEOREM FOR DIGRAPHS (ARC-FORM). *Let* D *be a connected digraph and let* s *and* t *be vertices of* D. *Then the maximum number of arc-disjoint* st-*paths is equal to the minimum number of arcs separating* s *from* t.

As with Menger's theorem for graphs, if we can find *k* arc-disjoint *st*-paths and *k* arcs separating *s* from *t* (for the same value of *k*), then *k* is the *maximum* number of arc-disjoint *st*-paths and the *minimum* number of arcs separating *s* from *t*.

Menger's Theorem for Graphs (Vertex-form)

We have seen how Menger's theorem (edge-form) relates the number of edge-disjoint *st*-paths in a graph to the smallest number of edges separating *s* from *t*, and how this result relates to edge-connectivity. We now state an analogous theorem for vertex-disjoint *st*-paths. This is the version of Menger's theorem actually proved by K. Menger in 1927. The corollary was proved five years later by H. Whitney. The edge-form and arc-form of Menger's theorem were proved in 1955 by L. R. Ford and D. R. Fulkerson. As before, we motivate our discussion with examples.

Example 1:

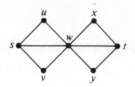

This graph has (vertex-)connectivity 1, and the vertex *w* separates *s* from *t*. It follows that *there cannot be two vertex-disjoint st-paths*, since all *st*-paths must include the vertex *w*.
Example 2:

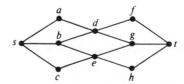

This graph has connectivity 2, and the vertices *d* and *e* separate *s* from *t*. It follows that *there are at most two vertex-disjoint st-paths*, since all *st*-paths must include one of these vertices.

More generally, consider a set of vertices separating non-adjacent vertices s and t in an arbitrary connected graph. Since the removal of these vertices destroys all paths between s and t, every st-path must include at least one of them. It follows that *the maximum number of vertex-disjoint st-paths cannot exceed the number of vertices in this set.*

As with the edge-form of Menger's theorem, these numbers are, in fact, equal. This is the *vertex-form of Menger's theorem,* which we state formally.

MENGER'S THEOREM FOR GRAPHS (VERTEX-FORM). *Let* G *be a connected graph and let* s *and* t *be non-adjacent vertices of* G. *Then the maximum number of vertex-disjoint* st-*paths is equal to the minimum number of vertices separating* s *from* t.

As before, it follows that, if we can find k vertex-disjoint st-paths and k vertices separating s from t (for the same value of k), then k is the *maximum* number of vertex-disjoint st-paths and the *minimum* number of vertices in a vertex-cutset separating s from t. Note that these k vertices separating s from t necessarily form a vertex-cutset. It follows that, when looking for them, we need consider only vertex-cutsets whose removal disconnects G into two or more components, one containing s and another containing t.

We can also use this theorem to obtain a result about vertex-connectivity.

COROLLARY OF MENGER'S THEOREM FOR GRAPHS (VERTEX-FORM). *A connected graph* G *is* k-*connected if and only if any two vertices of* G *are connected by at least* k *vertex-disjoint paths.*

Menger's Theorem for Digraphs (Vertex-form)

Finally, for completeness, we present the vertex-form of Menger's theorem for digraphs. This is almost identical to the vertex-form for graphs.

MENGER'S THEOREM FOR DIGRAPHS (VERTEX-FORM). *Let* D *be a connected digraph and let* s *and* t *be nonadjacent vertices of* D. *Then the maximum number of vertex-disjoint* st-*paths is equal to the minimum number of vertices separating* s *from* t.

9.5 THE PROOF OF MENGER'S THEOREM

We now prove Menger's theorem. We start by proving the arc-form for digraphs, and then show how the corresponding result for graphs follows immediately. Finally, we indicate how the vertex-forms for graphs and digraphs follow from the other versions.

MENGER'S THEOREM FOR DIGRAPHS (ARC-FORM). *Let* D *be a connected* *digraph and let* s *and* t *be vertices of* D. *Then the maximum number of arc-disjoint* st-*paths is equal to the minimum number of arcs separating* s *from* t.

Proof We have already shown that the maximum number k of arc-disjoint st-paths cannot exceed the minimum number of arcs separating s from t. To show that these numbers are actually equal, we need to find a set S of k arcs separating s from t.

Consider any set A of k arc-disjoint st-paths. Let X be the set of all vertices of D which can be reached from s by a path disjoint from those in A, and let Y be the remaining set of vertices. Then t must lie in Y, since if t were in X, then there would be another st-path, disjoint from the rest; this is impossible since A contains the maximum number of arc-disjoint st-paths.

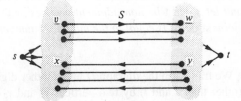

We now let S be the set of arcs of D directed from a vertex v in X to a vertex w in Y. Any such arc must be included in a path in A, since otherwise w (as well as v) could be reached from s by a path disjoint from those in A, and w would have to be in X, rather than Y. By a similar argument, any arc directed from a vertex in Y to a vertex in X cannot be included in a path in A. So the number of arcs in S is equal to the number of paths in A—that is, S is a set of k arcs separating s from t, as required. □

We can now deduce Menger's theorem for graphs (edge-form).

MENGER'S THEOREM FOR GRAPHS (EDGE-FORM). *Let* G *be a connected graph and let* s *and* t *be vertices of* G. *Then the maximum number of edge-disjoint* st-*paths is equal to the minimum number of edges separating* s *from* t.

Outline of Proof We transform the graph G into a digraph $D(G)$ by replacing each edge by two arcs, one in each direction, as indicated in the diagram

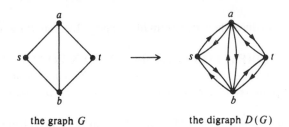

the graph G the digraph $D(G)$

It can be shown that

    a.   The maximum number of edge-disjoint st-paths in G is equal to the maximum number of arc-disjoint st-paths in $D(G)$.

  b. The minimum number of edges of G separating s from t is equal to the
      minimum number of arcs of $D(G)$ separating s from t.

By Menger's theorem for digraphs (proved above), the maximum number of arc-disjoint
st-paths in $D(G)$ is equal to the minimum number of arcs of $D(G)$ separating s from t,
and so the maximum number of edge-disjoint st-paths in G is equal to the minimum
number of edges of G separating s from t, as required. ☐

We can also deduce the vertex-form of Menger's theorem for digraphs.

MENGER'S THEOREM FOR DIGRAPHS (VERTEX-FORM). *Let* D *be a
connected digraph and let* s *and* t *be non-adjacent vertices of* D. *Then the maximum
number of vertex-disjoint* st-*paths is equal to the minimum number of vertices separating* s *from* t.

Outline of Proof   We transform the digraph D into another digraph D' by replacing
each vertex v of D (other than s and t) by two vertices v_1 and v_2 joined by an arc, as
indicated by

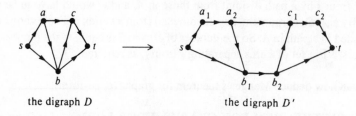

the digraph D the digraph D'

All arcs of D directed towards a vertex v become arcs of D' directed towards the vertex
v_1, and all arcs of D directed away from v become arcs of D' directed away from v_2.
   It is not difficult to see that two or more st-paths in D are vertex-disjoint if and only
if the corresponding st-paths in D' are arc-disjoint. Applying the arc-form of Menger's
theorem to D', we obtain the vertex-form of Menger's theorem for D. ☐

Finally, we can deduce the vertex-form of Menger's theorem for graphs.

MENGER'S THEOREM FOR GRAPHS (VERTEX-FORM). *Let* G *be a con-
nected graph and let* s *and* t *be non-adjacent vertices of* G. *Then the maximum number of
vertex-disjoint* st-*paths is equal to the minimum number of vertices separating* s *from* t.

Outline of Proof   This form of Menger's theorem is deduced from the vertex-form
for digraphs in the same way as the edge-form for graphs is deduced from the arc-form
for digraphs—namely, by considering the digraph $D(G)$. ☐

PROBLEMS

Edge-connectivity and Vertex-connectivity

⊃9.1. Write down the values of $\kappa(G)$ and $\lambda(G)$ for each of the following graphs G:

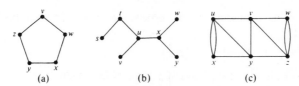

(a)   (b)   (c)

Which of these graphs are 2-connected? Which are 3-connected? Which are 2-edge-connected? Which·are 3-edge-connected?

9.2. Write down the values of $\kappa(G)$ and $\lambda(G)$ for each of the following graphs G:

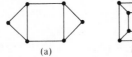

(a)   (b)   (c)

Which of these graphs are 2-connected? Which are 3-connected? Which are 2-edge-connected? Which are 3-edge-connected?

9.3. Find $\kappa(G)$ and $\lambda(G)$ for each of the following graphs G:

(a)   (b)   (c)

⊃9.4. Which of the following sets of edges are cutsets of the following graph G?

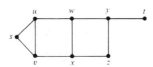

a. $\{su,sv\}$;   c. $\{ux,vx,wx,yz\}$;   e. $\{wx,xz,yz\}$;
b. $\{ux,wx,yz\}$;   d. $\{yt\}$;   f. $\{uw,wx,wy\}$.

9.5. In the Petersen graph, find a cutset with
   a. three edges;
   b. four edges;
   c. five edges;
   d. six edges.

○9.6. Which of the following sets of vertices are vertex-cutsets of the graph in Problem 9.4?
   a. $\{u,v\}$;   b. $\{v,w\}$;   c. $\{u,x,y\}$;   d. $\{w,z\}$.

9.7.[†] Give an example (if it exists) of a graph G for which
   a. $\kappa(G) = 2, \lambda(G) = 3, \delta(G) = 4$;
   b. $\kappa(G) = 3, \lambda(G) = 2, \delta(G) = 4$;
   c. $\kappa(G) = 2, \lambda(G) = 2, \delta(G) = 4$.

9.8.[†] Find a 4-connected graph with eight vertices and sixteen edges.

Menger's Theorem

○9.9. Consider the following graph:

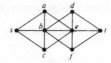

   Write down
   a. three edge-disjoint st-paths;
   b. two st-paths that are edge-disjoint, but not vertex-disjoint;
   c. two vertex-disjoint st-paths.
   Does this graph contain three vertex-disjoint st-paths?

9.10. Consider the following graph:

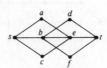

   a. Write down three edge-disjoint st-paths.
   b. Write down a set of three edges separating s from t.
   c. What is the maximum number of edge-disjoint st-paths?
   Give a brief reason for your answer.

⊙9.11. a. Prove that if two st-paths in a graph are vertex-disjoint, then they must also be edge-disjoint.

  b. Give an example of a graph in which no two edge-disjoint st-paths are vertex-disjoint.

⊙9.12. By finding k edge-disjoint st-paths, and k edges separating s from t (for the same value of k), and using the edge-form of Menger's theorem, find the maximum number of edge-disjoint st-paths for each graph

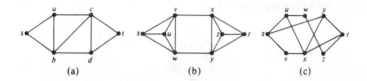

(a)   (b)   (c)

9.13. By finding k arc-disjoint st-paths, and k arcs separating s from t (for the same value of k), and using the arc-form of Menger's theorem, find the maximum number of arc-disjoint st-paths for each digraph

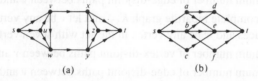

(a)   (b)

9.14. By finding k vertex-disjoint st-paths, and k vertices separating s from t (for the same value of k), and using Menger's theorem for digraphs (vertex-form), find the maximum number of vertex-disjoint st-paths for the digraph

9.15. a. By finding k arc-disjoint st-paths, and k arcs separating s from t (for the same value of k), find the maximum number of arc-disjoint st-paths for the digraph

b. Using similar reasoning, find the maximum number of vertex-disjoint st-paths.

9.16. By finding k vertex-disjoint st-paths, and k vertices separating s from t (for the same value of k), and using the vertex-form of Menger's theorem, find the maximum number of vertex-disjoint st-paths for the graph

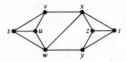

9.17. Consider the following graph G:

Find

a.   the maximum number of vertex-disjoint paths between v and w;

b.   the maximum number of edge-disjoint paths between v and w.

♥9.18. Consider the complete bipartite graph $K_{5,7}$, and let v be any vertex in the set with five vertices and w be any vertex in the set with seven vertices. Find

a.   the maximum number of vertex-disjoint paths between v and w;

b.   the maximum number of edge-disjoint paths between v and w.

9.19.[†]   Verify both the edge-form and the vertex-form of Menger's theorem for the Petersen graph, for all possible choices of the vertices s and t.

CHAPTER 10

TREES

In Chapter 3 we showed how tree structures arise in many different contexts, ranging from chemistry to linguistics. We now obtain several results on the properties of trees, and then turn our attention to some common algorithms associated with trees. We divide these into three types:

1. Algorithms for searching and labeling parts of a given tree;
2. Algorithms for constructing various types of tree;
3. Algorithms for counting trees of a particular type.

10.1 MATHEMATICAL PROPERTIES OF TREES

For the mathematician, the interest and importance of trees arises from the fact that in many ways a tree is the simplest non-trivial type of graph, and has several pleasing properties—for example, any two vertices are connected by exactly one path. In trying to prove a general result or test a general conjecture in graph theory, it is sometimes convenient to start by trying to prove the corresponding result for a tree. There are several conjectures which have not been proved for arbitrary graphs, but which are known to be true for trees.

We start by recalling the definition of a tree.

DEFINITION. *A **tree** is a connected graph which contains no cycles.*

For example, the following diagram depicts all the trees with at most six vertices:

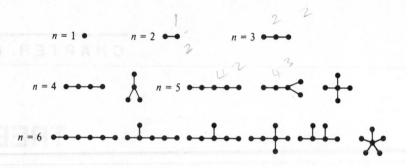

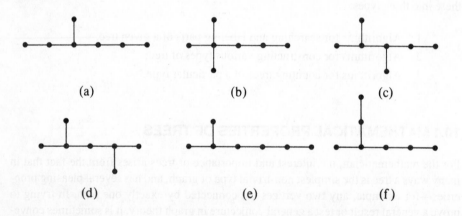

Suppose we now consider the following tree with six vertices:

By adding an edge joining a new vertex to an existing one, we can obtain a tree with seven vertices. This is a general procedure for increasing the size of a tree, since it creates no cycles and can be carried out systematically by adjoining the new edge to each vertex in turn. For example, we obtain the following trees with seven vertices from the above tree:

       (a)   (b)   (c)

       (d)   (e)   (f)

We can omit tree (f) from this list, since it is isomorphic to tree (a), and so we get five trees with seven vertices from our original tree with six vertices. The difficulty of producing trees in this way is in recognizing duplicates, but at least we know that each tree with seven vertices must be obtained at least once from some tree with six vertices.

Starting with the tree with just one vertex, we can build up any tree we wish by successively adding a new edge and a new vertex. At each stage the number of vertices exceeds the number of edges by 1, so that

every tree with n vertices has exactly $n-1$ edges.

At no stage is a cycle created, since each added edge joins an old vertex to a new one. It follows that

> any two vertices in a tree are connected by exactly one path.

There is at least one path, because at each stage the tree remains connected, and there is at most one, because if there were two or more paths joining two given vertices, these paths would contain a cycle (and possibly other edges as well).

In particular, any two adjacent vertices are connected by exactly one path—namely, the edge joining them. If this edge is removed, then there is no path between the two vertices. Therefore,

> each edge of a tree is a bridge.

Moreover,

> the addition of an edge between any two vertices of a tree creates exactly one cycle.

This is because any two vertices v and w are connected by just one path, and the addition of the edge vw produces a single cycle—the cycle consisting of the path and the edge vw.

Several of the properties just obtained can be used as alternative definitions of a tree. In the following theorem we state six of these alternative definitions. They are all *equivalent*: any one of them can be taken as the definition of a tree, and the other five can then be deduced. We leave you to check this if you wish (see Problem 10.3).

THEOREM 9.1. *Let* T *be a graph with* n *vertices. Then the following statements are equivalent*:

a. T *is connected and contains no cycles*;

b. T *is connected and has* n–1 *edges*;

c. T *has* n–1 *edges and contains no cycles*;

d. T *is connected and each edge is a bridge*;

e. *any two vertices of* T *are connected by exactly one path*;

f. T *contains no cycles, but the addition of any new edge creates exactly one cycle*.

10.2 SPANNING TREES

Later in this chapter we shall need the concept of a spanning tree. Recall the definition of a spanning tree in a connected graph.

DEFINITION. *Let* G *be a connected graph. A* **spanning tree** *in* G *is a subgraph of* G *that includes all the vertices of* G *and is also a tree. The edges of the tree are called* **branches.**

For example, the following diagram illustrates a graph and three of its spanning trees:

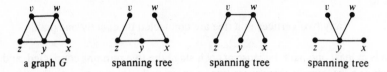

For any connected graph G, we can find a spanning tree systematically by using either of two methods.

Cutting-down Method   We start by choosing any cycle in G and removing one of its edges. (If there are no cycles, the graph G is itself a spanning tree.) Since we cannot disconnect a graph by removing just one edge from a cycle, we still have a connected graph. We now repeat this procedure until there are no cycles left; this gives our spanning tree. For example, from the above graph G, we can remove the edges

   vy (destroying the cycle $vwyv$),

   yz (destroying the cycle $vwyzv$),

   xy (destroying the cycle $wxyw$).

We thus obtain the second of the above spanning trees.

Building-up Method   We select edges of G one at a time in such a way that no cycles are created, and repeat this procedure until all vertices are included. For example, in the above graph G, we can choose the edges vz, wx, xy, and yz; then no cycles are created, and we obtain the first of the above spanning trees.

10.3 CENTERS AND BICENTERS

When proving results involving trees, we frequently find it convenient to start at the middle of a tree and move outwards, building up the tree as we proceed. This was the approach used by Arthur Cayley in the 1870s when he counted the number of chemical molecules with a given formula by building them up step by step. More recently, the concept of a *balanced tree* has been used in computing, where we build up a tree in such a way that the various subtrees emerging from each vertex are 'balanced'—that is, they involve the same number of vertices. But what do we mean by the 'middle' of a tree? For some trees this is easy to define.

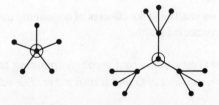

However, how do we define the 'middle' of the following trees?

There are at least two possible answers to this question:

Method 1   Remove all the vertices of degree 1, together with their incident edges; repeat this as often as you can until you obtain *either* a single vertex (the **center**) *or* two vertices joined by an edge (the **bicenter**).

A tree with a center is called a **central tree,** and a tree with a bicenter is called a **bicentral tree.** Every tree is either central or bicentral, but not both.

Examples: A *central tree* with center *e*.

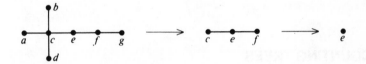

A *bicentral tree* with bicenter *cd*.

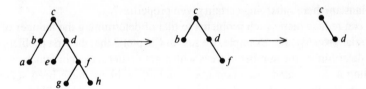

Method 2   For each vertex *v* of degree 2 or more, count the number of vertices in each of the subtrees emanating from *v*, and let n_v be the maximum of these numbers. If the tree has *n* vertices, it can be shown that *either* there is just one vertex *v* for which $n_v \leq \frac{1}{2}(n-1)$ (the **centroid**), *or* there are two adjacent vertices *v* and *w* for which $n_v = n_w = \frac{1}{2}n$ (the **bicentroid**).

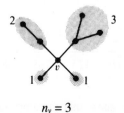

$$n_v = 3$$

We can think of the centroid or bicentroid as the 'center of gravity' of the tree. A tree with a centroid is called a **centroidal tree,** and a tree with a bicentroid is called a **bicentroidal tree.** Every tree is either centroidal or bicentroidal, but not both.

Examples: $n_c = 4$, $n_e = 4$, $n_f = 5$, and $n_g = 6$, so we have a bicentroidal tree with bicentroid ce.

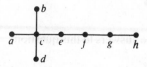

$n_b = 6$, $n_c = 5$, $n_d = 3$, and $n_f = 5$, so we have a centroidal tree with centroid d.

10.4 COUNTING TREES

How many chemical molecules are there with the formula C_8H_{18}? How many irrigation canal systems are there linking five locations with four canals? How many architectural floor plans are there satisfying certain given properties?

We can reduce many such problems to that of determining the number of trees with a particular property. For example, we saw in Chapter 3 that the first problem reduces to that of determining the number of trees with eight vertices, each of which has degree not exceeding 4. Since many standard tree-counting problems have been solved, we can sometimes use the results to deduce the solution of our original problem.

In general, counting problems for labeled graphs are much easier to solve than their analogs for unlabeled graphs; in fact, there are certain types of graph for which the former problem has been solved while the latter problem remains unsolved. However, the problems of counting the labeled and unlabeled trees have both been solved, although the former problem is easier to solve than the latter one. The following table lists the numbers of unlabeled and labeled trees with n vertices, for $n \leq 10$.

n	1	2	3	4	5	6	7	8	9	10
unlabeled trees	1	1	1	2	3	6	11	23	47	106
labeled trees	1	1	3	16	125	1296	16807	262144	4782969	10^8

Using this table, it is easy to guess that there are exactly n^{n-2} labeled trees with n

vertices. This fact is known as *Cayley's theorem*. We outline a proof of this result, which is due to H. Prüfer and involves the construction of a one-to-one correspondence between labeled trees with n vertices and sequences of $n-2$ numbers (called **Prüfer sequences**). We assume that $n \geq 3$, since the result is clearly true if $n = 1$ or 2.

First we describe Prüfer's construction.

Prüfer's Construction   We construct a one-to-one correspondence between the set of labeled trees with n vertices and the set of all sequences of the form $(a_1, a_2, a_3, \ldots, a_{n-2})$, where each a_i is one of the integers $1, 2, 3, \ldots, n$ (allowing repetition). In order to obtain the required one-to-one correspondence, we take a labeled tree with n vertices and apply three steps.

STEP 1   Look at the vertices of degree 1 and choose the one with the smallest label.

STEP 2   Look at the vertex adjacent to the one just chosen and place its label in the first available position in the sequence.

STEP 3   Remove the vertex chosen in STEP 1 and its incident edge, leaving a smaller tree.

Repeat STEPS 1–3 for the remaining tree, continuing until there are only two vertices left. By the time this happens, the required Prüfer sequence will have been constructed.

Example: Consider the labeled tree

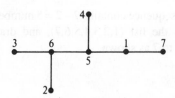

STEP 1   The vertices of degree 1 are vertices 3, 2, 4, and 7; the one with the smallest label is vertex 2.

STEP 2   The vertex adjacent to vertex 2 is vertex 6, so the sequence starts with **6.**

STEP 3   Removal of the vertex 2 and the edge 26 leaves.

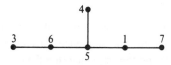

STEP 1   The vertices of degree 1 are vertices 3, 4, and 7; the one with the smallest label is vertex 3.

STEP 2   The vertex adjacent to vertex 3 is vertex 6, so the next term in the sequence is **6.**

STEP 3   Removal of the vertex 3 and the edge 36 leaves the tree

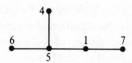

Continuing in this way, we successively remove the edges 45, 65 and 51, and obtain the Prüfer sequence (**6,6,5,5,1**).

In order to obtain the reverse correspondence, we take a Prüfer sequence and apply three steps.

STEP 1   Draw the *n* vertices, labeling them from 1 to *n* and make a list of the numbers from 1 to *n*.

STEP 2   Find the smallest number that is in the list but *not* in the Prüfer sequence, and also find the first number in the sequence; then add an edge joining the vertices with these labels.

STEP 3   Remove the first number of STEP 2 from the list and the other number of STEP 2 from the sequence, leaving a smaller list and sequence.

Repeat STEPS 2 and 3 for the remaining list and sequence, continuing until there are only two labels left in the list. Finally, join the vertices with these labels.

Example: Consider the Prüfer sequence (**6,6,5,5,1**).

STEP 1   Since the sequence contains $7 - 2 = 5$ numbers, we start with the list (1,2,3,4,5,6,7), and draw the vertices 1 to 7 as shown.

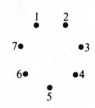

STEP 2   The smallest number in the list but not in the sequence is 2, and the first number in the sequence is **6**, so we add an edge joining the vertices 2 and 6.

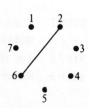

STEP 3   Removal of the number 2 from the list, and the number **6** from the sequence, leaves the list (1,3,4,5,6,7) and the sequence (**6,5,5,1**).

STEP 2   The smallest number in the new list which is not in the new sequence is 3, and the first number in the new sequence is **6**, so we add an edge joining the vertices 3 and 6.

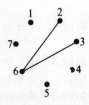

STEP 3   Removal of the number 3 from the list, and the number 6 from the sequence, leaves the list (1,4,5,6,7) and the sequence (**5,5,1**).

Continuing in this way, we successively add edges joining the vertices 4 and **5**, 6 and **5**, and 5 and **1**. The list is now (1,7), and we join the vertices with these labels. This gives the labeled tree shown on the right.

Note that this labeled tree obtained from the Prüfer sequence (**6,6,5,5,1**) is the same as the labeled tree which earlier gave rise to this sequence. This happens in general—if you start with any labeled tree, find the corresponding Prüfer sequence, and then find the labeled tree corresponding to this sequence, you should get back to the original tree. This gives the required one-to-one correspondence:

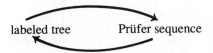

labeled tree   Prüfer sequence

CAYLEY'S THEOREM. *The number of labeled trees with* n *vertices is* n^{n-2}.

Proof (H. Prüfer, 1918)   We construct the above one-to-one correspondence between the set of labeled trees with n vertices and the set of all sequences of the form $(a_1, a_2, a_3, \ldots, a_{n-2})$, where each a_i is one of the integers 1, 2, 3, $\ldots$, n (allowing repetition). Since there are exactly n possible values for each number a_i, the total number of possible sequences is n^{n-2}. The result follows immediately. $\square$

10.5 SEARCHING TREES

A problem which frequently arises in practice is that of searching through some given tree structure in a systematic way. For example, a computer file is often organized as a tree-like data-structure in some form of random-access memory (RAM), and a systematic tree search is necessary whenever a particular piece of information is required. In practice, this usually involves examining every part of the tree until the desired vertex or edge is found; in order to avoid unnecessary wastage of time and processing resources, we need a search technique which is guaranteed to visit all parts of the tree eventually without visiting any particular vertex too often.

There are two well-known search methods, which differ in the pattern of search they employ. They are usually known as **depth-first search** (DFS) and **breadth-first search** (BFS). Each of these methods lists the vertices as they are encountered, and indicates the direction in which each edge is first traversed. The methods differ only in the way in which the vertex-lists are constructed. No good rule can be given as to which search method should be used for a particular problem. Both are in widespread use, but each method has its advantages and disadvantages, depending on the problem in hand. Although our discussion here is introduced in the context of trees, both methods can easily be applied to more general types of graph. In such applications, they effectively search the graph by searching through all the vertices of an appropriate spanning tree.

Depth-first Search (DFS)

The basic idea of depth-first search is to penetrate as deeply as possible into a tree before fanning out to other vertices.

Example: Consider the following tree:

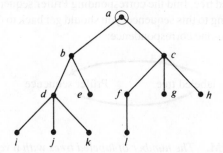

In order to perform a depth-first search starting at the vertex a, we start by choosing any vertex adjacent to a (b, say), then any vertex adjacent to b (d, say), and so on. At each stage, we choose a vertex not previously used, if it is possible to do so. We number the vertices as we go. Thus, we may start by assigning to a, b, d, and i the labels 1, 2, 3, and 4, respectively. Once we have reached i, since there are no new vertices to go to we are stuck. We must therefore backtrack to d, from which we can go to j, assigning it label 5. Backtracking to d again takes us to k, to which we assign label 6. We now have to backtrack via d to b, from which we can go to e, assigning it label 7. Backtracking to a takes us to c, f, and l, and (eventually) to g and h. (In choosing which adjacent vertex to take at each stage, we have selected the left-hand one in every case, although it is not necessary to be so systematic.) This gives us the labeled tree

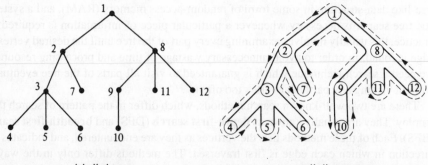

labelled tree   wall diagram

Another way of obtaining this labeling is to regard the tree as a solid wall, and to walk around it, always keeping the wall on our left-hand side. Whenever we reach a new vertex, we give it the next label, as shown in the above diagram. A similar idea arises in computer programming, where we sometimes use a binary tree to represent an arithmetic expression. For example, the expression $a+\{(b-c)\times d\}$ can be represented by the following tree; we retrieve this expression by walking around the tree, writing each vertex as we walk *underneath* it:

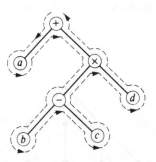

The above procedures can be extended to any connected graph, as the following example shows.

Example: Consider the graph:

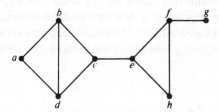

We can perform a depth-first search on this graph by starting at a, going to b, c, and d, backtracking to c, going to e, f, and g, backtracking to f, going to h, and returning to a. This gives us the labeling

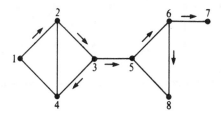

Note that we have marked with an arrow those edges we used when going to each new vertex. These edges form a spanning tree, called a **DFS spanning tree**.

A practical example of the use of depth-first search is the search for flow-augmenting paths in a capacitated network, as explained in the companion volume on *Networks*.

Breadth-first Search (BFS)

The basic idea of breadth-first search is to fan out to as many vertices as possible before penetrating deep into a tree. This means that we visit all the vertices adjacent to the current vertex before going on to another one, as the following example shows.

Example: Consider the tree

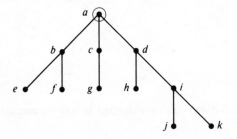

In order to perform a breadth-first search starting at the vertex a, we start by visiting the vertices b and c that are adjacent to a. We then visit the vertices d and e adjacent to b, and the vertices f, g, and h adjacent to c. If we label each new vertex as we come to it, we eventually obtain the following labeling of the vertices (the DFS labeling is shown for comparison):

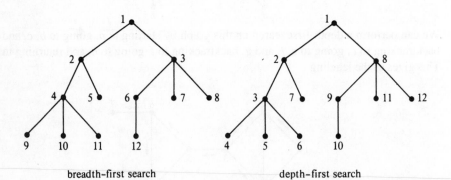

breadth–first search   depth–first search

Note that if the vertices are laid out in horizontal 'levels', as in this example, then in a breadth-first search we must complete each level before proceeding to the next one.

The above procedure can be extended to any connected graph, as the following example shows.

Example: Consider the graph

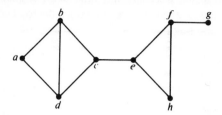

We can perform a breadth-first search on this graph by starting at *a*, visiting the vertices *b* and *d* adjacent to *a*, visiting the vertex *c* adjacent to *b*, and so on. This gives us the labeling

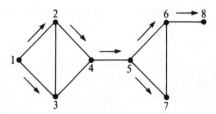

Note that we have marked with an arrow those edges we used when going to each new vertex. These edges form a spanning tree, called a **BFS spanning tree**.

A practical example of the use of breadth-first search is the shortest path algorithm (discussed in Chapter 8).

10.6 CONSTRUCTING TREES

There are two types of situation in which a tree-growing algorithm is useful. One of these involves problems in which we wish to construct large trees from smaller ones. As we saw earlier in this chapter, we can do this by taking the smaller tree and repeatedly adding a vertex and edge to it in all possible ways, removing duplicates as they occur. The second type of situation is more complicated, and arises when we need to find a particular kind of spanning tree in a given graph. A typical example of this kind is the *minimum connector problem*, which we now discuss.

The Minimum Connector Problem

Suppose that we wish to build an irrigation canal system connecting a number of given locations. The cost of digging and maintaining each canal is known, except that some pairs of locations cannot be joined by a canal for geographical or political reasons (for example, a gorge or a politically inviolate area). How do we design a canal system which connects all the locations at minimum possible total cost?

This problem can be interpreted in two different ways, depending on whether or not we allow extra 'locations' where canals may intersect. For example, in the case of the canal system shown below, we may be able to reduce the total cost by creating an extra location at the point E, and linking it to A.

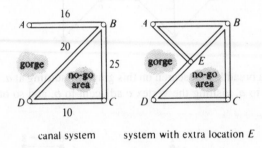

canal system   system with extra location E

Unfortunately, for many minimum connector-type problems, the cost of inserting an extra location (which may be a telephone exchange or power station) can greatly exceed the possible saving in cost, and the resulting mathematical analysis becomes rather complicated. In view of this, we adopt the second interpretation of the problem and assume that each connection joins two existing locations.

We can represent the minimum connector problem graphically by taking the locations as vertices and the canals as edges, giving us a weighted graph. The problem is then to find a subgraph of minimum total weight, passing through each vertex. Note that *such a subgraph must always be a spanning tree*, because if there is a cycle then we can lower the total cost by removing any one of its edges.

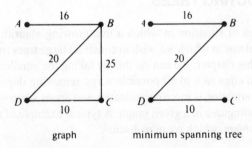

graph   minimum spanning tree

In our example, the graph has total weight 71. Removal of any one of the edges in the cycle BCD lowers the total weight, and gives us a spanning tree. Clearly, the spanning tree of minimum total weight is obtained by removing the edge BC, and the minimum total cost is, therefore, $16 + 20 + 10 = 46$.

DEFINITION. *Let* T *be a spanning tree of minimum total weight in a connected weighted graph* G. *Then* T *is a* **minimum spanning tree** *(or a* **minimum connector***) of* G, *and its weight is denoted by* **W(T)**.

We can now restate the minimum connector problem in graphical terms.

The Minimum Connector Problem   Given a weighted graph, find a minimum spanning tree in it.

A construction that works for the minimum connector problem is known as the *greedy algorithm,* or as *Kruskal's algorithm*; it first appeared in a Czech paper by Borůvka in 1928.

THE GREEDY ALGORITHM.   *To construct a minimum spanning tree in a connected weighted graph* G, *successively choose edges of* G *of minimum weight in such a way that no cycles are created.*

The name 'greedy algorithm' arises from the fact that at each stage we make the greediest choice available (that is, the edge involving the smallest weight) with no concern for what is happening elsewhere in the graph. Algorithms of this kind do not usually succeed in practice, but this is one algorithm which does, as we show below.

We illustrate the use of this algorithm by finding a minimum spanning tree in the weighted graph

First choice   We choose an edge of minimum weight; this is *AE* with weight 2.

Second choice   We choose an edge of next smallest weight; this is either *AC* or *CE* with weight 4. Let us choose *CE*.

Third choice   We cannot now include *AC* in the tree, since it would create a cycle (*ACEA*), so we choose an edge of next smallest weight; this is *BC* with weight 5.

Fourth choice   The edges of next smallest weight are *AB* and *BE* with weight 6. Since either of these would create a cycle (*ABCEA* or *BCEB*), we choose instead the edge *DE* with weight 7.

This completes the spanning tree, which is a minimum spanning tree of weight 18. (Note that if we had chosen the edge AC at the second stage, rather than the edge CE, then we should have obtained a different spanning tree, but its weight would still be 18.) We now prove that the greedy algorithm works.

Proof of the Greedy Algorithm   Let G be a connected graph with n vertices. Let T be a graph that results from applying the algorithm. By the way in which T was constructed, it has no cycles. Also, T is connected, since otherwise we could add another edge of G without creating a cycle. Also, T contains every vertex of G, since if it did not contain the vertex v, then we could add an edge incident with v without creating a cycle. Therefore, T is a spanning tree in G.

We must show that T is a minimum spanning tree of G. We do this by contradiction. Suppose that S is a spanning tree in G of smaller total weight than T; that is, $W(S) < W(T)$. Let e be the edge of smallest weight lying in T but not in S, and consider the subgraph obtained by adding e to S.

By adding the edge e to S we create a cycle C containing e. Since this cycle must contain an edge e' not contained in T, it follows that the subgraph obtained from S on replacing e' by e is still a spanning tree (S', say). By the construction of T, the weight of e cannot exceed the weight of e'; so $W(S') \leq W(S)$, and S' has one more edge in common with T than S. It follows, on repeating this procedure, that we can change S into T, one step at a time, with the weight decreasing at each stage. This shows that $W(T) \leq W(S)$, contradicting the definition of S. This contradiction establishes the result. $\square$

Although the greedy algorithm can easily be applied by hand when the graph is small, it is not particularly well suited for efficient computer implementation, owing to the need to arrange the edges in order of ascending weight, and the need to recognize cycles as they are created. Both of these difficulties can easily be overcome by a slight modification of the above algorithm; the result is known as **Prim's algorithm.**

Prim's Algorithm   To construct a minimum spanning tree T in a connected weighted graph G, build up T step by step by

    a.   putting an arbitrary vertex into T;

    b.   successively adding edges of minimum weight joining a vertex already in T to a vertex not in T.

The advantage of Prim's algorithm is that we can operate directly on the table of weights rather than on the graph itself. If the graph is large, this makes the method more suitable for computer implementation. All we need to do is to delete a row of the table whenever the corresponding vertex is placed in T, and then choose the smallest entry in the column corresponding to vertices in T. The following example illustrates the method.

Example: We use Prim's method to find a minimum spanning tree in the weighted graph

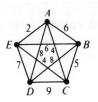

	A	B	C	D	E
A	–	6	4	8	2
B	6	–	5	8	6
C	4	5	–	9	4
D	8	8	9	–	7
E	2	6	4	7	–

First choice

We choose any vertex (say, B) and put it into T.

Delete row B from the table of weights. Look for the smallest entry in column B.

	A	B	C	D	E
A	–	6	4	8	2
C	4	⑤	–	9	4
D	8	8	9	–	7
E	2	6	4	7	–

Second choice

BC is the edge of minimum weight joining B to other vertices. Put the edge BC and the vertex C into T.

The smallest entry in column B occurs in row C, so delete row C. Look for the smallest entry in columns B and C.

	A	B	C	D	E
A	–	6	④	8	2
D	8	8	9	–	7
E	2	6	④	7	–

Third choice

CA and CE are the edges of minimum weight joining B and C to other vertices. Choose one of these (say CA), and put the edge CA and the vertex A into T.

The smallest entry in columns B and C occurs in rows A and E. Choose one of these (say, A), and delete row A. Look for the smallest entry in columns A, B, and C.

	A	B	C	D	E
D	8	8	9	–	7
E	②	6	4	7	–

Fourth choice

AE is the edge of minimum weight joining A, B, and C to other vertices. Put the edge AE and the vertex E into T.

The smallest entry in columns A, B, and C occurs in row E, so delete row E. Look for the smallest entry in columns A, B, C, and E.

	A	B	C	D	E
D	8	8	9	–	⑦

Fifth choice

ED is the edge of minimum weight joining A, B, C, and E to D. Put the edge ED and the vertex D into T.

The smallest entry in columns A, B, C, and E occurs in row D, so delete row D.

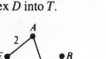

This completes the spanning tree, which is a minimum spanning tree of weight 18.

Application to the Traveling Salesman Problem

In Chapter 7 we described the traveling salesman problem, in which a salesman wishes to visit a number of cities and return to the starting-point, covering the minimum possible total distance on the way. In view of the simple nature of the greedy algorithm for solving the minimum connector problem, we might hope that there is a simple algorithm for solving the traveling salesman problem as well. Unfortunately, no such algorithm is known. We could, of course, try all possible Hamiltonian cycles and simply choose one with the smallest total weight, but this is a hopeless task, even on a computer, unless the number of vertices is very small. For a job-sequencing problem involving (say) 100 jobs, there would be 100! ($\approx 9.3 \times 10^{157}$) sequences to be considered, and no method along these lines would be worth attempting.

In view of this, we are forced to look for approximate solutions to the problem. One method, which often works well in practice, is to find a *lower bound* for the minimum weight Hamiltonian cycle by solving the minimum connector problem instead! To justify this method, we argue as follows:

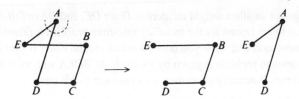

If we take a minimum-weight Hamiltonian cycle in a weighted complete graph, and remove a vertex A and its incident edges, we get a path passing through the remaining vertices. Such a path must be a spanning tree for the complete graph formed by these remaining vertices, and the weight of the Hamiltonian cycle is obtained by adding the weight of this spanning tree to the weights of the two edges incident to A. *We can therefore obtain a lower bound for the solution of the traveling salesman problem by adding the weight of a minimum spanning tree joining those vertices to the two smallest weights of edges incident to A.*

Example: Consider the weighted graph

If we remove the vertex A, then the remaining weighted graph has the four vertices $B, C, D,$ and E.

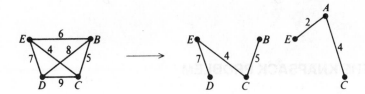

The minimum-weight spanning tree joining these four vertices is the tree whose edges are $BC, CE,$ and ED, with total weight 16. The two edges of smallest weight incident to A are AE and AC, with total weight 6. The required lower bound for the traveling salesman problem is therefore $16 + 6 = 22$.

A better lower bound is obtained by removing the vertex D. In this case, the remaining weighted graph has the four vertices $A, B, C,$ and E, and there are two minimum-weight spanning trees joining these vertices, each with total weight 11.

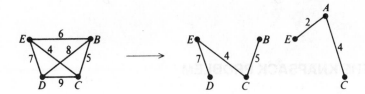

The two edges of smallest weight incident to D are DE, and DA or DB, with total weight 15. The required lower bound for the traveling salesman problem is therefore $11 + 15 = 26$. A little experimentation will show you how good this second lower bound is: the solution of the traveling salesman problem is given by the cycle $ACBDEA$ with total weight 26, so that removing the vertex D actually gives the correct answer in this case.

We can also find an upper bound for the minimum-weight Hamiltonian cycle. One method is to choose any cycle, and calculate its total weight. Alternatively, we can perform a depth-first search on a minimum spanning tree, giving a closed walk which visits each vertex at least once, so that the total distance traveled equals or exceeds the solution of the traveling salesman problem. But if we perform a depth-first search on a minimum spanning tree, we cover each edge of the tree exactly twice and travel a total distance equal to twice the weight of the tree. It follows that the solution of the traveling salesman problem is at most twice the solution of the minimum connector problem. The upper bound for the above example is $2 \times 18 = 36$.

We can improve this upper bound considerably by taking 'short cuts' wherever possible. For example, if in the above example we go directly from D to C, and from B and A, then we reduce the upper bound from 36 to 29.

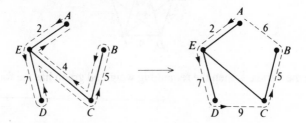

10.7 THE KNAPSACK PROBLEM

We conclude this chapter by solving a problem related to scheduling. Suppose that we have a container in which to pack a number of items of various sizes, and that each item has a value associated with it as well as a size. Which items should we choose to pack in the container so that the total value is as large as possible? This problem is called the **knapsack problem**, since it may be formulated in the following terms.

The Knapsack Problem A hiker is planning a trip, but has a knapsack that can accommodate only a certain total weight. There are a number of items the hiker wishes to take along, each of which has a particular value for the trip. Which items should be packed so that the total value is a maximum, subject to the weight restriction?

A more practical interpretation of this problem is the following:

A company has a certain limited resource which can be used for a number of applications. Each application has a certain value, and uses a certain amount of the resource. Which applications should be chosen so that the greatest total value is obtained from the use of the resource?

The technique we give for solving the knapsack problem is called the **branch-and-bound method**, and involves a search through a tree of possible solutions. We explain how this method works in the context of the following example.

Example: Suppose that five items are available whose weights and values are

Item	A	B	C	D	E
Weight	3	8	6	4	2
Value	2	12	9	3	5

The problem is to find a packing of largest possible total value with a total weight not exceeding 9. In this example, we can list all possible packings and choose one with a maximum total value, subject to the total weight restriction. However, this would obviously not be practical for an example with a large number of items. The branch-and-bound method, which we now describe, is a more efficient procedure in general.

The first step is to list the items in decreasing order of value per unit weight, as follows:

Order number i	1	2	3	4	5
Item	E	B	C	D	A
Weight w_i	2	8	6	4	3
Value v_i	5	12	9	3	2
Value per unit weight	2.5	1.5	1.5	0.75	0.67

We denote each possible packing by a *solution vector* of the form $(x_1, x_2, x_3, x_4, x_5)$, where each x_i takes the value 1 if item i is packed, and the value 0 if that item is not packed. For example, the solution vector $(0,0,1,1,0)$ denotes the packing which includes only items 3 and 4. The total weight w for this solution vector is $w_3 + w_4 = 10$, and the total value v is $v_3 + v_4 = 12$. A solution which satisfies the weight constraint ($w \leq 9$) is called a **feasible solution**. The **null solution** $(0,0,0,0,0)$ is obviously a feasible solution, but $(0,0,1,1,0)$ is infeasible.

Note that the above ordering of items is not essential for this particular type of problem. However, it is an important feature of the branch-and-bound method when used to obtain approximate solutions. In such cases we do not examine all possible feasible solutions.

The branch-and-bound method uses a branching procedure to search for an optimum solution. For example, if we take the solution vector $(0,1,0,0,0)$, we can branch out to other solution vectors:

$$(0, 1, 0, 0, 0) \begin{cases} (0, 1, 1, 0, 0) \\ (0, 1, 0, 1, 0) \\ (0, 1, 0, 0, 1) \end{cases}$$

The solutions produced by this branching procedure are those which have one more item than the starting solution, but the number of such new solutions is restricted; we may add a new item only if it has a higher order number than any item already packed—that is, we may change only those positions to the right of the last 1 in the starting solution. For example, if we start with the solution vector $(1,0,0,1,0)$, we can add only one item (item 5), so only one branch is permitted:

$$(1, 0, 0, 1, 0) \bullet\!\!\!-\!\!\!-\!\!\!-\!\!\!-\!\!\!-\!\!\!-\!\!\!\bullet (1, 0, 0, 1, 1)$$

The branch-and-bound method starts with the null solution and uses this branching procedure to examine possible solutions in a systematic way. At each stage, we calculate the total weight for each solution, and the total value for each feasible solution, and branching is then continued from a feasible solution which has not been previously used as a branching point, and which has the highest value of any such solution. Solutions which cannot be branched out further, either because the weight limit has already been reached, or because there is an item at the extreme right position in the solution vector, are marked with a square. The procedure is continued until all vertices of degree 1 are marked. A record is kept of the best solution obtained so far, and this is updated as necessary.

We illustrate this procedure by applying it to our example. First, we branch out from the null solution, as shown

$$(0, 0, 0, 0, 0) \Big\langle$$

$(1, 0, 0, 0, 0)$	$w = 2, v = 5$
$(0, 1, 0, 0, 0)$	$w = 8, v = \boxed{12}$
$(0, 0, 1, 0, 0)$	$w = 6, v = 9$
$(0, 0, 0, 1, 0)$	$w = 4, v = 3$
$\square\ (0, 0, 0, 0, 1)$	$w = 3, v = 2$

STORE $v = 12$, solution $= (0,1,0,0,0)$

[The highest value of any of these feasible solutions is 12, so we store this value, together with the corresponding solution. The vertex corresponding to the solution $(0,0,0,0,1)$ is marked with a square, to indicate that we cannot continue the branching process from this vertex.]

We delete the marked vertex and continue the branching process from the solution with the highest value—that is, $(0,1,0,0,0)$:

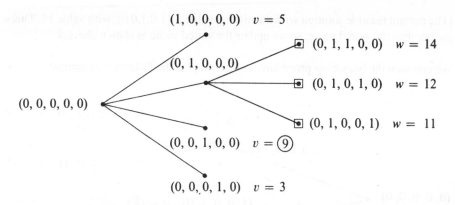

STORE $v = 12$, solution $= (0,1,0,0,0)$
[All three new solutions are infeasible, so we mark the corresponding vertices with squares.]

The current feasible solution with the highest value is $(0,0,1,0,0)$, so we branch out from this vertex:

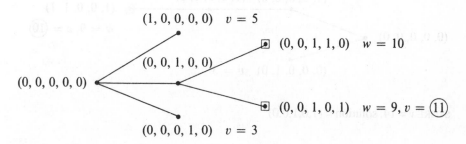

STORE $v = 12$, solution $= (0,1,0,0,0)$
[Although the new solution $(0,0,1,0,1)$ is feasible, we cannot branch further from it, because it has an item in the fifth place, and also because it has already reached the maximum allowable weight. We therefore mark this solution and also the infeasible solution $(0,0,1,1,0)$.]

We continue the branching process from the solution $(1,0,0,0,0)$:

$(0, 0, 0, 0, 0)$	$(1, 0, 0, 0, 0)$	▣ $(1, 1, 0, 0, 0)$ $w = 10$
		$(1, 0, 1, 0, 0)$ $w = 8, v = \textcircled{14}$
		$(1, 0, 0, 1, 0)$ $w = 6, v = 8$
		▣ $(1, 0, 0, 0, 1)$ $w = 5, v = 7$
	$(0, 0, 0, 1, 0)$ $v = 3$	

STORE $v = 14$, solution $= (1,0,1,0,0)$

[The current feasible solution with the highest value is (1,0,1,0,0), with value 14. This is greater than the stored value, so we update the stored value as shown above.]

We continue the branching procedure, as illustrated in the following diagrams:

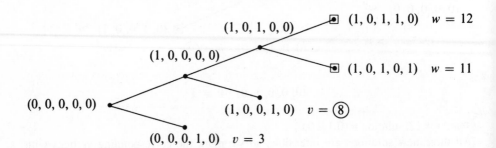

STORE $v = 14$, solution = (1,0,1,0,0)

STORE $v = 14$, solution = (1,0,1,0,0)

STORE $v = 14$, solution = (1,0,1,0,0)

The procedure has now been completed, and the required solution vector is (1,0,1,0,0). This corresponds to packing items C and E, with a total value of 14.

This branch-and-bound method always gives an optimum solution, since it examines all solutions which occur in the branching process. It is more efficient than simply listing and examining all possible solutions, since the branching process automatically excludes many solutions which are infeasible. For example, in the solution to the above problem, there are $2^5 = 32$ possible solutions, but only 18 of these are examined in the branch-and-bound procedure.

PROBLEMS

Mathematical Properties of Trees

◐10.1. By adding a new edge in all possible ways to each tree with six vertices, find all the trees with seven vertices.

10.2. By adding a new edge in all possible ways to each tree with seven vertices, find the 23 trees with eight vertices.

10.3.[†] Prove Theorem 9.1.

[*Hint*: One efficient way to proceed is to prove that (*a*) implies (*b*), (*b*) implies (*c*), . . . , (*e*) implies (*f*), and (*f*) implies (*a*).]

Spanning Trees

◐10.4. A **forest** is a (not necessarily connected) graph, each of whose components is a tree.

    a. Let *G* be a forest with *n* vertices and *k* components. How many edges does *G* have?

    b. Construct a forest with 12 vertices and 9 edges.

    c. Is it true that every forest with *k* components has at least 2*k* vertices of degree 1 (see Problem 2.35)?

10.5. A **spanning forest** in a (not necessarily connected) graph *G* is obtained by constructing a spanning tree for each component of *G*.

    a. Find a spanning forest for the following graph:

    b. Let *G* be a graph, and let *F* be a subgraph of *G*. If *F* is a forest which includes all vertices of *G*, is *F* necessarily a spanning forest of *G*?

Centers and Bicenters

10.6. Classify each of the following trees as central or bicentral, and as centroidal or bicentroidal, and locate the center/bicenter and centroid/bicentroid in each case:

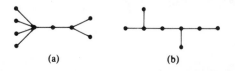

(a)   (b)

10.7. Classify each of the following trees as central or bicentral, and as centroidal or bicentroidal, and locate the center/bicenter and centroid/bicentroid in each case:

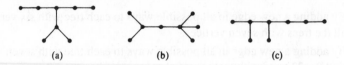

(a)   (b)   (c)

10.8. Classify all the trees with five and six vertices as central or bicentral, and as centroidal or bicentroidal, and locate the center/bicenter and centroid/bicentroid in each case.

10.9.[†] Classify all the trees with seven vertices as central or bicentral, and as centroidal or bicentroidal, and locate the center/ bicenter and centroid/bicentroid in each case.

Counting Trees

⊙10.10. Draw the sixteen labeled trees with four vertices.

10.11. a. Verify directly that there are exactly 125 labeled trees with five vertices.
b. Explain why the complete graph K_n has exactly n^{n-2} spanning trees.
c. How many spanning trees has the complete bipartite graph $K_{2,s}$?

⊙10.12. Find the Prüfer sequence corresponding to each of the following labeled trees:

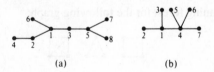

(a)   (b)

10.13. Find the Prüfer sequence corresponding to each of the following labeled trees:

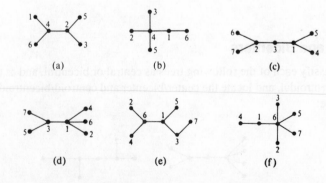

(a)   (b)   (c)

(d)   (e)   (f)

10.14. Find the labeled tree corresponding to each of the following Prüfer sequences:
    a. $(2, 1, 1, 3, 5, 5)$;
    b. $(1, 1, 4, 4, 4)$.

10.15. Find the labeled tree corresponding to each of the following Prüfer sequences:
    a. $(1, 2, 3, 4)$;   d. $(1, 1, 5, 1, 5)$;
    b. $(3, 3, 3, 3)$;   e. $(1, 1, 5, 2, 5)$;
    c. $(1, 3, 7, 2, 1)$;   f. $(1, 3, 2, 3, 5)$.

Searching Trees

◌10.16. Perform (a) a depth-first search and (b) a breadth-first search on the following rooted tree:

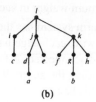

10.17. Perform (a) a depth-first search and (b) a breadth-first search on each of the following rooted trees:

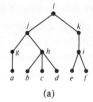

(a)

(b)

10.18. Find a rooted tree which represents the expression $(ab + c) \times (d - e) \times f$.

10.19. Find a DFS spanning tree and a BFS spanning tree in each of the following graphs:

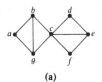

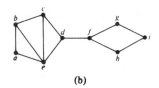

(a)   (b)

Constructing Trees

○10.20. Use the greedy algorithm to find a minimum spanning tree in the following weighted graph:

10.21. The following table gives the distances (in miles) between six places in Ireland. Use the greedy algorithm to find a minimum spanning tree connecting these places.

	Athlone	Dublin	Galway	Limerick	Sligo	Wexford
Athlone	—	78	56	73	71	114
Dublin	78	—	132	121	135	96
Galway	56	132	—	64	85	154
Limerick	73	121	64	—	144	116
Sligo	71	135	85	144	—	185
Wexford	114	96	154	116	185	—

10.22.[†] a. Describe an alternative algorithm for the minimum connector problem which involves the removal from the graph of edges of greatest weight.

   b. Show how to adapt the proof of the greedy algorithm to show that a spanning tree of *maximum* weight can be constructed by successively choosing edges of maximum weight in such a way that no cycles are created.

10.23.[†] A burglar alarm system has the form of a graph whose edges consist of valuable copper wire, each edge having a different value. The alarm will sound if the graph is disconnected. A burglar wishes to steal as many edges as possible without sounding the alarm. Which edges should he steal so as to maximize the value of his haul?

○10.24. In the example of the traveling salesman problem on page 203, we obtained a lower bound of 22 by removing vertex A, and one of 26 by removing vertex D. Find the corresponding lower bounds obtained by removing

   (a) vertex B;   (b) vertex E.

10.25. Consider the traveling salesman problem for the six places in Ireland in Problem 10.21. Find the lower bound obtained by removing the vertex *Athlone*.

10.26. The following table gives the distance (in miles) between five towns:

	A	B	C	D	E
A	—	9	7	5	7
B	9	—	9	9	8
C	7	9	—	7	6
D	5	9	7	—	6
E	7	8	6	6	—

a. Find a minimum spanning tree joining these towns, using (i) the greedy algorithm and (ii) Prim's algorithm.

b. Find lower bounds for the solution of the traveling salesman problem for these towns, obtained by removing (i) the vertex B and (ii) the vertex E.

Find the correct solution by inspection.

10.27. The following table gives the distances (in hundreds of miles) between six European cities:

	Berlin	London	Madrid	Moscow	Paris	Rome
Berlin	—	7	15	11	7	10
London	7	—	11	18	3	12
Madrid	15	11	—	27	8	13
Moscow	11	18	27	—	18	20
Paris	7	3	8	18	—	9
Rome	10	12	13	20	9	—

a. Find a minimum spanning tree joining these cities, using (i) the greedy algorithm and (ii) Prim's algorithm.

b. Find lower bounds for the solution of the traveling salesman problem for these cities, obtained by removing (i) the vertex *London* and (ii) the vertex *Moscow*.

10.28. The following table gives the distances (in miles) between six places in Scotland:

	Aberdeen	Edinburgh	Fort William	Glasgow	Inverness	Perth
Aberdeen	—	120	147	142	104	81
Edinburgh	120	—	132	42	157	45
Fort William	147	132	—	102	66	105
Glasgow	142	42	102	—	168	61
Inverness	104	157	66	168	—	112
Perth	81	45	105	61	112	—

a. Find a minimum spanning tree joining these places, using (i) the greedy algorithm and (ii) Prim's algorithm.

b. Find lower bounds for the solution of the traveling salesman problem for these places, obtained by removing (i) the vertex *Glasgow* and (ii) the vertex *Aberdeen*.

What is the correct solution?

10.29. Obtain an upper bound for the solution to the traveling salesman problem for each of the graphs in Problems 10.24–10.28 by performing a depth-first search on a minimum spanning tree for each of these graphs. How can you improve these upper bounds?

The Knapsack Problem

10.30. A hiker wishes to take some of the following items on a trip:

Item	A	B	C	D
Weight	5	4	3	2
Value	5	3	6	1

Use the branch-and-bound procedure to determine which items should be taken if the total value is to be as large as possible and the total weight should not exceed nine units.

10.31. A traveler wishes to buy some books to take along on a journey. The estimated time to read each of the five books is shown in the following table:

Book	A	B	C	D	E
Cost ($)	4	6	3	2	5
Reading time (hours)	5	9	4	4	4

Use the branch-and-bound method to determine which books should be bought so as to provide the maximum amount of reading material without spending more than $8.

○10.32. A machine in a factory can be used to make any of five items *A, B, C, D,* and *E*. The time taken to produce each item, and the value of each item, are

Item	A	B	C	D	E
Production time (in days)	3	7	2	4	4
Value	3	14	3	7	8

If the machine is available for only 10 days, which of the items should be produced so that the total value is as large as possible?

10.33.† A hiker wishes to take some of the following items on a journey:

Item	A	B	C	D
Weight	5	3	6	1
Value	5	4	3	2

By modifying the branch-and-bound procedure, determine which items should be taken if the total value is at least 9 but the total weight is a minimum.

CHAPTER 11

PLANARITY

11.1 INTRODUCTION

In this chapter we consider the problem of determining whether a given graph can be drawn in the plane without edges crossing, and we present important results of Euler and Kuratowski.

We have seen several instances of graphs which are commonly drawn in several different ways. For example, the complete graph K_4 and the complete bipartite graph $K_{3,3}$ can be drawn as

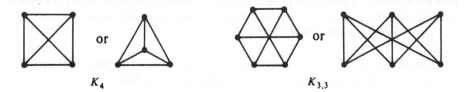

K_4 $K_{3,3}$

The particular drawing we choose often depends on the use to which the graph is to be put. For example, in tree-branching problems we often put the root at the top and let the branches hang down from it. Another example occurs in architecture, where we use a graph to depict the layout of rooms in a building, as follows:

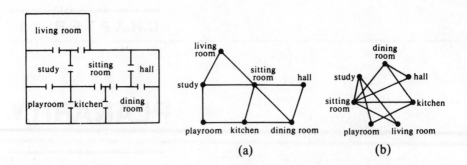

(a)   (b)

Although the graph representation in diagram (a) gives us no information about the size or shape of each room, it does show clearly how the walls and rooms relate to each other geographically, and provides a useful way of describing the floor plan of the building. A different drawing of the same graph, such as the one in diagram (b), still tells us which pairs of rooms are adjacent, but gives us no idea of the spatial relationships between the various rooms.

11.2 PLANAR GRAPHS

In many problems, such as the printed circuits problem described on page 119, it is useful to be able to draw graphs in such a way that no two edges cross each other. For example, the above drawing of the architectural graph in diagram (a) has this property, whereas the equivalent drawing in diagram (b) does not. For some graphs, such as K_4, it is possible to find a drawing which involves no 'crossings', whereas for others, such as $K_{3,3}$, there are no such drawings, as we shall see. This leads us to make the following definitions.

DEFINITIONS. *A graph G is* **planar** *if it can be drawn in the plane in such a way that no two edges meet each other except at a vertex to which they are both incident. Any such drawing is called a* **plane drawing** *of* G.

For example, the graph K_4 is planar, since it can be drawn in the plane without edges crossing. The following diagram shows three plane drawings of K_4:

K_4 plane drawings of K_4

Similarly, the five Platonic graphs are all planar, since they can be drawn as

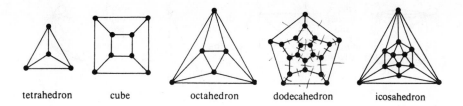

tetrahedron   cube   octahedron   dodecahedron   icosahedron

On the other hand, the complete bipartite graph $K_{3,3}$ is not planar, since every drawing of it contains at least one crossing. To see why this is, note that $K_{3,3}$ has a cycle of length 6 (namely, $uavbwcu$) which must appear in any plane drawing as a hexagon (not necessarily regular).

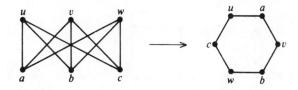

We must now insert the edges ub, vc, and wa. Only one of them can be drawn inside the hexagon, since two or more would cross. Similarly, only one of them can be drawn outside, since two or more would cross.

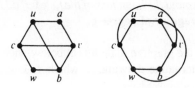

It is therefore impossible to insert all three of these edges without creating a crossing, and so $K_{3,3}$ is not a planar graph. A similar proof can be given to show that K_5 is not planar (see Problem 11.4).

We can use the fact that $K_{3,3}$ is not planar to settle the utilities problem mentioned in Chapter 1. In this problem there are three houses A, B, and C which need to be connected to three utilities, gas, water and electricity, using non-crossing connections. If we regard the three houses and the three utilities as the vertices of $K_{3,3}$, we see immediately that any solution of the utilities problem would yield a plane drawing of $K_{3,3}$. Since no such drawing exists, the utilities problem has no solution.

Note that in studying planar graphs, we can restrict our attention to simple graphs whenever it is convenient to do so. If a planar graph has multiple edges or loops, we collapse the multiple edges to a single edge and remove the loops. After drawing the resulting simple graph without crossings, we can then insert the loops and multiple edges.

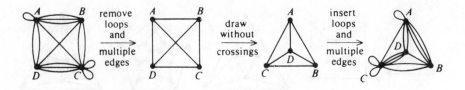

11.3 EULER'S FORMULA

Every plane drawing of a planar graph divides the plane into a number of regions. For example, any plane drawing of K_4 divides the plane into four regions—three triangles, and one 'infinite region'.

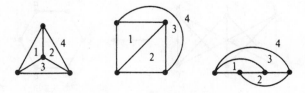

DEFINITIONS. *If G is a planar graph, then any plane drawing of G divides the plane into regions, called* **faces.** *One of these faces is unbounded, and is called the* **infinite face.** *If* f *is any face, then the* **degree of** f *(denoted by deg* f*) is the number of edges encountered in a walk around the boundary of the face* f. *If all faces have the same degree* (g, *say), then G is* **face-regular of degree g.**

For example, if G is the graph in diagram (a) below, then G has four faces, f_4 being the infinite face. An alternative drawing, in which f_2 is the infinite face, is given in diagram (b). In each drawing we have

$$\deg f_1 = 3, \ \deg f_2 = 4, \ \deg f_3 = 9, \ \deg f_4 = 8.$$

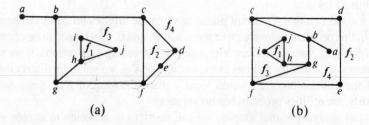

$$(a) \hspace{6cm} (b)$$

Note that *the sum of all the degrees of the faces is equal to twice the number of edges in the graph,* since each edge either borders two different faces (such as the edges bg, cd, and cf) or occurs twice when we walk around a single face (such as the edges ab and gh). This result can be regarded as a sort of *handshaking lemma* for the faces of a planar graph (a face-shaking lemma?), and we shall refer to it as the **handshaking lemma for planar graphs**.

There is a remarkable formula that relates to the number of vertices, edges, and faces of a planar graph. If *n, m,* and *f* denote the numbers of vertices, edges, and faces of a connected planar graph, then we get $n - m + f = 2$. This result is true for any plane drawing of a connected planar graph, and is known as **Euler's formula**. In particular, it tells us that all plane drawings of a connected planar graph have the same number of faces—namely, $2 + m - n$. In our proof of Euler's formula, we start with a spanning tree and build up the graph edge by edge.

THEOREM 11.1 (EULER'S FORMULA).   *Let G be a connected planar graph, and let* n, m, *and.*f *denote, respectively, the numbers of vertices, edges, and faces in a plane drawing of* G. *Then*

$$n - m + f = 2.$$

Proof Any connected graph *G* can be constructed by taking a spanning tree and adding edges to it, one at a time, until the graph *G* is obtained. We prove the result by showing that:

   a.   for a spanning tree, $n - m + f = 2$;
   b.   at each stage, the addition of an edge does not change the value of $n - m + f$.

First, we prove a. If *T* is any spanning tree of *G*, we may draw *T* in the plane—for example,

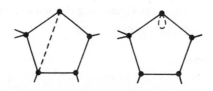

Since *T* has *n* vertices and *n*–1 edges, and there is only 1 face, we have

$$n - m + f = n - (n-1) + 1 = 2,$$

as required.

We now prove b. Whenever we add an edge, such an edge must either connect two different vertices, or connect a vertex to itself (if it is a loop), but in both cases it cuts an existing face in two, as shown

This leaves n unchanged, increases m by 1, and increases f by 1, thereby leaving $n - m + f$ unchanged. Since $n - m + f = 2$ throughout the process, the result follows. □

Historical note. This result is often called *Euler's polyhedral formula*, since it relates the numbers of vertices, edges, and faces of a polyhedron. (For example, a cube has eight vertices, twelve edges and six faces, and $8 - 12 + 6 = 2$.) It appeared in this form in a letter from Euler to the number theorist Christian Goldbach in November 1750. (Goldbach is chiefly remembered for *Goldbach's conjecture*, that every even number $n \geq 4$ can be written as the sum of two prime numbers.)

At this time Euler was unable to prove the result, but he presented a proof two years later. Unfortunately, Euler's proof was deficient, but a correct proof for polyhedra was obtained by A. M. Legendre in 1794. The corresponding formula for graphs drawn in the plane was first obtained by A.–L. Cauchy in 1813. (It is sometimes claimed that René Descartes obtained the formula around the year 1640; in fact, Descartes obtained an expression for the sum of the angles of all thé faces of a polyhedron, from which the required formula can be deduced, but Descartes apparently never made this deduction.)

Using Euler's formula, we can obtain a number of useful results. In particular, we can give alternative proofs of the fact that K_5 and $K_{3,3}$ are non-planar.

COROLLARY 1. *Let G be a connected planar simple graph with* n (≥ 3) *vertices and* m *edges. Then* m $\leq$ 3n $-$ 6.

Proof For a plane drawing of G with f faces, it follows from the handshaking lemma for planar graphs that $2m \geq 3f$ (since the degree of each face of a simple graph is at least 3), so that $f \leq \frac{2}{3}m$. Combining this with Euler's formula, $f = m - n + 2$, we get $m - n + 2 \leq \frac{2}{3}m$, and hence $m \leq 3n - 6$. □

Example: K_5 is non-planar.

Proof Suppose that K_5 is a planar graph. Since K_5 has five vertices and ten edges, it follows from Corollary 1 that $10 \leq (3 \times 5) - 6 = 9$. This contradiction shows that K_5 is non-planar. □

Since $K_{3,3}$ has six vertices and nine edges, and it is true that $9 \leq (3 \times 6) - 6 = 12$, we cannot use Corollary 1 to prove that $K_{3,3}$ is non-planar. However, we can use the following corollary.

COROLLARY 2. *Let G be a connected planar simple graph with* n *vertices and* m *edges, and no triangles. Then* m $\leq$ 2n $-$ 4.

Proof For a plane drawing of G with f faces, it follows from the handshaking lemma for planar graphs that $2m \geq 4f$ (since the degree of each face of a simple graph without triangles is at least 4), so that $f \leq \frac{1}{2}m$. Combining this with Euler's formula $f = m - n + 2$, we get $m - n + 2 \leq \frac{1}{2}m$, and hence $m \leq 2n - 4$. □

Example: $K_{3,3}$ is non-planar.

Proof   Suppose that $K_{3,3}$ is a planar graph. Since $K_{3,3}$ has six vertices and nine edges and no triangles, it follows from Corollary 2 that $9 \leq (2 \times 6) - 4 = 8$. This contradiction shows that $K_{3,3}$ is non-planar. $\Box$

We can also prove the following result which is obtained in a similar way.

COROLLARY 3.   *Let G be a connected planar simple graph. Then G contains at least one vertex of degree 5 or less.*

Proof   By Corollary 1, we get $m \leq 3n - 6$. Suppose that every vertex in G has degree 6 or more. Then we have $2m \geq 6n$ (since $2m$ is the sum of the vertex-degrees), and so $m \geq 3n$. This contradiction shows that at least one vertex has degree 5 or less. $\Box$

We now use Euler's formula to show why there are only five regular convex polyhedra—namely, the tetrahedron, cube, octahedron, dodecahedron, and icosahedron (see page 38); a polyhedron is *convex* if the straight line segment joining any two of its vertices lies entirely within it. We use the fact that we can represent any polyhedron as a planar graph by projecting it down onto a plane:

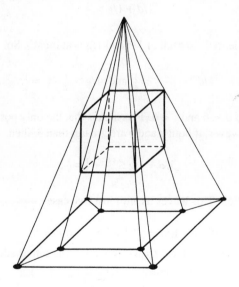

This method of projection is called *stereographic projection,* and was used by A.–L. Cauchy in 1813 in his paper *Recherches sur les polyèdres* (*Researches on polyhedra*). In this paper he derived the planar graph formulation of Euler's formula, and used it to prove that there are only five regular convex polyhedra.

THEOREM 11.2.   *There are only five regular convex polyhedra.*

Proof   We prove this theorem by showing that there are only five connected planar graphs G with the following properties:

    a. G is regular of degree d (where $d \geq 3$);

b.   any plane drawing of G is face-regular of degree g (where $g \geq 3$).

Let n, m, and f be the numbers of vertices, edges, and faces of such a planar graph G. Then, by properties a and b, we get

$$m = \tfrac{1}{2}dn = \tfrac{1}{2}gf, \text{ giving } n = 2m/d \text{ and } f = 2m/g.$$

Since G is a planar graph, Euler's formula holds—that is, $n - m + f = 2$. Thus

$$2m/d - m + 2m/g = 2,$$

which can be written

$$1/d - \tfrac{1}{2} + 1/g = 1/m.$$

Since $1/m > 0$, it follows that

$$1/d + 1/g > \tfrac{1}{2}.$$

Each of d and g is at least 3, so each of $1/d$ and $1/g$ is at most $\tfrac{1}{3}$. So,

$$1/d > \tfrac{1}{2} - \tfrac{1}{3} = \tfrac{1}{6} \text{ and } 1/g > \tfrac{1}{2} - \tfrac{1}{3} = \tfrac{1}{6},$$

and we conclude that $d < 6$ and $g < 6$. This means that the only possible values of d and g are 3, 4, and 5. However, if both d and g are greater than 3, then

$$1/d + 1/g \leq \tfrac{1}{4} + \tfrac{1}{4} = \tfrac{1}{2},$$

which is a contradiction. This leaves us with just five cases:

Case 1: $d = 3$, $g = 3$. We get $1/m = \tfrac{1}{3} - \tfrac{1}{2} + \tfrac{1}{3} = \tfrac{1}{6}$, so $m = 6$;
          it follows that $n = 8$ and $f = 4$—this gives the **tetrahedron**.

Case 2: $d = 3$, $g = 4$. We get $1/m = \tfrac{1}{3} - \tfrac{1}{2} + \tfrac{1}{4} = \tfrac{1}{12}$, so $m = 12$;
          it follows that $n = 8$ and $f = 6$—this gives the **cube**.

Case 3: $d = 3$, $g = 5$. We get $1/m = \tfrac{1}{3} - \tfrac{1}{2} + \tfrac{1}{5} = \tfrac{1}{30}$, so $m = 30$;
          it follows that $n = 20$ and $f = 12$—this gives the **dodecahedron**.

Case 4: $d = 4$, $g = 3$. We get $1/m = \tfrac{1}{4} - \tfrac{1}{2} + \tfrac{1}{3} = \tfrac{1}{12}$, so $m = 12$;
          it follows that $n = 6$ and $f = 8$—this gives the **octahedron**.

Case 5: $d = 5$, $g = 3$. We get $1/m = \tfrac{1}{5} - \tfrac{1}{2} + \tfrac{1}{3} = \tfrac{1}{30}$, so $m = 30$;
          it follows that $n = 12$ and $f = 20$—this gives the **icosahedron**. $\square$

11.4 TESTING FOR PLANARITY

The restrictions on the number of edges in a planar graph given in Corollaries 1 and 2, and their generalizations in Problems 11.12 and 11.13, are often useful for showing that a graph is not planar. For example, we used them to show that K_5 and $K_{3,3}$ are not planar. Unfortunately, this method does not work the other way round—there are many graphs which satisfy these inequalities but which are not planar. Because of this, we now turn our attention to other ways of determining whether or not a given graph is planar.

We begin with some simple, but important, observations:

    a. *not all graphs are planar*: in particular, we have already seen that the graphs K_5 and $K_{3,3}$ are not planar;

    b. *if* G *is a planar graph, then every subgraph of* G *is planar*; this is often stated in the following form:

    c. *if* G *contains a non-planar graph as a subgraph, then* G *is non-planar*: for example, the following graphs are non-planar, since the first contains K_5 and the second contains $K_{3,3}$.

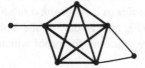

The next two observations involve the insertion of vertices of degree 2 into the edges of a graph G, as shown in the diagram

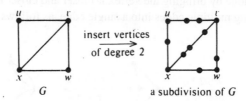

Any graph formed from G in this way is called a **subdivision** of G. Since the insertion of a vertex of degree 2 cannot affect the planarity or non-planarity of a graph, we deduce the following result:

    d. *if* G *is a planar graph, then every subdivision of* G *is planar*; this is often stated in the following alternative form:

    e. *if* G *is a subdivision of a non-planar graph, then* G *is non-planar*: for example, the following graphs are non-planar, since the first is a subdivision of K_5 and the second is a subdivision of $K_{3,3}$:

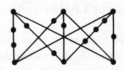

It follows from observations c and e that *if G is any graph which contains a subdivision of K_5 or $K_{3,3}$ as a subgraph, then G must be non-planar*. For example, the following graph is non-planar, since it contains a subdivision of K_5 as a subgraph:

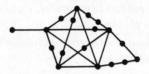

By now you may be wondering why we are so concerned with K_5 and $K_{3,3}$ and their subdivisions. The reason is that *all* non-planar graphs can be obtained in the way we have just described—namely, by adding vertices and edges to a subdivision of K_5 or $K_{3,3}$. In other words, *every non-planar graph contains as a subgraph a subdivision of K_5 or $K_{3,3}$*. This remarkable result appeared in 1930, and is due to the Polish mathematician K. Kuratowski. We state it formally here, but omit the proof which is rather long and complicated.

THEOREM 11.3 (KURATOWSKI'S THEOREM).   *A graph is planar if and only if it does not contain a subdivision of K_5 or $K_{3,3}$ as a subgraph.*

A similar characterization of planar graphs involves the notion of 'contracting' an edge vw. This is done by bringing the vertex w closer and closer to v until they coincide, and then coalescing multiple edges into a single edge, as follows:

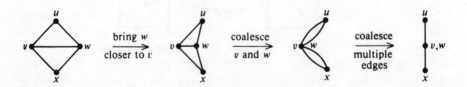

A **contraction** of a graph is the result of a sequence of edge-contractions. For example, K_5 is a contraction of the Petersen graph, since it is the result of contracting each of the five 'spokes'.

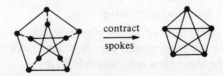

THEOREM 11.4. *A graph is planar if and only if it does not contain a subgraph which has K_5 or $K_{3,3}$ as a contraction.*

The importance of Theorems 11.3 and 11.4 is that they give us necessary and sufficient conditions for a graph to be planar in purely graph-theoretic terms (*subgraph, subdivision, $K_{3,3}$*, etc.) rather than geometrical terms (*crossing, drawing in the plane*, etc.). They also provide a convincing demonstration that a given graph is non-planar, if we happen to spot a subgraph which is a subdivision of K_5 or $K_{3,3}$, or a subgraph which contracts to K_5 or $K_{3,3}$. What they do not do is to provide an easy way of showing that a given graph is planar, since this would involve looking at a large number of subgraphs and verifying that none of them is a subdivision of, or contracts to, K_5 or $K_{3,3}$. For this reason, no currently used algorithm for testing the planarity of a graph uses these two theorems.

We next consider a concept which will be needed in Chapter 14. The **thickness** of a graph G is defined to be the minimum number of planar graphs which can be superimposed to form the given graph G, and is denoted by $t(G)$. For example, the thickness of any planar graph is 1, whereas the thickness of K_5 or $K_{3,3}$ is 2, since K_5 can be formed by superimposing

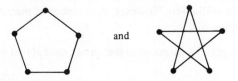

and $K_{3,3}$ can be formed by superimposing

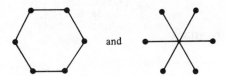

In general, there is no known formula which gives the thickness of any given graph. However, we can easily obtain a *lower bound* for $t(G)$ which very often gives the correct value. We restrict our attention to simple graphs, since loops and multiple edges can be dealt with as shown earlier. We adopt the following notation.

NOTATION. *If* x *is any positive number, then*

$$\lfloor x \rfloor \ is \ the \ 'next \ integer \ down' \ from \ x$$

(for example, $\lfloor \tfrac{7}{2} \rfloor = 3, \lfloor 6.2 \rfloor = 6, \lfloor 4 \rfloor = 4$),

$$and \ \lceil x \rceil \ is \ the \ 'next \ integer \ up' \ from \ x$$

(for example, $\lceil \tfrac{7}{2} \rceil = 4, \lceil 6.2 \rceil = 7, \lceil 4 \rceil = 4$).

Note that if x is an integer, then $\lfloor x \rfloor = \lceil x \rceil = x$.

The connection between these functions is given by the equation

$$\lceil a/b \rceil = \lfloor (a+b-1)/b \rfloor.$$

for example, $\lceil 7/5 \rceil = 2 = \lfloor (7+5-1)/5 \rfloor = \lfloor 11/5 \rfloor$.

We can now prove the following result.

THEOREM 11.5. *Let G be a connected simple graph with* n *vertices and* m *edges. Then*

(a) $t(G) \geq \lceil m/(3n-6) \rceil$;

(b) *if* G *has no triangles,* $t(G) \geq \lceil m/(2n-4) \rceil$.

Proof (a) It follows from Corollary 1 that the number of edges in each planar subgraph of G is at most $3n-6$. Since there are m edges altogether, the number of planar graphs must be at least $m/(3n-6)$. However, the number of planar graphs is an integer, and so $t(G) \geq \lceil m/(3n-6) \rceil$.

(b) This part of the proof is identical to that in (a), except that we use Corollary 2. $\square$

Example 1: If $G = K_n$, then $m = \frac{1}{2}n(n-1)$. It follows from part(a) of Theorem 11.5 that

$$t(K_n) \geq \frac{n(n-1)/2}{3n-6}$$

We can simplify this by writing

$$\lceil n(n-1)/2\,(3n-6) \rceil = \lfloor \{n(n-1) + 2(3n-6)-1\}/2\,(3n-6) \rfloor$$
$$= \lfloor (n^2+5n-14)/2\,(3n-6) \rfloor = \lfloor (n+7)(n-2)/6\,(n-2) \rfloor = \lfloor (n+7)/6 \rfloor.$$

Thus, $t(K_n) \geq \lfloor \frac{1}{6}(n+7) \rfloor$.

It can be shown that $t(K_n) = \lfloor \frac{1}{6}(n+7) \rfloor$ for *all n,* except for $n = 9$ and $n = 10$, in which case $t(K_n) = 3$.

Example 2: If $G = K_{r,s}$, then $m = rs$ and G has no triangles. It follows from part (b) of Theorem 11.5 that

$$t(K_{r,s}) \geq \lceil rs/(2r + 2s - 4) \rceil.$$

It is not known whether this inequality is always an equality, but it is certainly so for complete bipartite graphs with less than 48 vertices.

11.5 DUALITY

We conclude this chapter by introducing the idea of duality. This concept will be of importance when we discuss the coloring of maps in Chapter 13.

Given a connected planar graph G, we shall define a corresponding **dual graph** G^*. Its construction is in three stages:

1. first take a plane drawing of G;
2. choose one point inside each face of the plane drawing—these points are the vertices of G^*;
3. for each edge e of the plane drawing, draw a line connecting the vertices of G^* on each side of e.

This procedure is illustrated as follows: the vertices of G^* are represented by small circles, and the edges of G^* are indicated by dashed lines:

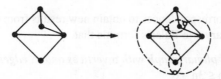

Note that each plane drawing of G gives rise to just one dual graph G^*. However, different plane drawings of G can give rise to different dual graphs G^*; an example which illustrates this is given in Problem 11.34. We shall always assume that we have already been presented with a particular plane drawing of G. There is a simple relationship between the number of vertices, faces and edges of a graph and its dual. In the above example, G has five vertices, four faces (including the infinite face), and seven edges, and G^* has four vertices, five faces, and seven edges. In general, we have the following simple result, which we ask you to prove in Problem 11.36.

THEOREM 11.6. *If G is a connected planar graph with n vertices, f faces and m edges, then G* has f vertices, n faces and m edges.*

Note also that if G is a connected planar graph, then so is G^*, and we can thus construct $(G^*)^*$, the dual of G^*. However, a glance at the above figure shows that the construction which gives rise to G^* from G can be reversed to give G from G^*. It follows that $(G^*)^*$ is isomorphic to G, and that there really is a duality between G and G^*.

Using this duality, we can draw up a list of dual concepts; for example,

an edge of G	corresponds to	an edge of G^*
a vertex of degree k in G	corresponds to	a face of degree k in G^*
a face of degree k in G	corresponds to	a vertex of degree k in G^*

We can continue this list as follows:

a cycle of G	corresponds to	a cutset of G^*
a cutset of G	corresponds to	a cycle of G^*

These last correspondences are most easily seen from the following figure. To obtain the first correspondence, we take a cycle in G (with solid edges); the corresponding edges of G^* (the dashed edges) from a cutset whose removal separates the set of vertices inside the cycle from those outside. To obtain the second correspondence, we simply interchange the roles of G and G^*.

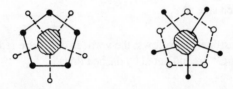

We can use these correspondences to obtain new results from old ones. For example, it follows from Corollary 1 to Euler's formula that

if G is a connected planar graph with n vertices and m edges, and with no loops or multiple edges, then m ≤ 3n − 6.

Since loops (cycles of degree 1) and pairs of multiple edges (cycles of degree 2) correspond to vertices of degree 1 and 2 in the dual graph, we deduce from the above correspondence that

if G is a connected planar graph with f faces and m edges, and with no vertices of degree 1 or 2, then m ≤ 3f − 6;

conversely, we can dualize this last result to obtain the previous one. Similarly, we know from Corollary 3 to Euler's formula that

if G is a simple connected planar graph, then G has a vertex of degree 5 or less.
Dualizing this result, we deduce that

if G is a connected planar graph with no vertices of degree 1 or 2, then G has a face of degree 5 or less.

Our final example was mentioned at the beginning of this section; although it uses concepts from the next two chapters, all you need to know here is that a map is a connected planar graph with no bridges. The celebrated four-color theorem can then be stated as follows.

THE FOUR-COLOR THEOREM FOR MAPS. *The countries (faces) of any map can be colored with four colors in such a way that neighboring countries are differently colored.*

Dualizing this result, we get the following result on vertex-colorings, a topic to be discussed in Chapter 12:

THE FOUR-COLOR THEOREM FOR PLANAR GRAPHS. *The vertices of any connected planar graph can be colored with four colors in such a way that adjacent vertices are differently colored.*

PROBLEMS

Planar Graphs

11.1 There was once a king with five sons. In his will he stated that after his death each son should build a castle, and that the five castles should be connected in pairs by non-intersecting roads. Can the terms of the will be satisfied? (This is a form of the 'Möbius problem', first stated around 1840.)

○11.2 By finding a plane drawing, show that each of the following graphs is planar:

     (a)   (b)   (c)

11.3 By finding a plane drawing, show that the following graph is planar:

○11.4 Give an argument, similar to that used for $K_{3,3}$ on page 217, to show that the complete graph K_5 is not planar.

○11.5 Classify the following statements as TRUE or FALSE, giving your reasons in each case:

  a. every subgraph of a planar graph is planar;

  b. every subgraph of a non-planar graph is non-planar;

  c. every graph which contains a planar graph (as a subgraph) is planar;

  d. every graph which contains a non-planar graph is non-planar.

11.6 a. For which values of n is the complete graph K_n planar?

  b. For which values of r and s (with $r \leq s$) is the complete bipartite graph $K_{r,s}$ planar?

11.7. Find plane drawings of the graph in diagrams (a) and (b) on page 218 in which
   a. f_3 is the infinite face;
   b. f_1 is the infinite face.

○11.8. Verify the 'handshaking lemma for planar graphs' (given on pages 218–219) for each of the following graphs:

   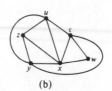

(a)   (b)   (c)

Euler's Formula

○11.9. Verify Euler's formula for each of the graphs in Problem 11.8.

11.10. Verify Euler's formula for each of the five Platonic graphs:

        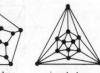

tetrahedron   cube   octahedron   dodecahedron   icosahedron

11.11. Verify Euler's formula for:
   a. the 'wheel' with k spokes (the following diagram illustrates the case $k = 5$);

   b. the complete bipartite graph $K_{2,s}$;
   c. the graph formed by the vertices, edges and faces of a $k \times k$ chessboard.

○11.12. (a) Let G be a connected planar simple graph with n (≥ 3) vertices and m edges whose shortest cycle length is 5. Use the method of proof of Corollaries 1 and 2 to prove that

$$m \leq \tfrac{5}{3}\,(n{-}2).$$

(b) Use this result to show that the Petersen graph is non-planar.

11.13. If G is a graph whose shortest cycle length is g, then we say that the **girth** of G is g. Use the method of proof of Corollaries 1 and 2 to prove that, if G is a simple connected planar graph with n (≤ 3) vertices, m edges, and girth g, then

$$m \leq g(n-2)/(g-2).$$

Prove that this inequality is an equality if each face of G has degree g.

○11.14. Give examples of:
   a. a simple planar graph in which every vertex has degree 5;
   b. a planar graph with minimum vertex-degree 3, in which every face has degree 5;
   c. a planar graph in which every vertex has degree 6;
   d. a planar graph in which every face has degree 6.

○11.15. Let G be a connected planar graph with n vertices and f faces in a plane drawing of G. Show that
   a. if $n < 12$, and if G is a simple graph, then G contains at least one vertex of degree 4 or less;
   b. if $f < 12$, and if G has no vertices of degree 1 or 2, then G contains at least one face of degree 4 or less.

11.16. a. Give an example of a polyhedron all of whose faces are pentagons and hexagons.
   b. Use Euler's formula to prove that any such polyhedron must have at least 12 pentagonal faces.
   c. Prove that if, in addition, there are exactly three faces meeting at each vertex, then the polyhedron must have exactly 12 pentagonal faces.
   d. What does this have to do with the game of soccer?

11.17. a. Give an example of a polyhedron all of whose faces are squares and hexagons.
   b. Use Euler's formula to prove that any such polyhedron must have at least six square faces.
   c. Prove that if, in addition, there are exactly three faces meeting at each vertex, then the polyhedron must have exactly six square faces.

11.18.[†] Let G be a connected simple planar graph which is regular of degree 3, and let g_k denote the number of faces with face-degree k in a plane drawing of G. Show that
$$12 = 3g_3 + 2g_4 + g_5 - g_7 - 2g_8 - 3g_9 - \dots .$$
Use this result to deduce part c of Problems 11.16 and 11.17.

11.19.[†] a. Prove that there exists no graph G with 11 vertices for which both G and its complement $\overline{G}$ are planar.
   b. Give an example of a graph G with eight vertices for which both G and $\overline{G}$ are planar.

Testing for Planarity

⊕**11.20.** Use Kuratowski's theorem to prove that the following graph is non-planar:

11.21. Prove that the Petersen graph is non-planar

    a. by using Theorem 11.4;

    b. by using Kuratowski's theorem.

    (Hint for part b.: Delete the two 'horizontal' edges.)

⊕**11.22.** Which of the following graphs on the graph cards (see Chapter 1) are planar?

             (a) card 181; (b) card 195; (c) card 203; (d) card 207.

    For any that are planar; give a plane drawing and verify Euler's formula; for any that are non-planar, verify Theorem 11.3 by finding appropriate subgraphs.

11.23. Repeat Problem 11.22 for the following graph cards:

        (a) card 186;   (c) card 201;   (e) card 205;

        (b) card 197;   (d) card 202;   (f) card 206.

11.24. We say that two graphs are **homeomorphic** if each is a subdivision of a third graph. Let n_1 and m_1 denote the numbers of vertices and edges in a graph G_1, and let n_2 and m_2 denote the numbers of vertices and edges in a graph G_2. Prove that if G_1 and G_2 are homeomorphic, then $m_1 - m_2 = n_1 - n_2$.

⊕**11.25.** By showing how three planar graphs can be superimposed to form K_9, show that $t(K_9) \leq 3$. [In fact, $t(K_9) = 3$.]

11.26. a. By using Theorem 11.5, show that the 4-cube Q_4 is non-planar.

       b. Find two planar graphs which can be superimposed to form Q_4, and hence show that the thickness of Q_4 is 2.

⊕**11.27.** By splitting $K_{r,s}$ into a number of copies of $K_{2,s}$, show that if r is even, then $t(K_{r,s}) \leq \frac{1}{2}r$. Using this result, together with Theorem 11.5, prove that, if r is even and $s > \frac{1}{2}(r-2)^2$, then $t(K_{r,s}) = \frac{1}{2}r$.

11.28.[†] The **crossing number** cr(G) of a graph G is the smallest number of crossings that are possible in a plane drawing of G (where the word 'crossing' refers to the crossing of exactly *two* edges).

a. Show that cr(K_5) = cr($K_{3,3}$) = 1.

b. Draw the complete graph K_6 with as few crossings as you can.

c. Find the crossing numbers of the Petersen graph and the four-cube Q_4.

d. If r and s are both even, show that

$$cr(K_{r,s}) \le \tfrac{1}{16} rs(r-2)(s-2).$$

(Hint for part d: Place the r vertices along the x-axis, with an equal number on each side of the origin, and place the s vertices along the y-axis in a similar way—now count the crossings.)

11.29.[†] a. Draw each of the following graphs on a torus (that is, a doughnut) in such a way that there are no crossings:

  1. the complete graph K_5;

  2. the complete bipartite graph $K_{3,3}$;

  3. the Petersen graph.

b. Make a conjecture for the value of $n - m + f$ for any non-planar connected graph with n vertices, m edges, and f faces that can be drawn without crossings on a torus, and check your conjecture for K_5, $K_{3,3}$, and the Petersen graph.

11.30.[†] Draw the complete graph K_7 on a torus with as few crossings as you can.

Duality

11.31. Draw the dual of each of the following graphs:

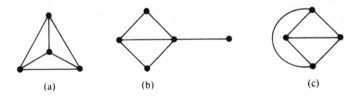

(a)   (b)   (c)

○11.32. Find the duals of each of the following graphs of your graph cards (see Chapter 1), and give the corresponding graph card number in each case:

(a) card 50; (b) card 174; (c) card 189.

11.33. Show that the graph on graph card 188 can be drawn in the plane in two different ways, but that the corresponding dual graphs are isomorphic.

✷11.34. The following diagrams show two different plane drawings of the same planar graph. Show that their duals are not isomorphic.

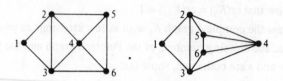

11.35. Show that the dual of the cube graph is the octahedron graph, and that the dual of the dodecahedron graph is the icosahedron graph.

✷11.36. Prove Theorem 11.6.

✷11.37. Let G be a connected plane graph. Prove that G is bipartite if and only if its dual G^* is Eulerian.

11.38. Dualize the statements of the following problems above:

(a) Problem 11.16; (b) Problem 11.17; (c) Problem 11.18.

11.39.[†] How would you define the dual of a graph (such as K_5 or $K_{3,3}$) drawn on the surface of a torus?

CHAPTER 12

COLORING GRAPHS

In this chapter we consider a number of problems involving the coloring of the vertices or edges of a graph. This leads, in the next chapter, to a discussion of map-coloring problems, including the famous four-color problem mentioned in the Introduction to Part II.*

12.1 VERTEX-COLORINGS

We start with some definitions.

DEFINITIONS. *Let* G *be a graph without loops. A* **k-coloring** *of* G *is an assignment of* k *colors to the vertices of* G *in such a way that adjacent vertices are assigned different colors. If* G *has a* k-*coloring, then* G *is said to be* **k-colorable.** *The* **chromatic number** *of* G, *denoted by* χ*(G)*, *is the smallest number* k *for which* G *is* k-*colorable.*

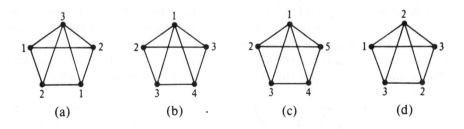

(a)   (b)   (c)   (d)

---

*Materials in this chapter are reprinted, with permission, from The Proof of the Four-Color Theorem by Kenneth Appel, in *New Scentist,* Vol. **72**, No. 1023, 21 October 1976, p. 155.

We usually display a k-coloring by writing the numbers 1, 2, 3, ..., k next to the appropriate vertices. For example, diagrams (a), (b), and (c) above illustrate a 3-coloring, a 4-coloring and a 5-coloring of a graph G with five vertices; diagram (d) is not a permissible coloring, since one of the edges has color 2 at both ends. It follows that $\chi(G) \leq 3$, since G has a 3-coloring [diagram (a)]. On the other hand, $\chi(G) \geq 3$, since G contains three mutually adjacent vertices (forming a triangle), which must be assigned different colors. So $\chi(G) = 3$.

Note that the above definitions are given only for graphs without loops, since in any k-coloring the vertices at the ends of each edge must be assigned different colors, and so the vertex at the ends of a loop would have to be assigned a different color from itself! We may also assume that there are no multiple edges, since the presence of one edge between two vertices forces these vertices to be colored differently, and the addition of further edges between these vertices is then irrelevant to the coloring. We can therefore restrict our attention to simple graphs.

There is a simple method for obtaining a lower bound for $\chi(G)$—namely, look for the largest complete subgraph in G. For example, the following graph contains the complete graph K_4, and so $\chi(G) \geq 4$:

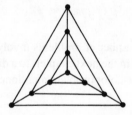

To obtain an upper bound for $\chi(G)$, we note that if G has n vertices, then $\chi(G) \leq n$. However, this upper bound is generally very poor, and we can improve it considerably if we know the largest vertex-degree in G, as the following theorem shows.

THEOREM 12.1.   *If G is a simple graph whose maximum vertex-degree is* d, *then*

$$\chi(G) \leq d + 1.$$

Proof   We prove this result by mathematical induction on n, the number of vertices of G. When $n = 1$, the graph is K_1, for which $\chi(G) = 1$ and $d = 0$, and the result is true.

Now we show that if the result is true for all graphs with less than n vertices, then it must also be true for all graphs with n vertices. So suppose that the result is true for all graphs with less than n vertices. Let G be a graph with n vertices and maximum vertex degree d, and let H be the graph obtained from G by removing any vertex v and the edges incident to v:

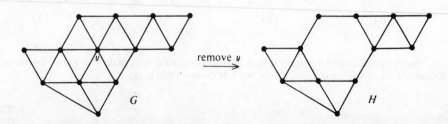

Since H has less than n vertices and maximum vertex-degree d (or less), it follows from the induction assumption that $\chi(H) \leq d + 1$—that is, H is $(d+1)$-colorable. We can now obtain a $(d+1)$-coloring of G by coloring v with any color not assigned to the (at most d) vertices adjacent to v. (Note that these vertices involve at most d colors.) It follows that $\chi(G) \leq d + 1$, and so the result is true for graphs with n vertices. This completes the proof. $\Box$

With a lot more effort, we can prove the following slightly stronger theorem, which was proved by L. Brooks in 1941; we omit the proof.

THEOREM 12.2 (BROOKS' THEOREM).   *Let* G *be a connected simple graph whose maximum vertex-degree is* d. *If* G *is neither a cycle graph with an odd number of vertices, nor a complete graph, then* $\chi(G) \leq d$.

To illustrate the use of Brooks' theorem, we consider the graph G on page 236. Since G contains the complete graph K_4, we observed that $\chi(G) \geq 4$. On the other hand, G satisfies the conditions of Brooks' theorem (with $d = 4$), and so $\chi(G) \leq 4$. It follows that $\chi(G) = 4$.

Unfortunately, the situation is not always as satisfactory as this. In particular, if G contains a few vertices of high degree, then the bound given by Brooks' theorem may be very poor. For example, if G is the bipartite graph $K_{1,100}$, then $\chi(G) = 2$, whereas Brooks' theorem gives us the upper bound $\chi(G) \leq 100$.

12.2 CHROMATIC POLYNOMIALS

It follows from the above discussion that the lower and upper bounds do not always give a good estimate for the chromatic number. In such cases we must look for other ways of finding $\chi(G)$. One method is to look at all possible ways of coloring the vertices, increasing the number of available colors until a valid coloring is obtained. Unfortunately, this is a hopelessly time-consuming way of proceeding. In fact, all known algorithms for finding the chromatic number of a graph are somewhat inefficient, and may take a long time to implement. This is in contrast to, say, the greedy algorithm for solving the minimum connector problem. However, there are algorithms which are substantially better than trying all possibilities, and we consider one of these now. It involves the idea of a *chromatic polynomial*, which is of some interest and importance in its own right.

DEFINITION.   *Let* G *be a simple graph, and let* $P_G(k)$ *be the number of ways of coloring the vertices of* G *with* k *colors in such a way that no two adjacent vertices are assigned the same color. The function* $P_G(k)$ *is called the* **chromatic polynomial** *of* G.

Note that, although we have called $P_G(k)$ the chromatic *polynomial* of G, it is not at all clear from the above definition why the number of k-colorings of G must necessarily by a polynomial in k. Before explaining this, we look at a few examples.

Example 1: If G is the complete graph K_3, then the top vertex can be assigned any of the k

colors, the left-hand vertex can be assigned any of the $k-1$ colors not assigned to the top vertex, and the right-hand vertex can then be assigned any of the $k-2$ colors not assigned to the other two vertices. The chromatic polynomial of K_3 is therefore $k(k-1)(k-2)$. We can extend this immediately to give the following result:

if G *is the complete graph* K_n, *then* $P_G(k) = k(k-1)(k-2) \cdots (k-n+1)$.

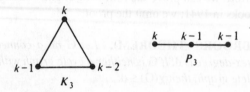

Example 2: If G is the path graph P_3, then the left-hand vertex can be assigned any of the k colors, the middle vertex can be assigned any of the $k-1$ colors not assigned to the left-hand vertex, and the right-hand vertex can then be assigned any of the $k-1$ colors not assigned to the middle vertex. The chromatic polynomial of P_3 is therefore $k(k-1)^2$. We can extend this to give the following result:

if G *is any tree with* n *vertices, then* $P_G(k) = k(k-1)^{n-1}$.

It follows from this result that non-isomorphic graphs can have the same chromatic polynomial.

We can easily calculate the chromatic number of a graph if we know its chromatic polynomial, since the chromatic number of a graph G is the smallest positive integer k for which $P_G(k) > 0$. So if we can find a routine method for determining the chromatic polynomial, then we can derive an algorithm for determining the chromatic number.

In order to motivate such a method we observe that

$$k(k-1)(k-2) = k(k-1)^2 - k(k-1)$$

—that is,

$$P_G(k) = P_{G'}(k) - P_{G''}(k),$$

where G, G', and G'' are the following graphs:

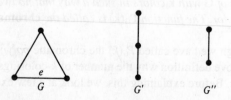

Note that G' is obtained from G by *deleting the edge e*. Also, G'' is obtained from G by *contracting the edge e* (see Chapter 11). This idea suggests the following result, known as the deletion-contraction theorem.

THEOREM 12.3 (THE DELETION-CONTRACTION THEOREM). *Let* G *be a simple graph, and let* G′ *and* G″ *be the graphs obtained from* G *by deleting and contracting an edge* e. *Then*

$$P_G(k) = P_{G'}(k) - P_{G''}(k).$$

Proof Let $e = vw$ be the edge in question, and consider the possible k-colorings of G'. The number of k-colorings of G' in which v and w are assigned different colors remains unchanged if the edge e is drawn joining v and w, and is therefore equal to the number of k-colorings of G. The number of k-colorings of G' in which v and w are assigned the same color remains unchanged if the vertices v and w are made to coalesce, and is therefore equal to the number of k-colorings of G''. The total number of k-colorings of G' is therefore

$$P_G(k) + P_{G''}(k),$$

as required. □

The importance of the deletion-contraction theorem lies in the fact that it expresses the chromatic polynomial of a graph G in terms of the chromatic polynomials of two graphs with fewer edges. By continuing this process as often as necessary, we can eventually express the chromatic polynomial of G in terms of chromatic polynomials we can calculate. We illustrate this process in the following example.

Notation For convenience, we draw the graph itself, rather than its chromatic polynomial; thus the above example can be expressed in the form:

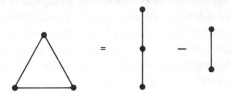

Example: We use this deletion-contraction process to calculate the chromatic polynomial of the following graph G, and hence find $\chi(G)$:

G

We have

$$k(k-1)(k-2)(k-3)$$

and

$$k(k-1)^3(k-2) \qquad k(k-1)^2(k-2)$$

It follows that

$$P_G(k) = [k(k-1)^3(k-2) - k(k-1)^2(k-2)] - k(k-1)(k-2)(k-3)$$

$$= k(k-1)(k-2)(k^2-4k+5)$$

$$= k^5 - 7k^4 + 19k^3 - 23k^2 + 10k.$$

Since $P_G(1) = 0$, $P_G(2) = 0$, and $P_G(3) = 12$, we have $\chi(G) = 3$.

It is now clear why the number of k-colorings of a graph G is always a polynomial. By continuing the above deletion-contraction process until there are no edges left, we eventually obtain the chromatic polynomial of G by adding and subtracting the chromatic polynomials of null graphs. However, the chromatic polynomial of the null graph N_n is simply k^n, and so the chromatic polynomial of G is obtained by adding and subtracting terms of this form, and is therefore a polynomial.

12.3 EDGE-COLORINGS

Again, we start with some definitions.

DEFINITIONS. *Let G be a graph without loops. A **k-edge-coloring** of G is an assignment of* k *colors to the edges of G in such a way that any two edges meeting at a common vertex are assigned different colors. If G has a k-edge-coloring, then G is said to be **k-edge colorable**. The **chromatic index** of G, denoted by $\chi'(G)$, is the smallest number* k *for which G is k-edge-colorable.*

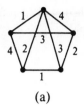
(a)

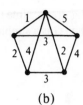
(b)

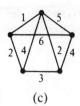
(c)

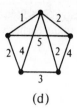
(d)

We usually display a k-edge-coloring by writing the numbers $1, 2, 3, \ldots, k$ next to the appropriate edges. For example, diagrams (a), (b), and (c) above illustrate a 4-edge-coloring, a 5-edge-coloring, and a 6-edge-coloring of a graph G with eight edges; diagram (d) is not a permissible coloring, since two of the edges colored 2 meet at a common vertex. It follows that $\chi'(G) \leq 4$, since G has a 4-edge-coloring [diagram (a)]. On the other hand, $\chi'(G) \geq 4$, since G contains four edges meeting at a common vertex (that is, a vertex of degree 4), which must be assigned different colors. So $\chi'(G) = 4$.

Note that the above definitions are given only for graphs without loops, since in any k-edge-coloring the edges meeting at a vertex must be assigned different colors. On the other hand, we often wish to consider graphs with multiple edges, since the introduction of multiple edges can significantly alter the chromatic index.

There is an obvious lower bound for $\chi'(G)$—namely, if d is the largest vertex-degree in G, then $\chi'(G) \geq d$. To obtain an upper bound for $\chi'(G)$, we note that if G has m edges, then $\chi'(G) \leq m$. However, this upper bound is very poor, and has been improved considerably by V. G. Vizing and by C. E. Shannon. For simple graphs, Vizing proved the following very strong result in 1963, which we state without proof:

THEOREM 12.4 (VIZING'S THEOREM). *If G is a simple graph whose maximum vertex-degree is* d, *then*

$$d \leq \chi'(G) \leq d+1.$$

This remarkable result tells us that if G is any simple graph, then the chromatic index of G is either d or $d+1$. This gives us a way of classifying simple graphs into two classes—those for which $\chi'(G) = d$, and those for which $\chi'(G) = d+1$. Both possibilities can occur, but it is not known in general which graphs belong to which class.

Before investigating this problem of classifying simple graphs into those with $\chi'(G) = d$ and those with $\chi'(G) = d+1$, we state (without proof) two results which give upper bounds for the chromatic index of a graph with multiple edges. The first of these is an extension of Vizing's theorem.

THEOREM 12.5 (VIZING'S THEOREM—EXTENDED VERSION). *If G is a graph whose maximum vertex-degree is* d, *and if* h *is the maximum number of edges joining a pair of vertices, then*

$$d \leq \chi'(G) \leq d + h.$$

For example, if G is the following graph, then $d = 6$ and $h = 3$, and so these bounds are

$6 \leq \chi'(G) \leq 9$; in fact, $\chi'(G) = 8$ for this particular graph. Note that Theorem 12.5 reduces to the earlier version of Vizing's theorem when G is a simple graph.

The second upper bound for the chromatic index of a graph was obtained by Shannon in a paper on electrical networks.

THEOREM 12.6 (SHANNON'S THEOREM). *If G is a graph whose maximum vertex-degree is* d, *then*

$$d \leq \chi'(G) \leq \tfrac{3}{2}d.$$

For example, if G is the above graph, then $d = 6$, and so these bounds are $6 \leq \chi'(G) \leq 9$. If d is odd, then $\tfrac{3}{2}d$ is not an integer. In this case we can strengthen the bound to $\tfrac{3}{2}d - \tfrac{1}{2}$.

We now return to the problem of classifying simple graphs into two classes—those with $\chi'(G) = d$ and those with $\chi'(G) = d+1$. For some types of graph, this question is very straightforward—for example, it can easily be checked that for the cycle graphs C_n ($n \geq 3$), we have

$$\chi'(C_n) = 2 \text{ if } n \text{ is even, and } \chi'(C_n) = 3 \text{ if } n \text{ is odd}.$$

A similar result holds for complete graphs K_n.

THEOREM 12.7. *For the complete graph* K_n,

$$\chi'(K_n) = n - 1 \text{ if } n \text{ is even, and } \chi'(K_n) = n \text{ if } n \text{ is odd}.$$

Proof Since each vertex has degree $n-1$, it follows from Vizing's theorem that $\chi'(K_n)$ is either $n-1$ or n.

If n is odd, then the maximum number of edges that can be assigned the same color is $\tfrac{1}{2}(n-1)$, since otherwise two of these edges meet at a common vertex. However, K_n has exactly $\tfrac{1}{2}n(n-1)$ edges, so the number of colors must be at least n. Hence $\chi'(K_n) = n$. In fact, we can obtain an explicit n-edge-coloring of K_n by drawing the vertices in the form of a regular n-gon, and coloring the edges around the boundary using a different color for each edge. The remaining edges are then assigned the same colors as the boundary edges parallel to them. The first diagram below illustrates this procedure in the case $n = 5$.

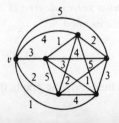

If n is even, we can prove that $\chi'(K_n) = n-1$ by explicitly constructing an $(n-1)$-edge-coloring of the edges of K_n. If $n = 2$, this is trivial. If $n > 2$, we choose any vertex v and remove it (together with its incident edges). This leaves a complete graph K_{n-1} with an odd number of vertices, whose edges can be colored with $n-1$ colors, using the above construction. At each vertex there is exactly one color missing, and these missing colors are all different. The edges of K_n incident to v can therefore be colored using these missing colors. The second diagram above illustrates this procedure in the case $n = 6$. $\square$

We conclude this chapter with an important theorem of Dénes König (1884–1944), a Hungarian mathematician who wrote the first comprehensive treatise on graph theory. König's theorem tells us that every *bipartite* graph (not necessarily simple) with maximum vertex-degree d can be edge-colored with just d colors.

THEOREM 12.8 (KÖNIG'S THEOREM).   *If G is a bipartite graph whose maximum vertex degree is* d, *then $\chi'(G) = d$.*

Proof   We prove this result by mathematical induction on m, the number of edges of G. When $m = 1$, we have $\chi'(G) = 1$ and $d = 1$. The result is therefore true when $m = 1$.

Suppose that the result is true for all bipartite graphs with less than m edges. Let G be a bipartite graph with m edges and maximum vertex-degree d, and let H be the graph obtained from G by removing an edge e adjacent to the vertices v and w:

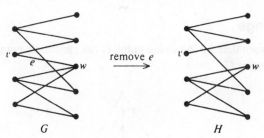

Since H has less than m edges and maximum vertex-degree d (or less), it follows from our induction assumption that $\chi'(H) \leq d$—that is, H is d-edge-colorable. We now color the edges of H with d colors, and replace the edge e. If we can color e with one of the d colors, then we obtain a d-edge-coloring of G, as required.

To show that the edge e can always be colored in this way, we argue as follows. Since H is obtained from G by removing the edge e, there must be at least one color missing at v, and at least one color missing at w. If there is some color missing at *both* v and w, then we can assign this color to the edge e, thereby completing the d-edge-coloring of G. If this is not the case, suppose that the color blue (say) is missing at v, and the color red (say) is missing at w, and consider all the vertices of H which can be reached from v by a path consisting entirely of red and blue edges.

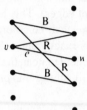

Since the edges in such a path must alternate in color, and since the color red is missing at w, it follows that w *cannot* be reached from v by a red–blue path. (This is where we use the fact that G, and hence H, is bipartite.)

If we now interchange the colors on this path, so that the blue edges become red, and the red edges become blue, then the colors appearing at w are unchanged, and the color red is now missing at both v and w. We can therefore assign the edge e the color red, thereby completing the coloring of G. This completes the proof. □

PROBLEMS

Vertex-Colorings

◌12.1. We have seen that the following graph G has chromatic number 4. Write down a 4-coloring of G.

12.2. Find $\chi(G)$ for the following graphs:

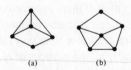

(a)   (b)

12.3. Find $\chi(G)$ for each of the following graphs G on the graph cards (see Chapter 1):

a. card 51;   c. card 130;   e. card 146;   g. card 178;

b. card 128   d. card 143;   f. card 152;   h. card 194.

○12.4. Find the chromatic numbers of:
  a. the complete graph K_7;
  b. the complete bipartite graph $K_{3,5}$;
  c. the cycle graph C_9;
  d. the 4-cube Q_4;
  e. the Petersen graph.

○12.5. What can you say about graphs G for which
  (a) $\chi(G) = 1$;   (b) $\chi(G) = 2$?

○12.6. Classify each of the following statements as TRUE or FALSE, giving your reasons:
  a. if G contains the complete graph K_r as a subgraph, then $\chi(G) \geq r$;
  b. if $\chi(G) \geq r$, then G contains the complete graph K_r as a subgraph.

12.7. Let G be the graph obtained by removing an edge from the complete graph K_n. By Brooks' theorem, we know that $\chi(G) \leq n-1$. Give a method for $(n-1)$-coloring G. Test your method for the case $n = 7$.

12.8. Consider the following graph G;

  a. Obtain upper and lower bounds for $\chi(G)$.
  b. What is the correct value of $\chi(G)$?

12.9.[†] Let G be a connected planar graph of girth g. By finding an inequality for the average vertex-degree in G, prove that
  a. if $g = 5$, then $\chi(G) \leq 4$;
  b. if $g = 6$, then $\chi(G) \leq 3$.

12.10. If G is a graph with n vertices which is regular of degree d, prove that
  $$\chi(G) \geq n/(n-d).$$

12.11.[†] Let χ and $\overline{\chi}$ denote the chromatic numbers of a simple graph G with n vertices, and its complement $\overline{G}$. Prove that

$$2\sqrt{n} \leq \chi + \overline{\chi} \leq n+1 \quad \text{and} \quad n \leq \chi\,\overline{\chi} \leq \tfrac{1}{4}(n+1)^2.$$

Give examples to show that these bounds can all be achieved.

Chromatic Polynomials

○12.12. Write down the chromatic polynomials of
    a. the complete graph K_5;
    b. the complete bipartite graph $K_{1,4}$.

12.13. For each of the following graphs G depicted on the graph cards (see Chapter 1), find the chromatic polynomial $P_G(k)$:
    a. card 42;
    b. card 46.

12.14. *All but one* of the following polynomials are chromatic polynomials of graphs with four vertices. Find the polynomial which is *not* the chromatic polynomial of any graph.
    a. $k^2(k-1)(k-2)$;   d. $k(k-1)(k^2-2k+2)$;
    b. $k(k-1)^2(k-2)$;   e. $k(k-1)(k^2-3k+3)$;
    c. $k(k-1)(k-2)^2$;   f. $k(k-1)(k-2)(k-3)$.

○12.15. Find the chromatic polynomial of each of the following graphs directly—that is, without using the deletion-contraction theorem:

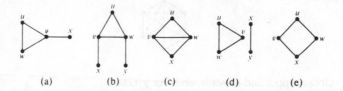

    (a)   (b)   (c)   (d)   (e)

○12.16. Multiply out the polynomials in parts (a) and (b) of Problem 12.15, and verify in each case that:
    a. the polynomial has the form $k^n - mk^{n-1} + \ldots$, where n and m are the numbers of vertices and edges in G;
    b. the signs of the terms are alternately + and − ;
    c. there is no constant term.

    (These observations, which are true in general, are a useful check on whether you have obtained the correct polynomial.)

12.17.[†] Let G be a simple graph with n vertices and m edges, and let $P_G(k)$ be its chromatic polynomial. Use mathematical induction on m and the deletion-contraction theorem to prove that
    a. the terms of $P_G(k)$ are alternately + and − ;
    b. the coefficient of k^{n-1} is $-m$.

○12.18. Use the deletion-contraction theorem to find the chromatic polynomials of each of the following graphs:

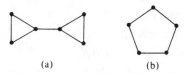

(a)   (b)

12.19. Use the deletion-contraction theorem to find the chromatic polynomials of each of the following graphs. In how many ways can these graphs be colored with five colors?

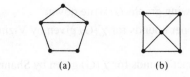

(a)   (b)

Edge-Colorings

○12.20. Find $\chi'(G)$ for each of the following graphs G:

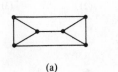

(a)   (b)

12.21. Find $\chi'(G)$ for the graphs G in Problem 12.2.

12.22. Find $\chi'(G)$ for each of the following graphs G on the graph cards (see Chapter 1):

a. card 128;   c. card 143;   e. card 152;   g. card 182;
b. card 130;   d. card 146;   f. card 178;   h. card 194.

○12.23. What can you say about graphs G for which
(a) $\chi'(G) = 1$;   (b) $\chi'(G) = 2$?

○12.24. Classify each of the following statements as TRUE or FALSE, giving your reasons:
a. if G contains a vertex of degree r, then $\chi'(G) \geq r$:
b. if $\chi'(G) \geq r$, then G contains a vertex of degree r.

○12.25. For each of the following simple graphs, write down:
- a. the lower and upper bounds for $\chi'(G)$ given by Vizing's theorem;
- b. the correct value of $\chi'(G)$:
  - (1) the cycle graph C_7;
  - (2) the complete graph K_6;
  - (3) the complete bipartite graph $K_{3,4}$.

Justify your answers to (2) and (3) by producing an explicit coloring of the edges of the graph.

12.26. For the graph G in Problem 12.8:
- a. Use Vizing's theorem to obtain lower and upper bounds for $\chi'(G)$.
- b. What is the correct value of $\chi'(G)$?

12.27. For each of the following graphs G, write down:
- a. the lower and upper bounds for $\chi'(G)$ given by Vizing's theorem (extended version);
- b. the lower and upper bounds for $\chi'(G)$ given by Shannon's theorem;
- c. the exact value of $\chi'(G)$:

   (1)   (2)   (3)

12.28. Consider the following graph G:

- a. Use the theorems of Vizing and Shannon to obtain lower and upper bounds for $\chi'(G)$.
- b. What is the correct value of $\chi'(G)$?

12.29.† Obtain bounds corresponding to those in Problem 12.10 for $\underline{\chi'}$ and $\overline{\chi'}$, the chromatic indices of a simple graph G and its complement $\overline{G}$.

○12.30. Use the graph cards in Chapter 1 to locate all of the connected simple graphs G with at most five vertices that satisfy $\chi'(G) = d + 1$, where d is the maximum vertex-degree in G.

12.31.† Of the 112 connected simple graphs G with six vertices, only three satisfy $\chi'(G) = d + 1$, where d is the maximum vertex-degree in G. Use the graph cards in Chapter 1 to locate these three graphs.

12.32. Prove that if G is a Hamiltonian graph which is regular of degree 3, then
$\chi'(G) = 3$.

12.33.[†] a. Show that the Petersen graph has chromatic index 4.
   (*Hint:* Assume that the chromatic index is 3; then there is essentially only one
   way to 3-edge-color the outside pentagon.)

   b. What is the chromatic index of the graph obtained from the Petersen graph
   by deleting any vertex (and its incident edges)?

   c. What is the chromatic index of the graph obtained from the Petersen graph
   by deleting any edge?

12.34. Use König's theorem to write down the chromatic index of

   a. the complete bipartite graph $K_{r,s}$ $(r \le s)$;

   b. the graph of the cube;

   c. the k-cube Q_k.

   Give an explicit edge-coloring for the graph in part a.

⊘12.35. Suppose that n teams take part in a competition in which each team is required
to play exactly one match against each of the other $n-1$ teams. Assuming that
any matches which involve different pairs of teams may be played simultaneously, how many rounds of matches are necessary?

⊘12.36. At the end of an academic year, each student has to take an examination with
each of his tutors. If (a) there are 8 tutors and 50 students; (b) each student can
be examined by up to 3 tutors; (c) the tutors are available for 6, 6, 7, 8, 9, 12,
15, and 15 periods, how many examination periods are required?

12.37. The line graph $L(G)$ of a graph G was defined in Problem 2.39. If G is not a
null graph, show that $\chi'(G) = \chi(L(G))$.

CHAPTER 13

COLORING MAPS

13.1 INTRODUCTION

Consider the following map of the United States of America (excluding Alaska and Hawaii):

It is very common for maps of this kind to be colored in such a way that neighboring regions (states or countries) are colored differently. This enables us to distinguish easily between the various regions, and to locate the state boundaries. The question arises as to *how many colors are needed to color the entire map,* since the larger and more complicated the map, the more colors we might expect to need.

In fact, it is not difficult to show that five colors are sufficient to color any map, however complicated, and it is also possible, but very difficult, to show that four colors are always sufficient. However, we cannot reduce this number any further, since there are some maps, such as the above map of the USA, which cannot be colored with three colors. To see this, look at the ring of five states surrounding Nevada—namely, California, Oregon, Idaho, Utah, and Arizona. This ring of states needs at least three colors, and Nevada will then need yet another color, making four colors in all.

A 4-coloring of the above map is as follows:

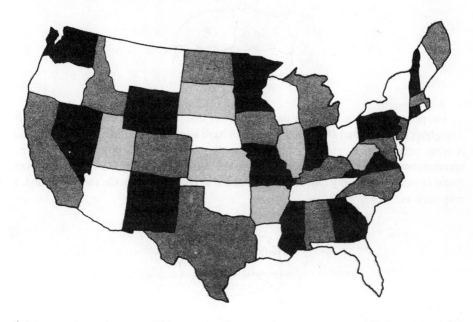

13.2 THE FOUR-COLOR PROBLEM

About a hundred years ago, some schoolchildren were challenged by their headmaster to solve the following problem:

Show that all maps can be colored with just four colors so that neighboring countries are differently colored.

The headmaster said that he would accept no proof that exceeded 30 lines of manuscript and one page of diagrams. It seemed to him that the problem was too simple to merit a longer solution. How disappointed he must have been at the unsuccessful attempts of his pupils, for it was not until 1976 that a solution to the problem was found! Two mathematicians from the University of Illinois, Kenneth Appel and Wolfgang Haken, used over

1000 hours of computer time to produce a proof running to several hundred pages and some 10,000 diagrams. But why should such a simple problem be so difficult to solve?

In 1852, the Professor of Mathematics at University College, London, was Augustus De Morgan. An ex-student of his, Francis Guthrie, had noticed that the counties of England can be colored with four colors in such a way that neighboring counties have different colors. Through his brother, he asked De Morgan whether or not four colors would suffice for all maps. The professor considered it fairly obvious that four colors must be enough, but he could not prove it. Nor could anyone else, for more than a century.

On June 13, 1878, at a meeting of the London Mathematical Society, Arthur Cayley asked if anyone could solve the problem. From that moment on, what was known as the **four-color problem** became one of the most famous unsolved problems in the whole of mathematics.

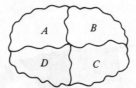

To appreciate the nature of the problem, notice that in the above map the country A is a neighbor of both B and D, because they each have a common boundary with A, but that A is not regarded as a neighbor of C, because they meet only at a point and so have no common boundary. We could color both A and C red and, similarly, we could color both B and D blue, so that only two colors are needed to color this map. On the other hand, a map such as

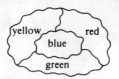

shows that four colors are sometimes necessary, because every country has a common boundary with every other country.

The *four-color conjecture* is that four colors are always sufficient. Note that it is immaterial whether or not we include the outside region in our coloring, since the outside region can be regarded (from a coloring point of view) as an extra ring-shaped country, as shown below. We shall not usually bother to include this outside region.

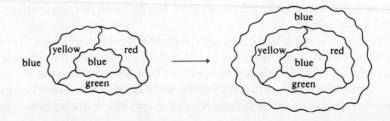

In 1879, the four-color conjecture was 'proved' by Alfred Kempe, a London barrister and keen amateur mathematician. Kempe produced what purported to be a proof of the fact that every map can be 4-colored. Although this attempted proof contains a fatal flaw, it also contains a number of ideas which appeared, in much more complicated form, in the eventual solution. In view of this, we spend some time analyzing Kempe's proof and extracting the main ideas.

The first idea is to use mathematical induction on the number of countries. It is clear that all maps with at most four countries can be 4-colored. The question is, if we can 4-color all maps with less then k countries, can we extend these colorings so as to 4-color all maps with k countries—and if so, how?

To answer this question, we need to look more closely at the maps that we are considering. We consider a map to be a connected planar graph whose faces (apart from the infinite face) correspond to the countries. We also assume that the graph contains no bridges (since the colors on each side of an edge have to be different), and contains no vertices of degree 1 or 2 (since these do not affect the coloring of the faces).

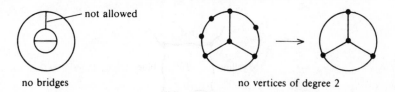

no bridges   no vertices of degree 2

It follows from Corollary 3 of Euler's formula (see page 221) and the section on dual graphs that every map contains at least one country (face) bounded by five edges or fewer—that is, one of the following:

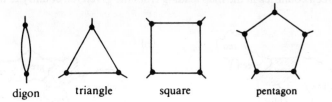

digon   triangle   square   pentagon

Since every map contains at least one of these configurations, we call such a set of configurations an **unavoidable set**. Another unavoidable set is

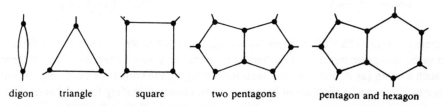

digon   triangle   square   two pentagons   pentagon and hexagon

Returning to our first unavoidable set, we look at the four types of country in turn, and try to show by induction that any map containing any of them can be 4-colored—that is, we assume that any map with less than k countries can be 4-colored and we try to extend these colorings so as to color all maps with k countries.

Digon   If there is a digon in the map, we can shrink it down to a point. The resulting map has one fewer country, and our induction hypothesis is that this map can be 4-colored. We now reinstate the digon, and color it with one of the two available colors. This gives a 4-coloring of the original map.

Triangle   If there is a triangle in the map, we can shrink it down to a point. The resulting map has one fewer country, and our induction hypothesis is that this map can be 4-colored. We now reinstate the triangle, and color it with the single available color. This gives a 4-coloring of the original map.

Square   If there is a square we shrink it down to a point, and 4-color the resulting map. The difficulty arises when we try to reinstate the square, since it may be surrounded by four different colors, so that there is no spare color with which to color the square.

To get out of this difficulty, we use a **Kempe-chain argument**. We consider the red and green countries adjacent to the square, and investigate whether or not there is a chain of red and green countries in the map leading from the given red country to the given green country.

If there is no such chain of countries [as in diagram (a)], then we can interchange the colors in the red–green part at the top, thereby enabling the square to be colored red. If there is such a chain [as in diagram (b)], then interchanging the colors does not help. But in this case there can be no chain of blue and yellow countries leading from the given blue country to the given yellow country. We interchange the colors in the blue–yellow part on the right-hand side of the map, thereby enabling the square to be colored blue as required. So in either case we get a 4-coloring of the original map.

In each of the above cases, we shrank the configuration to a point, 4-colored the remaining map, and reinstated the configuration. In each case we can extend the coloring to the configuration, either directly or after a number of color-interchanges. We express this by saying that these configurations are **reducible**.

Where Kempe went wrong was in trying to extend the same idea to the case in which there is a pentagon. In doing this, he had to consider the case where two simultaneous color-interchanges are necessary. Although either of these color-interchanges is permissible on its own, to do them both is not, as was shown in 1890 by a mathematician named Percy Heawood.

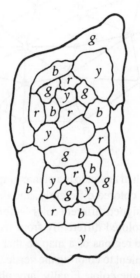

Heawood gave the above counter-example to refute Kempe's proof. The error is a fundamental one, and it soon became clear that the problem is extremely difficult, so that Appel and Haken's achievement in solving it is a major one. What Appel and Haken had to do was to replace the pentagon by other configurations, until they had found an *unavoidable set of reducible configurations*—*unavoidable* means that every map contains at least one of them, and *reducible* means that whichever one it is then the proof can be completed by the methods outlined above. The question is, how is this set constructed?

Professors Appel and Haken did this by constructing a set of almost 2000 reducible configurations. An account of how they did this is given in an article from the *New Scientist* of 21 October 1976, part of which is reproduced in the Appendix at the end of this chapter.

13.3 EQUIVALENT FORMS OF THE FOUR-COLOR THEOREM

It was recognized early on that it is useful to state the four-color problem in terms of graphs. Let M be a map drawn in the plane. Place a vertex in each region, and join two vertices with an edge if the regions they represent share a common border. The result is the **dual graph** of the map (see Chapter 11). For example, the dual graph of the map of the United States on page 250 is as follows:

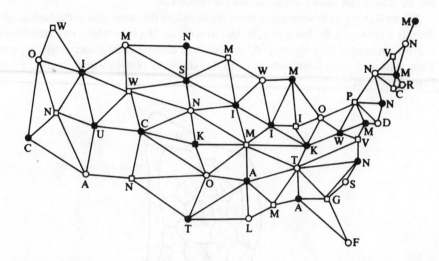

It is clear that the dual graph of any map is a planar graph. Further, any two neighboring states in the original map are colored differently, and thus, any two adjacent vertices in the dual graph must also be assigned different colors—for example, the bottom right-hand vertex F (Florida) must be colored differently from its neighbors A (Alabama) and G (Georgia). Thus, coloring the regions of a map so that regions with a common border have different colors is equivalent to coloring the vertices of its dual graph so that no two adjacent vertices have the same color. Finally, any plane drawing of a graph can be thought of as the dual graph of *some* map—namely, the map formed by its own dual.

Recall that a graph is *k-colorable* if its vertices can be colored with k colors so that adjacent vertices have different colors. The four-color theorem can thus be restated as follows:

THEOREM 13.1 (THE FOUR-COLOR THEOREM).   *Every planar graph is 4-colorable.*

The next theorem is a much weaker result, but its proof is a nice illustration of a proof by induction.

THEOREM 13.2.   *Every planar graph is 6-colorable.*

Proof   We use mathematical induction on the number of vertices. It is clear that all planar graphs with at most six vertices can be 6-colored. We must now show that if all planar graphs with less than k vertices can be 6-colored, then so can all planar graphs with k vertices.

So let G be a planar graph with k vertices. It follows from Corollary 3 of Theorem 11.1 that G contains a vertex v of degree at most 5. If we delete v (and its incident edges), then the resulting planar graph has less than k vertices, and by our induction hypothesis we assume that this planar graph can be 6-colored.

We now reinstate the missing vertex v. Since v has at most five neighbors, there is a spare color which can be used for coloring v. This gives a 6-coloring of our original planar graph. The result is therefore true for planar graphs with any number of vertices. □

The next theorem was proved by Heawood, in trying to salvage what he could from Kempe's incorrect proof of the four-color theorem:

THEOREM 13.3.   *Every planar graph is 5-colorable.*

Proof   As before, we prove this result by induction on the number of vertices. Proceeding as in the proof of Theorem 13.2, we find a vertex v of degree at most 5, delete it, and 5-color the resulting planar graph. The difficulty arises when we try to reinstate v, since it may be surrounded by five different colors, so that there is no spare color with which to color v.

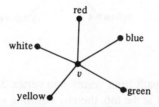

To get around this difficulty, we use a Kempe-chain argument. We consider the red and green vertices adjacent to v, and investigate whether or not there is a path of red and green vertices between the given red vertex and the given green one.

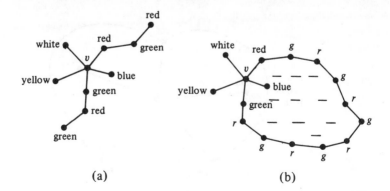

(a)   (b)

If there is no such path [figure (a)], we can interchange the colors in the red–green part at the top, thereby enabling v to be colored red. If there is such a path [figure (b)], then there can be no path of yellow and blue vertices between the yellow and blue vertices adjacent to v. We interchange the colors in the blue–yellow part of the right-hand side of the graph, thereby enabling v to be colored blue, as required. So in each case we get a

5-coloring of the original graph. The result is therefore true for planar graphs with any number of vertices. □

We now present the essence of Kempe's proof of the four-color theorem. We leave it to you to discover the flaw in it (see Problem 13.5).

KEMPE'S 'PROOF' OF THE FOUR-COLOR THEOREM.

The inductive argument is as before. The difficulty arises when v is surrounded by four different colors, as follows:

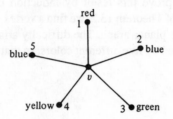

If there is no red–green path from vertex 1 to vertex 3, then we can interchange the colors in the red–green part at the top, thereby enabling v to be colored red, and we are done. We therefore assume that there is a red–green path from vertex 1 to vertex 3.

Similarly, if there is no red–yellow path from vertex 1 to vertex 4, then we can interchange the colors in the red–yellow part at the top, thereby enabling v to be colored red, and we are done. We therefore assume that there is a red–yellow path from vertex 1 to vertex 4.

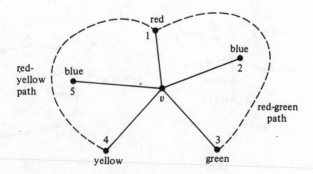

Since there cannot be a blue–yellow path from vertex 2 to vertex 4, we can begin a blue–yellow color switch at vertex 2, and this does not change the color of vertex 4. Similarly, we can begin a blue–green color switch at vertex 5, and this does not change the color of vertex 3. The vertices around v are now all colored red, green, and yellow, so that v can be colored blue. This completes the 'proof'. □

We now turn to a form of the four-color theorem involving chromatic polynomials. Since the chromatic polynomial $P_G(k)$ counts the number of ways of coloring a graph with k colors, we can restate the four-color theorem in terms of chromatic polynomials.

THE FOUR-COLOR THEOREM.   *If* G *is a planar graph, then* $P_G(4) > 0$.

Another form of the four-color theorem was found by P. G. Tait, who thought that he had proved it in 1880. Since we are concerned with vertex-colorings of dual graphs of planar maps, we need consider only planar graphs with no bridges. Tait realized that it is sufficient to look at edge-colorings of cubic graphs of that form.

THEOREM 13.4 (TAIT'S THEOREM).   *The four-color theorem is equivalent to the statement that any connected bridgeless planar cubic graph is 3-edge-colorable.*

Proof   We first assume the four-color theorem—that is, that the regions of any map can be 4-colored so that regions with a common border have different colors. Let G be a connected bridgeless planar cubic graph. If we draw G in the plane without crossings, then the faces of G can be colored with four colors A, B, C, and D, so that no two adjacent faces have the same color. We can then use the following table to color the edges of G:

	A	B	C	D
A	$\cdots$	b	c	d
B	b	$\cdots$	d	c
C	c	d	$\cdots$	b
D	d	c	b	$\cdots$

To color an edge bordering two faces colored B and C (say), we look up the entry in row B and column C, and then use color d to color the edge. Since the table has distinct entries in each row and column, we can never color two adjacent edges the same color. Thus, G is 3-edge-colorable.

To prove the converse result, we assume that any connected bridgeless planar cubic graph is 3-edge-colorable. Let M be a map that we wish to color with four colors. This map is already a bridgeless planar graph, and we must turn it into a cubic graph. At each vertex whose degree is greater than 3 we perform the following replacement:

It is clear that if we can color the faces in the right-hand figure so that no two faces which share a common border have the same color, then we can similarly color the faces in the left-hand figure as well. By our assumption, we can 3-edge-color the right-hand graph, and we can then use the above table in reverse to color the faces of this graph with the colors A, B, C, and D, beginning with an arbitrary color and face. This gives us a 4-coloring of the faces of the original map, as required. ☐

Yet another variation of the four-color theorem was given by Heawood who cast it in an algebraic setting.

THEOREM 13.5 (HEAWOOD'S THEOREM). *A bridgeless planar cubic graph is 3-edge-colorable if and only if its vertices can be labeled +1 or −1 so that the sum for the vertices around the boundary of any face is divisible by 3.*

Proof Let G be such a graph that has been 3-edge-colored with colors a, b, and c. We label a vertex +1 if the three edges incident to it are colored a, b, and c in clockwise order, and label the vertex −1 if the coloring is counter-clockwise. We now begin at an edge of a face and move counter-clockwise along the boundary of the face. When we come to a vertex labeled +1, we go from an edge colored a to one colored b, or from b to c, or c to a. When we come to a vertex labeled −1, then we change colors in the opposite order. After a full circuit around the face, we return to the original edge, and so the total of the +1's and −1's must be divisible by 3.

Conversely, if the graph has been labeled +1 and −1 in the prescribed fashion, then we can reverse the foregoing procedure to find a 3-edge-coloring for the graph. ☐

13.4 GRAPH EMBEDDINGS AND THE HEAWOOD MAP-COLORING THEOREM

The four-color theorem states that four colors are sufficient to color any map drawn in the plane. Since any map drawn on the surface of a sphere can be stereographically projected to a map in the equatorial plane of the sphere (see page 221), it follows that four colors are sufficient to color any map drawn on the surface of a sphere. This is not true, as we shall see, for maps drawn on other surfaces. This leads to the notion of graph 'embeddings'.

DEFINITION. *A graph is said to be* **embedded** *on a surface if it has been drawn on that surface without crossings.*

For example, a planar graph can be embedded on the plane.

Since K_5 and $K_{3,3}$ cannot be drawn in the plane without crossings, it is natural to ask whether there are any other surfaces on which they can be drawn without crossings. That K_5 can be embedded on a torus is shown in figure (a):

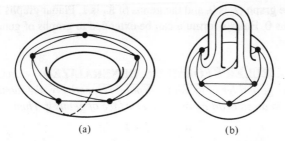

(a)   (b)

We can also think of a torus as a sphere with one handle [see figure (b)], since we can gradually deform the torus into a sphere with one handle without tearing it. (An old joke defines a topologist as a mathematician who cannot tell the difference between a doughnut and a coffee cup!)

A third representation of a torus is as a rectangle in which the top and bottom edges have been identified, and the right and left edges have been identified. You can think of glueing the top and bottom of the rectangle to form a tube, and then glueing the two ends of the tube together to form a torus. This representation is shown in figure (a) below, and in figure (b) we use this representation to embed K_5 on a torus.

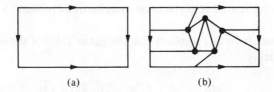

(a)   (b)

The above representation of the torus is used in many video games. In these games the screen is a rectangle. If a moving figure goes off the top of the screen it reappears at the bottom, and if it goes off the right edge of the screen it reappears on the left. In other words, Pac Man lives on a torus!

By an (orientable) **surface of genus g** we mean a sphere with g handles or, equivalently, a torus with g holes. For example, a sphere has genus 0, and a torus has genus 1.

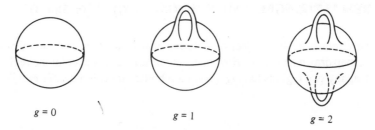

$g = 0$ $g = 1$ $g = 2$

It is clear that any graph can be embedded on some such surface, because by adding enough handles you can easily eliminate all crossings. The **genus of a graph** is the smallest genus of a surface on which the graph can be embedded. For example, the genus of the cube graph Q_3 is 0, and the genus of K_5 is 1. Planar graphs are precisely the graphs with genus 0. Euler's formula can be extended to graphs of genus g, as follows: we omit the proof.

THEOREM 13.6 (EULER'S FORMULA, GENERALIZED). *Let* G *be a connected graph with genus* g, *and let* n, m, *and* f *denote, respectively, the numbers of vertices, edges, and faces in an embedding of* G *on a surface of genus* g. *Then*

$$n - m + f = 2 - 2g.$$

Note that $g = 0$ for planar graphs, and that the above theorem then reduces to the original Euler's formula. This theorem gives us a lower bound for the genus of a graph.

COROLLARY. *Let* G *be a simple graph with* n *vertices and* m *edges. Then the genus* g(G) *of the graph* G *satisfies*

$$g(G) \geq \lceil \tfrac{1}{6}(m-3n) + 1 \rceil,$$

where $\lceil x \rceil$ *denotes the smallest integer greater than or equal to* x.

Proof This result follows from Theorem 13.6 since each face is bounded by at least three edges. The details are left to you as an exercise (see Problem 13.16). ☐

We can conclude from this corollary that the genus $g(K_n)$ of the complete graph K_n satisfies the inequality

$$
\begin{aligned}
g(K_n) \quad &\geq \quad \lceil \tfrac{1}{6}(\tfrac{1}{2}n(n-1) - 3n) + 1 \rceil \\
&= \quad \lceil \tfrac{1}{12}(n(n-1) - 6n + 12) \rceil \\
&= \quad \lceil \tfrac{1}{12}(n^2 - 7n + 12) \rceil \\
&= \quad \lceil \tfrac{1}{12}(n-3)(n-4) \rceil.
\end{aligned}
$$

For example, $g(K_8) \geq \lceil \tfrac{20}{12} \rceil = 2$, and hence, K_8 cannot be embedded on a torus.

We have just proved the easy half of a remarkable theorem that was proved in 1968:

THEOREM 13.7 (RINGEL AND YOUNGS). $g(K_n) = \lceil \tfrac{1}{12}(n-3)(n-4) \rceil.$

We now return to the subject of coloring maps on other surfaces. Consider the following map drawn on a torus. How many colors are needed to color the regions of this map so that any two regions having a common border are colored differently?

The rather surprising answer, as you can see, is that seven colors are required, since each of the seven regions has a border in common with all the other regions. The dual graph of this map is the complete graph K_7. Heawood proved that no graph embedded on the torus could need more than seven colors—that is, he proved the seven-color theorem for the torus.

We define the **chromatic number of a surface** S to be the largest chromatic number among the graphs that can be embedded on the surface S. We denote this number by $\chi(S)$. For example, the chromatic number of the plane or the sphere is 4, and the chromatic number of the torus is 7. Heawood believed he had proved a formula for the chromatic number of a surface with an arbitrary number of handles, but he had in fact only established an upper bound. Ringel and Youngs finally finished the proof in 1968, and the result is sometimes known as the Heawood Map-Coloring Theorem.

THEOREM 13.8 (THE HEAWOOD MAP-COLORING THEOREM). *If* S_g $(g \geq 1)$ *denotes the sphere with g handles, then the chromatic number of* S_g *is given by*

$$\chi(S_g) = \left\lfloor \tfrac{1}{2}\{7 + (1+48g)^{1/2}\} \right\rfloor,$$

where $\lfloor x \rfloor$ *denotes the greatest integer less than or equal to* x.

For example, for the torus ($g = 1$), the theorem gives $\chi(S_1) = 7$. If we also put $g = 0$, then the above formula yields $\chi(S_0) = 4$, which is nothing more nor less than the four-color theorem for the sphere!

PROBLEMS

The Four-Color Problem

◦13.1. Find a 4-coloring of the following map (excluding the outside region):

13.2. The following map is to be colored with the colors red, blue, yellow, and green in such a way that neighboring countries are differently colored. If three countries are colored blue, green and yellow as indicated, show that country A must be colored red. What can you say about the color of country B?

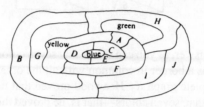

13.3.[†] Find a 4-coloring of the following map:

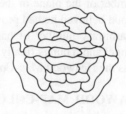

(This map is a re-drawing of the map used by Heawood to point out the flaw in Kempe's 'proof' of the four-color theorem.)

◦13.4. The map on page 252 requires four colors because each region is adjacent to all the other regions. Without using the four-color theorem, prove that no map in the plane can have five mutually adjacent regions. This does not prove the four-color theorem. Why?

Equivalent Forms of the Four-Color Theorem

13.5.[†] The following graph is the dual of the map used by Heawood to illustrate the mistake in Kempe's 'proof' of the four-color theorem. Show exactly where Kempe's argument fails.

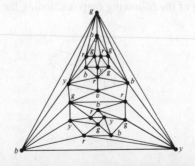

⊘13.6. Let G be a map. Prove that

    a. if the faces of G can be 2-colored, then G is an Eulerian graph;

    b. if the faces of G can be 3-colored, and if G is regular of degree 3, then every face of G has even degree.

13.7. Verify Heawood's Theorem (Theorem 13.5) for each of the following graphs:

    a. the graph of the cube;

    b. the graph of the dodecahedron.

Graph Embeddings and the Heawood Map-Coloring Theorem

13.8. Find an embedding of $K_{3,3}$ on

    a. a torus;

    b. a sphere with one handle;

    c. a rectangle with opposite sides identified.

13.9. Embed K_7 on a torus. How do you know this is possible?

13.10. Show that the Petersen graph has genus 1 by

    a. proving that it is not planar; and

    b. embedding it on a surface of genus 1.

⊘13.11. Calculate $g(K_7)$ and $g(K_{11})$.

13.12.[†] Give an example of a graph of genus 2, and show how it can be embedded on a sphere with two handles.

13.13. a. Using Theorem 13.7, prove that there is no value of n for which $g(K_n) = 7$.

    b. What is the next integer which is not the genus of any complete graph?

13.14.[†] A **Möbius strip** is formed by taking a rectangle and glueing together one pair of opposite ends after giving it a half-twist. Embed K_5 and $K_{3,3}$ on a Möbius strip

    a. by actually making two Möbius strips and drawing the two graphs on them;

    b. by using the following representation of a Möbius strip in which the arrows indicate the half-twist.

⊘13.15. Verify that the generalized Euler's formula (Theorem 13.6) holds for the graphs K_5 and $K_{3,3}$ embedded on a torus.

⊘13.16. Prove the corollary to Euler's formula.

13.17. Show that there is no graph G of genus g (≥ 1) such that

    a. G is regular of degree 4, and

    b. on a surface of genus g, every face of G is a triangle.

13.18. Prove that

$$g(K_{r,s}) \geq \left\lceil \tfrac{1}{4}(r-2)(s-2) \right\rceil.$$

(Ringel has shown that this inequality is actually an equality.)

13.19. Calculate $\chi(S_2)$ and $\chi(S_{10})$.

APPENDIX TO CHAPTER 13

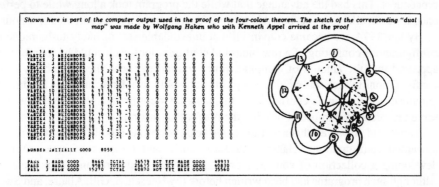

Shown here is part of the computer output used in the proof of the four-colour theorem. The sketch of the corresponding "dual map" was made by Wolfgang Haken who with Kenneth Appel arrived at the proof

Dr. Kenneth Appel

The Proof of the Four-Colour Theorem

New Scientist, 21 October 1976

Enter the Fast Digital Computer   Even though a great deal of progress was made in the study of reducibility, the goal of proving the four colour theorem by demonstrating the existence of an unavoidable set of reducible configurations seemed extremely far off. The critical problem was this: No one had any reasonable intuition of a set of configurations which was unavoidable and seemed to contain configurations which were likely to be reducible. In particular, if there were such a set it was not clear that it was small enough so that its members could be tested for reducibility.

With the advent of large, fast digital computers, a new tool was made available to workers in the field. Heesch formalised the ideas of Kempe and he and his students used computers to show a great many configurations reducible. Heesch strongly believed that an unavoidable set of configurations could be found and used a method which has since come to be known as the principle of discharging (by analogy with the idea of moving charges in an electrical network) to find an unavoidable set of reducible configurations for maps with certain restrictions.

Wolfgang Haken, in the late 1960s, noticed that Heesch's discharging arguments could be greatly improved and simplified. He argued that since the study of reducibility had proceeded much farther than that of unavoidable sets, one should spend a great deal more effort on the study of unavoidable sets. From the work on reducibility, especially the many configurations studied by Heesch, it became evident that configurations with certain easily checkable properties were rather likely to be reducible while those without these properties were unlikely to be reducible.

In 1972, Haken and I began to search for unavoidable sets of configurations which were likely to be reducible. We did this by examining various discharging procedures to see what sort of sets of configurations would be generated. A drawback to this approach had been that the study of a single discharging procedure would take several months and would not help greatly in simplifying the study of a second procedure. We overcame this difficulty by creating a very large sophisticated computer program which could, by minor variations in input and certain parameters, be used to study a great many discharging procedures. This had the advantage that while the program took a long while to perfect, once it was available it was possible to study the results of a procedure in a few hours.

By late 1974, we became convinced that unavoidable sets of likely-to-be-reducible configurations consisting of a few thousand configurations each could be found. It also appeared that the amount of computer time required to check the reducibility of the configurations in such sets would be large but not prohibitive. Unfortunately, the problem remained that if a single configuration in such a set were irreducible the set would not serve the intended purpose of proving the four colour theorem.

It appeared, however, that a method could be developed to modify such sets to replace unwanted configurations, Haken, and John Koch, and I then combined efforts on developing a collection of computer programs to test configurations for reducibility. Although such programs had been written before (by Heesch, S. Gill, Allaire, and Swart, and others), because of technical differences in purpose it was thought advisable to have a new set.

By January 1976 it appeared that the study of discharging procedures had reached a point in which a serious attempt on the four colour theorem could be made. The final attempt used a rather flexible technique in which one configuration at a time was generated for the potential unavoidable set. When it was generated an immediate attempt was made to show it reducible. If this could not be done with reasonable effort (up to 30 minutes on an IBM 370–168 computer) it was discarded and the procedure was modified to avoid its use. Previous work had given us confidence that this method would converge to an unavoidable set of reducible configurations. In June 1976, after analysis of 10,000 configurations, over 2000 of which were tested for reducibility, and after using over 1000 hours of computer time on various computers owned by the University of Illinois, an unavoidable set of under 2000 reducible configurations was produced.

(Reprinted, with permission, from *New Scientist*, 21 October 1976.)

CHAPTER 14

DECOMPOSITION PROBLEMS

14.1 INTRODUCTION

In Chapter 6 we introduced the idea of an Eulerian graph, and we investigated conditions under which a given connected graph is Eulerian. In particular, we saw that every Eulerian graph can be split into disjoint cycles—this means that we can divide up the set of edges in such a way that each edge of the graph belongs to one, and only one, of the subsets. In this chapter we adopt a similar approach for several other problems. Each of these problems can be formulated in graph-theoretical terms, and involves splitting either the set of vertices or the set of edges into disjoint subsets with particular graph-theoretical properties.

Some of the most interesting problems in graph theory involve the decomposition of a graph G into subgraphs of a particular type. In many of these problems, we split the set of *vertices* of G into a number of disjoint subsets, and this is called a **vertex decomposition** of G. In other problems, we split the set of *edges* of G into a number of disjoint subsets, and this is called an **edge decomposition** of G. For example, if our graph G is disconnected, as illustrated below, then a natural vertex decomposition is to split the vertex-set into the disjoint subsets

$$\{1,2,3\}, \{4,5,6,7\}, \{8\},$$

corresponding to the components of G. A corresponding edge decomposition of G is

$\{a, b, c\}, \{d, e, f, g, h\}.$

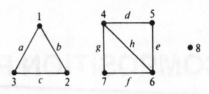

Another example of an edge decomposition, as mentioned above, is to take an Eulerian graph and split the edges into disjoint cycles. For example, if G is the Eulerian graph shown below, then there are five possible edge decompositions of G into disjoint cycles:

$\{a, b, c, d, e, f\}, \{g, h, i\};$ $\{a, f, i\}, \{b, c, g\}, \{d, e, h\};$

$\{a, f, h, g\}, \{b, c, d, e, i\};$ $\{b, c, h, i\}, \{a, f, e, d, g\};$

$\{d, e, i, g\}, \{a, b, c, h, f\}.$

In this chapter we consider a few of the most important graph decomposition problems. Some of these have arisen out of practical considerations, such as the New York sanitation problem and the printed circuits problem, whereas others are of a recreational nature, such as the map-coloring problem and the queens-on-a-chessboard problem.

14.2 VERTEX DECOMPOSITION PROBLEMS

We consider three types of problem—map-coloring problems, a sanitation problem (which can also be reformulated as a coloring problem), and some domination problems, including a recreational problem involving queens on a chessboard.

Map-Coloring Problems

Our first decomposition problem involves the coloring of maps. Recall that the map of the United States (excluding Alaska and Hawaii) can be colored with just four colors, as follows:

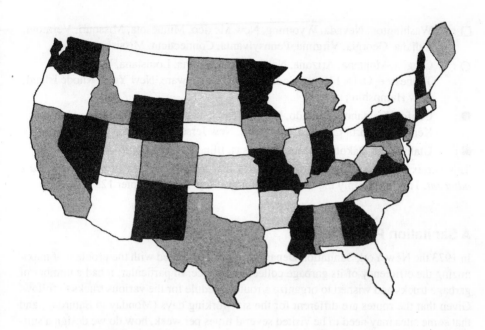

We can represent this as a vertex decomposition problem by considering the dual graph, in which each state is represented by a vertex, and two vertices are joined whenever the corresponding states share a common boundary line. This gives the following graph, in which each vertex has been assigned a symbol to represent the color of the corresponding state. Since any two neighboring states in the original map were colored differently, any two adjacent vertices in this dual graph are assigned different colors.

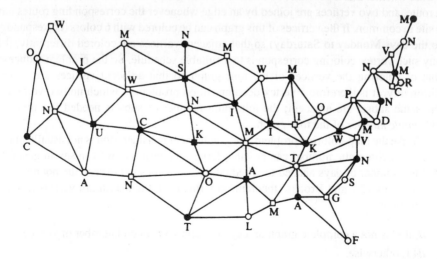

Such a coloring of the vertices of the graph splits the vertex-set into four subsets, corresponding to the four colors, as following.

□ :   Washington, Nevada, Wyoming, New Mexico, Minnesota, Missouri, Vermont, Indiana, Georgia, Virginia, Pennsylvania, Connecticut, Mississippi;

○ :   Oregon, Montana, Arizona, Nebraska, Oklahoma, Louisiana, Wisconsin, Tennessee, Ohio, Florida, South Carolina, Delaware, New York, Rhode Island, New Hampshire;

● :   California, Idaho, Colorado, North Dakota, Texas, Iowa, Michigan, Alabama, Kentucky, North Carolina, Maryland, New Jersey, Massachusetts, Maine;

■ :   Utah, South Dakota, Kansas, Arkansas, Illinois, West Virginia.

This vertex decomposition has the property that *no two vertices in the same set are adjacent*. They are simply the **vertex-colorings** discussed in Chapter 12.

A Sanitation Problem

In 1973 the New York Sanitation Department was concerned with the problem of maximizing the efficiency of its garbage collection service. In particular, it had a number of garbage trucks and wished to organize a route schedule for the various trucks to follow. Given that the routes are different for the six working days (Monday to Saturday) and that some sites may need to be visited several times per week, how do we design a suitable schedule?

In its full complexity, this problem is far too difficult to be considered here, so we look at just one aspect of it. Suppose that a weekly schedule of routes has been constructed, in which no route is too short or long, every truck is used on every working day, and every site is visited the required number of times. Is the problem now solved?

The answer to this question is likely to be *No,* unless we can arrange a schedule in such a way that two different garbage trucks do not visit the same site on the same day! To see whether this is possible, we construct a **tour graph** in which each vertex represents a route, and two vertices are joined by an edge whenever the corresponding routes have a site in common. If the vertices of this graph can be colored with 6 colors (corresponding to the days Monday to Saturday) so that adjacent vertices are colored differently, then any such vertex-coloring corresponds to a suitable schedule. So the problem reduces to that of coloring the vertices of the tour graph so that adjacent vertices are colored differently. It is therefore a vertex decomposition problem in which no two vertices in the same subset are adjacent; the minimum number of subsets needed is simply the *chromatic number* of the tour graph.

Unlike the map-coloring problem, the graph under consideration is not usually planar, and so its chromatic number can be quite large. The best that we can say in general is that the number of days needed to schedule the tours does not exceed the bounds given by Theorem 12.1 and Brooks' theorem, in terms of d, the maximum vertex-degree of G—namely,

d, if G is not a complete graph or a cycle graph with an odd number of vertices;

$d+1$, otherwise.

An exact determination of the number of days needed to schedule the tours requires a method for finding the chromatic number of the tour graph G. We presented such a method in Chapter 12, involving the calculation of the chromatic polynomial $P_G(k)$. The smallest value of k for which the chromatic polynomial of G is non-zero is the chromatic number of G, and the value of $P_G(k)$ for this number k gives the number of different ways of coloring the vertices of G with k colors. Thus a knowledge of the chromatic polynomial of the tour graph tells us the number of days needed to schedule the tours, and the number of different ways of scheduling the tours in this number of days.

Domination and Independence Problems

Communication links are to be set up between a number of cities, and transmitting stations are to be built in some of these cities so that every city can receive messages from at least one transmitting station. For reasons of economy, we require the number of transmitting stations to be as small as possible. How can this be done?

We can represent this situation by a graph whose vertices correspond to the cities, and whose edges correspond to pairs of cities which can communicate with each other. Since every city must either contain a transmitting station or communicate with a city containing a transmitting station, we wish to find a set of vertices which (between them) are adjacent to all other vertices of the graph. For example, if the graph

represents the communication links between six cities, then we can locate the transmitting stations at $A, C,$ and $E,$ since each of the other vertices $(B, D,$ and $F)$ is adjacent to at least one of these vertices. However, a more economical solution is to take just two transmitting stations and locate them at A and D; as before, each of the other vertices $(B, C, E,$ and $F)$ is adjacent to at least one of these vertices.

A set S of vertices with the property that every vertex of the graph either is in S or is adjacent to a vertex of S is called a **dominating set** of vertices, and a dominating set of smallest possible size is called a **minimum dominating set**. The number of vertices in a minimum dominating set in a graph G is called the **dominating number** of G. For example, the sets $S = \{A, C, E\}$ and $S = \{A, D\}$ are both dominating sets in the above graph, but of these only $\{A, D\}$ is a minimum dominating set. Other minimum dominating sets in the above graph are $\{B, E\}, \{C, F\},$ and $\{D, F\}$. Therefore, the dominating number is 2. It follows that the above communications problem reduces to that of finding a minimum dominating set in the corresponding graph.

Such problems occur in many different guises. For example, suppose that a number of locations in a nuclear power plant are fitted with warning lights, and the security guards are to be stationed in various places to watch for these lights. We can minimize the number of guards needed, by finding a minimum dominating set in the corresponding graph and positioning the guards accordingly. Any light which comes on can then be seen by at least one of the guards, who can then take appropriate action.

A recreational problem of this kind is to find the smallest number of queens that can be placed on a chessboard in such a way that every unoccupied square is attacked. In chess, a queen attacks all squares in the same row or column and all squares in either diagonal through the square on which she is placed. For example, if we place the first queen as shown in diagram (a), then 25 unoccupied squares are attacked. How many more queens are needed?

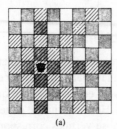

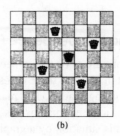

(a)   (b)

In fact, only four more queens are needed; an arrangement of five queens which attack all unoccupied squares is shown in diagram (b). Furthermore, it can be shown (although we shall not do so) that no arrangement of four queens will do, but that five queens are also sufficient for chessboards of size 9×9, 10×10, and 11×11.

We can represent this problem graphically by taking the squares as vertices, and joining two vertices by an edge whenever a queen can move from one of the squares to the other. A solution of the problem then corresponds to finding a dominating set with 5 vertices, and showing that it is a minimum dominating set. Since the graph corresponding to an 8×8 chessboard has 64 vertices and 728 edges, we shall not attempt to draw it, but look instead at the analogous problem of a bishop on a 4×4 chessboard. (A bishop can move only diagonally.)

In this case, the graph splits into two parts, corresponding to the black squares and the white squares. There are several minimum dominating sets—for example, $\{6,11,7,10\}$, which corresponds to placing a bishop on each of the central four squares. Other minimum dominating sets are $\{5,6,7,8\}$ and $\{9,10,11,12\}$.

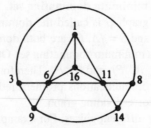

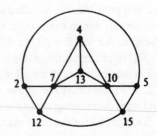

By now you are probably wondering what this has to do with vertex decomposition problems. To answer this, we take a dominating set, one vertex at a time, and write down each of its neighbors (omitting vertices in the dominating set, or those which have already been recorded). For example, the dominating set {6, 11, 7, 10} in the above graph gives us the following subsets:

for vertex 6, we take the vertices 1, 3, 9, and 16, giving the subset {6, 1, 3, 9, 16} (we have omitted vertex 11, since it lies in the dominating set);

for vertex 11, we take the vertices 8 and 14, giving the subset {11, 8, 14} (we have omitted vertices 1 and 16, since they have already been recorded);

for vertex 7, we take the vertices 2, 4, 12, and 13, giving the subset {7, 2, 4, 12, 13};

for vertex 10, we take the vertices 5 and 15, giving the subset {10, 5, 15}.

This gives us the vertex decomposition

{6, 1, 3, 9, 16}, {11, 8, 14}, {7, 2, 4, 12, 13}, {10, 5, 15}.

Note that this type of decomposition is very different from that produced in our discussion of coloring problems. For those problems, the subsets have the property that no two vertices in the same subset are adjacent. For domination problems, the subsets have the property that *each subset contains a vertex adjacent to all the other vertices in the subset.*

A related problem, known as the **independence problem**, is that of finding the largest set of queens that can be placed on a chessboard so that none of them is attacked by any other. Clearly, the number of queens cannot exceed 8, since at least two queens would then appear in the same row. On the other hand, it is certainly possible to place 8 queens in the required manner, as shown in the following diagram.

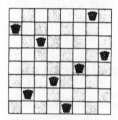

(This problem was studied by C. F. Gauss, who believed that there were 76 solutions. In 1854, the *Schachzeitung,* a Berlin chess journal, published 40 solutions. The correct number of solutions is 92.)

As with the domination problem, we can represent this situation by a graph whose vertices correspond to the squares, and whose edges join those pairs of squares which are connected by a queen's move. More generally, the *independence problem for a graph G* is that of finding the largest possible set of vertices of *G,* no two of which are adjacent.

A set of vertices no two of which are adjacent is called an **independent set** of vertices, and an independent set of largest possible size is called a **maximum independent set**. For example, the sets {A, D} {A, E}, and {A, C, E} are all independent sets in the graph below, but of these only {A, C, E} *is a maximum independent set.*

In order to solve the domination and independence problems for a graph G, we need to find the size of a minimum dominating set and the size of a maximum independent set in G. We denote these numbers by *dom G* and *ind G*, respectively. For example, if G is the graph above, then dom $G = 2$ and ind $G = 3$, whereas if G is the chessboard graph referred to above, then dom $G = 5$ and ind $G = 8$.

Unfortunately, there is no general formula which gives the values of dom G and ind G for a general graph. However, the following theorem gives two inequalities involving dom G and ind G.

THEOREM 14.1. *For any graph* **G** *with* n *vertices,*
   a. dom $G \le$ ind G;
   b. $\chi(G) \times$ ind $G \ge n$.

Proof a. Let S be a maximum independent set in G. Then S must be a dominating set, since otherwise there would be a vertex v in G which is not adjacent to any of the vertices in S; this vertex v could then be added to S to produce a larger independent set, which is impossible. The result follows.

   b. By the definition of $\chi(G)$, we can color the vertices of G with $\chi(G)$ colors in such a way that no two adjacent vertices are assigned the same color. It follows that the set of vertices of any given color must form an independent set, and hence that there are at most ind G vertices of any given color. Since there are $\chi(G)$ colors, the total number of vertices must be at most $\chi(G) \times$ ind G. $\square$

14.3 EDGE DECOMPOSITION PROBLEMS

We consider three types of problem—the printed circuits problem (which leads to the idea of a planar graph), matching problems (such as a problem on electrical networks and a scheduling problem), and various edge decomposition problems arising from a problem involving the bus routes between a number of towns.

The Printed Circuits Problem

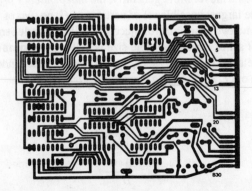

In printed circuits, electronic components are constructed by means of conducting strips printed directly onto a flat board of insulating material. Such printed connectors may not cross, since this would lead to undesirable electrical contact at crossing points. When necessary, insulated wires may be used to cross over conducting strips, but printed circuits are designed to avoid this as far as possible. Circuits in which large numbers of crossings are unavoidable may be printed on several boards which are then sandwiched together. Each board consists of a printed circuit without crossings. What is the smallest number of such layers for a given circuit?

We illustrate the printed circuits problem with a particular example. Suppose that the circuit has 36 interconnections and is represented by the complete graph K_9. Then it is impossible to arrange all these interconnections in one layer, or even two. Three layers are needed, and a solution is given below. Note that every edge of K_9 is included in exactly one of the layers—for example, the edge 28 appears on layer 2, and the edge 69 appears on layer 3.

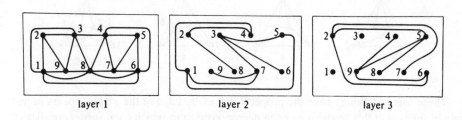

layer 1   layer 2   layer 3

Recall that a graph which can be drawn in the plane without crossings is called a **planar graph**. For example, each of the graphs appearing on one of the layers in the above diagram is a planar graph. The printed circuits problem therefore reduces to the problem of decomposing the graph into smaller graphs, all of which are planar. In other words, it is an edge decomposition problem in which *the edges in each subset form a planar graph*. In the case of K_9, we get the following edge decomposition corresponding to the three layers shown above:

$$\{12,13,16,18,19,23,29,34,38,39,45,46,47,48,56,57,67,68,78,89\},$$

$$\{14,15,17,24,28,35,36,37,79\}, \{25,26,27,49,58,59,69\}.$$

The minimum number of planar graphs which can be superimposed to form a given graph G is the **thickness** of G, discussed in Chapter 11. Although we cannot solve the printed circuits problem in general, we obtained a lower bound for the solution in Theorem 11.5 and this bound happens to give the correct answer surprisingly often.

Matching Problems

A **matching** in a graph G is a set of edges of G, no two of which have a vertex in common. For example, the following diagram shows a bipartite graph and one of its matchings:

In the above graph, we have 'matched' the vertices 1, 2, and 3 from the left-hand set of vertices with the vertices A, B, and D from the right-hand set of vertices. In fact, the idea of a matching applies equally well to graphs in general. For example, the graph of the octahedron has several matchings, four of which are

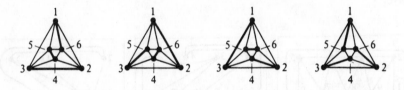

These four matchings have the property that every edge of the graph appears in just one of them, and this leads to an edge decomposition in which each subset consists of the edges in a matching—namely,

$$\{16,23,45\}, \{12,35,46\}, \{13,24,56\}, \{15,26,34\}.$$

It is clear that every graph can be decomposed into matchings, since if G has m edges then we can simply take m matchings, each consisting of a single edge. However, the problem of determining the *minimum* number of matchings needed to decompose a given graph may be much more difficult, and is unsolved in general. This question is of more than academic interest, and has arisen in a number of contexts, two of which we now consider.

A Wire-Coloring Problem

Suppose that we have an electrical unit, such as a relay panel, and that there are a number of relays, switches, and other devices $A, B, \ldots$, to be interconnected. The connecting wires are first formed into a cable, with the wires to be connected to A emerging at one point, those connected to B emerging at another, and so on. In order to distinguish them, it is necessary that all those wires which emerge from the same point be colored differently. What is the minimum number of colors necessary for the whole network? (This problem was posed by C. E. Shannon in 1949, in a paper on electrical networks.)

In order to see the connection between this problem and the matching problem described above, we represent the connection points by the vertices of a graph and the wires by edges. For example, the graph below represents a relay panel with six relays, $A, B, \ldots, F$.

Since the point C has five wires emerging from it, and since these wires must all be colored differently, we certainly need at least five colors to color the wires in the network. In fact, five colors are enough, as the following diagrams show—the numbers on the edges correspond to the five colors:

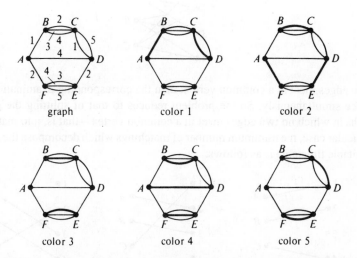

Since the edges of each color form a matching, the problem of finding the smallest number of colors needed to color the wires of the network is the same as the problem of determining the minimum number of matchings needed to decompose the graph. It follows that the wire-coloring problem is also an edge decomposition problem, and that the subsets consist of all the edges with the same color. The edge decomposition corresponding to the above wire-coloring is

$$\{AB,CD\}, \ \{AF, BC, DE\}, \ \{BC, EF\}, \ \{AD, BC, EF\}, \ \{CD, EF\}.$$

In these problems the graphs under consideration usually have multiple edges, and so the best we can say is that the number of matchings is limited by the bounds for the chromatic index given by the extended version of Vizing's theorem (Theorem 12.5) and by Shannon's theorem (Theorem 12.6)—namely,

$$d \leq \chi'(G) \leq d + h \ \text{ and } \ d \leq \chi'(G) \leq \tfrac{3}{2}d,$$

where d is the maximum vertex-degree in G, and h is the maximum number of edges joining a pair of vertices. Since it is possible to find graphs attaining any of these bounds, we cannot obtain better results than this in general.

A Scheduling Problem

At the end of an academic year, each student has to take an examination with each of his or her teachers. How many examination periods are required?

We can see what is involved if we consider a simple example with four students and three teachers. We represent the students and teachers by the vertices of a bipartite graph, and join a student-vertex to a teacher-vertex whenever the student needs to be examined by the teacher. An example of such a graph is

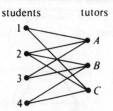

If two edges meet at a common vertex, then the corresponding examinations cannot take place simultaneously. So the problem reduces to that of splitting the graph into subgraphs in which no two edges meet in a common vertex—that is, into matchings. In this particular case, the minimum number of matchings which decompose the graph is 3, and a suitable timetable is as follows:

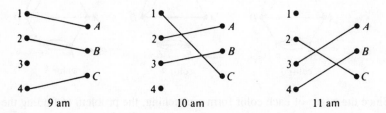

The corresponding edge decomposition is

$$\{1A, 2B, 4C\}, \{1C, 2A, 3B\}, \{2C, 3A, 4B\}.$$

Note that this can also be thought of as an edge-coloring problem. If we color the 9 *am* edges red, the 10 *am* edges yellow, and the 11 *am* edges blue, then the colors appearing at each vertex (student or teacher) are different.

In these scheduling problems the graphs under consideration are all bipartite graphs. The problem therefore reduces to that of finding the chromatic index of a bipartite graph, and this problem is answered completely by König's theorem (Theorem 12.8)—the smallest number of matchings needed is equal to the largest vertex-degree in the bipartite graph. Thus the matching problem is solved in this case.

Bus Route Problems

In a certain county there are a number of rival bus companies. Each company wishes to run a service that includes every town in the county, in such a way that passengers using that company can get from any town to any other town. However, the County Council will not allow different companies to operate along the same stretch of highway. How many different bus companies can be accommodated?

We can solve this problem by drawing a graph whose vertices correspond to the towns and whose edges correspond to the roads joining them. For example, the following graph represents a county containing 11 towns joined by 22 roads:

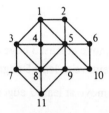

Each bus company needs a network which connects all the 11 towns, and so each company must be assigned at least 10 of the interconnecting roads. Since there are only 22 roads, the maximum number of companies that can be accommodated is 2. The following diagram shows an appropriate allocation of roads to the two companies:

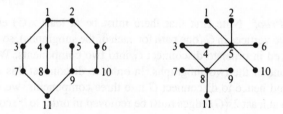

Such an allocation of roads to companies produces an edge decomposition of the original graph. Each of the subgraphs in this decomposition must include edges incident to all the vertices, and must be connected, so that a passenger can travel from any town to any other by the buses of each company. So the problem reduces to that of decomposing the graph into the maximum possible number of subgraphs, each of which is connected and includes every vertex of the graph.

To solve this problem, we denote the required number of subgraphs by $s(G)$. An expression for the number $s(G)$ was obtained by W. T. Tutte, who proved the following result in 1961.

THEOREM 14.2. *Let G be a connected graph with* n *vertices. Then* s(G) *is the largest integer for which the following statement is true:*

for each integer k = 1,2, ... , n − 1, *at least* k × s(G) *edges must be removed in order to disconnect* G *into* k + 1 *components.*

To illustrate this theorem, we consider the following graph G for which $s(G) = 2$:

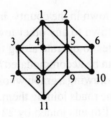

In order to disconnect G into

two components, we must remove at least 3 edges,   so $s(G) \leq 3$;

three components, we must remove at least 5 edges,   so $s(G) \leq \frac{5}{2}$;

four components, we must remove at least 7 edges,   so $s(G) \leq \frac{7}{3}$;

...

11 components, we must remove all 22 edges,   so $s(G) \leq \frac{22}{10}$.

The largest integer $s(G)$ which satisfies all these inequalities is 2, as required.

The formal proof of Theorem 14.2 is too complicated to be included here, but the following remarks indicate why the result is a reasonable one.

Outline of Proof   Note first that there must be at least $s(G)$ edge-disjoint paths between any two vertices in G (one path for each of the subgraphs), so at least $s(G)$ edges must be removed in order to disconnect G into two components. We now repeat this argument for one of the two subgraphs. In order to disconnect this subgraph into two components, and hence to disconnect G into three components, we must remove $s(G)$ more edges; so at least $2s(G)$ edges must be removed in order to disconnect G into three components. Carrying on in this way, we eventually obtain the result for every value of k. ☐

There are several variations of the above problem which lead to interesting mathematical results. We consider one of these. Suppose that each bus company operates from a depot in one of the towns and chooses each of its routes to be a path out to another vertex, returning the same way. This means that *each of the connected subgraphs must be a tree*—in other words, the graph can be decomposed into spanning trees. Note that such a decomposition is possible only if the number of edges in the graph is a multiple of the number of edges in a spanning tree; if the graph has n vertices and m edges, this means that m is a multiple of $n-1$. In the above example, where $n = 11$ and $m = 22$, this can be accomplished only if two roads are not used by either company. For example, if the roads 3–8 and 5–6 are removed from the graph, then the resulting graph can be decomposed into the following spanning trees:

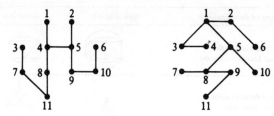

A necessary and sufficient condition for the existence of a solution of this problem is as follows:

THEOREM 14.3. *Let* G *be a connected graph with* n *vertices and* s(n – 1) *edges. Then* G *can be decomposed into* s *spanning trees if and only if, for each integer* k = 1,2, … , n–1, *at least* ks *edges must be removed in order to disconnect* G *into* k + 1 *components.*

Proof By Theorem 14.2, this theorem amounts to saying that G can be decomposed into s spanning trees if and only if $s(G) = s$. However, if G can be decomposed into s connected subgraphs, then they must all have $n - 1$ edges, and must therefore be spanning trees since there are no edges left over to form any cycles. ☐

14.4 SUMMARY

We conclude this chapter with a table showing the different types of decomposition problems described in this chapter.

problem	type of decomposition	typical graph	decomposition
Eulerian graph	edge decomposition into disjoint cycles		
coloring problems (map-coloring, sanitation problem).	vertex decomposition (no two vertices in the same subset are adjacent)		{1,3,8,11} {2,10} {4,6,9,12} {5,7,13}
domination problems (communication links, queens on a chessboard).	vertex decomposition (each subset contains a vertex adjacent to the other vertices in the subset)		{A,B,F} {D,C,E}

problem	type of decomposition	typical graph	decomposition
printed circuits problem	**edge decomposition** into planar subgraphs		
matching problems (wire-coloring, scheduling)	**edge decomposition** into matchings (no two edges have a vertex in common)		
bus-route problem	**edge decomposition** into connected subgraphs which include every vertex		
bus-route problem (variation)	edge decomposition into spanning trees		

PROBLEMS

14.1. Consider the octahedron graph:

Find (if they exist):

a. a vertex decomposition for which no two vertices in the same subset are adjacent;

b. a vertex decomposition for which each subset contains a vertex adjacent to the other vertices in the subset;

c. an edge decomposition into disjoint cycles;

d. an edge decomposition into planar subgraphs;

e. an edge decomposition into matchings;

f. an edge decomposition into connected subgraphs which include every vertex;

g. an edge decomposition into spanning trees.

To which of the problems discussed in this chapter does each of these decompositions correspond?

Vertex Decomposition Problems

○14.2. Consider the following map:

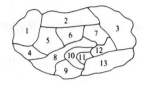

a. Find a 4-coloring of this map.

b. Draw the corresponding graph, and show how the 4-coloring in part a leads to a vertex decomposition of this graph in which no two vertices in the same subset are adjacent.

14.3. A youth club organizer wishes to organize some outings to the Zoo for nine children: Andrew, Bill, Catherine, Deirdre, Edward, Fiona, Gina, Harry, and Iris. Catherine refuses to go on an outing with any of the boys, Andrew will not go if there are any girls (except Deirdre), Edward and Harry must not be allowed to go together since they will cause havoc, Fiona cannot stand Bill or Gina, and Bill and Edward both dislike Iris. Express this information in terms of a suitable graph, and use this graph to find the minimum number of outings needed.

14.4. A chemical manufacturer wishes to store some chemicals in a warehouse. Some chemicals react violently when in contact with each other, and the manufacturer decides to divide the warehouse into a number of rooms so as to separate dangerous pairs of chemicals. In the following table, an asterisk (*) indicates those pairs of chemicals which must be kept separate:

	A	B	C	D	E	F	G
A	—	*	*	*			*
B	*	—	*	*	*		*
C	*	*	—	*		*	
D	*	*	*	—		*	
E		*			—		
F			*	*		—	*
G	*	*				*	—

By drawing an appropriate graph and regarding this as a vertex decomposition problem, find the smallest number of rooms needed to store these chemicals safely.

○14.5. Draw the tour graph for the following tourist bus routes in New York City, and use it to find the minimum number of days needed to ensure that no place is visited more than once in the same day. What is the corresponding vertex decomposition?

route 1 visits the Empire State Building, Rockefeller Center, Greenwich Village, and Pier 42;

route 2 visits Rockefeller Center, Lincoln Center, Central Park, and Columbia University;

route 3 visits Madison Square Garden, Rockefeller Center, and the United Nations;

route 4 visits the Metropolitan Museum of Art, Central Park, and Rockefeller Center;

route 5 visits the Metropolitan Museum of Art, Columbia University, and Lincoln Center;

route 6 visits Columbia University, the Bronx Zoo, and Yankee Stadium;

route 7 visits Shea Stadium, Yankee Stadium, and the Brooklyn Botanical Gardens;

route 8 visits the Bronx Zoo and the Brooklyn Botanical Gardens;

route 9 visits the Empire State Building, Madison Square Garden, Pier 42, and the United Nations;

route 10 visits Pier 42 and the Statue of Liberty;

route 11 visits the Statue of Liberty, Wall Street, and Greenwich village;

route 12 visits Wall Street, Greenwich Village, and City College.

14.6. Find a minimum dominating set in each of the following graphs, and use it to write down a vertex decomposition with the property that each subset contains a vertex adjacent to all the other vertices in the subset.

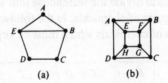

(a)   (b)

14.7. Draw the graph corresponding to a knight's move on a 3×3 chessboard, and find a minimum dominating set and the corresponding vertex decomposition. Hence find the smallest number of knights that can be placed on such a chessboard in such a way that every unoccupied square is attacked.

14.8.[†] a. Show that it is possible to place five queens on an 11×11 chessboard in such a way that every unoccupied square is attacked.

b. Is it possible to place eleven queens on an 11×11 chessboard in such a way that no queen attacks any other?

14.9. Let G be the Grötzsch graph depicted below.

Find (a) dom G; (b) ind G.

14.10. Let G be the 4-cube Q_4. Find (a) dom G; (b) ind G.

14.11. Verify the results dom $G \le$ ind G, and $\chi(G) \times$ ind $G \ge n$ of Theorem 14.1 when G is

a. the cube graph Q_3; b. the octahedron graph.

Edge Decomposition Problems

14.12. Show that K_6 and K_7 can be printed in two layers, and write down a corresponding edge decomposition in each case.

⊙14.13. Let G be a graph whose largest vertex-degree is k. What can you say about the number of matchings needed to decompose G?

⊙14.14. How many matchings are needed to decompose each of the following graphs?

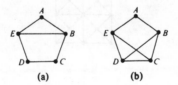

(a)   (b)

Write down a corresponding edge decomposition in each case.

14.15. How many colors are needed to color the wires of the following network so that any two wires emerging from the same point are colored differently?

⊙14.16. Five students have arranged separate tutorials on the same morning with three tutors A, B, and C. Tutor A wishes to teach students 1, 2, and 4; tutor B will be teaching students 1, 3, 4, and 5; and tutor C is to teach students 2, 3, and 5. By finding an edge decomposition of the corresponding bipartite graph into matchings, devise a suitable schedule for the tutorials.

14.17. Five students are to be examined by five tutors:

tutor 1 must examine students B and D;

tutor 2 must examine students A, B, and E;

tutor 3 must examine students B, C, and E;

tutor 4 must examine students A and C;

tutor 5 must examine students B, D, and E.

If each examination takes the same amount of time, find the minimum number of examination periods needed.

14.18. Five students are to be examined by four tutors:

tutor A must examine students 1, 2, and 5;

tutor B must examine students 1, 3, and 4;

tutor C must examine students 2, 3, and 5;

tutor D must examine students 2, 3, and 4.

If each examination takes the same amount of time, how many examination periods are needed, and how may the examinations be scheduled?

☉14.19. Consider the original bus route problem for a road network containing n towns and m interconnecting roads.

   a. Let k be the maximum number of bus companies that can be accommodated in such a network. Show that $k \leq m/(n-1)$.

   b. Find the value of k for the following road network:

☉14.20. Decompose the following graph into disjoint spanning trees:

14.21. Decompose the following graph into disjoint spanning trees:

14.22.[†] Verify the statement of Theorem 14.3 for the wheel with five spokes:

CHAPTER 15

CONCLUSION

15.1 PRIMARY AND SECONDARY APPLICATIONS

Throughout this book we have presented both the theory and the applications of graphs and digraphs. As an academic discipline, graph theory has become a rich and varied area of study, and we have endeavored to reflect this in the more theoretical parts of the book. But we have also tried to illustrate the very widespread use of graphs in different fields, ranging from chemistry and linguistics to operations research and the social sciences. This dichotomy between theory and applications is an important feature of graph theory, which we have tried to present in this book.

The reason for the widespread use of graphs and digraphs is undoubtedly due to their extreme simplicity. A graph or digraph is a very convenient and natural way of representing information involving the relationships between objects—all we need to do is to represent the objects by vertices and the relationships between them by undirected or directed lines. Examples of such representations are many and varied, as illustrated by the diagrams on the next page.

example	diagram	graph or digraph
chemical molecule		
phasing traffic lights		
bracing a framework		
signal-flow graphs		
Königsberg bridges		
tracing a maze		
coloring a map		

For many applications, such a pictorial representation may be all that is needed. By representing a situation in such a simple diagrammatic form, we may be able to derive all the information we require. The use of such a representation helps us to highlight the relevant features of the problem in hand and to play down the others. Such applications may be termed **secondary applications**—they are widespread and useful, but involve only the diagrammatic form of the graph or digraph.

Contrasted with these are the **primary applications.** These often go much deeper than the secondary applications, since they use the *properties* of the graph or digraph, or results concerning them, to solve the problem in hand. In these primary applications, we take the graph or digraph as our mathematical model, solve the appropriate graph-theoretic problem, and then interpret the solution in terms of the original problem. If the graph or digraph has been a good model, then the graph-theoretic solution will yield a good solution of the original problem. We can illustrate this modeling procedure as follows:

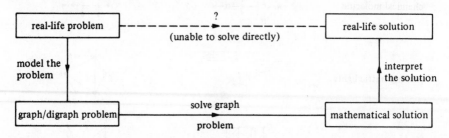

A good example of this modeling process was provided by the bracing of rectangular frameworks in Chapter 3. The problem was to determine whether or not a given braced framework is rigid and, if so, whether the bracing is a minimum bracing. In order to answer these questions, we modeled the braced framework by a bipartite graph whose vertices correspond to the rows and columns of the original framework, and whose edges correspond to the braced cells. By answering the graph-theoretic questions

> *Is this bipartite graph connected?*
> *Does it contain any cycles?*

we were able to answer our original questions, as follows:

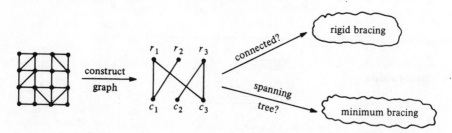

Graph theory abounds with such startling and elegant solutions to seemingly difficult problems.

Another example of a primary application was the solution of the Königsberg bridges problem in Chapter 6. In order to determine whether there exists a closed trail crossing each bridge exactly once, we constructed a graph whose vertices correspond to the parts of the city and whose edges represent the bridges. This graph is then the appropriate mathematical model, and we solved the original problem by determining whether it is an Eulerian graph. This was done very easily by checking whether all of the vertex-degrees in the graph are even, and the solution then followed immediately.

On the other hand, there are circumstances where a graph model may be too simplistic for the problem in hand. For example, if we wish to model the flow of traffic through the streets of a small town, then we may have to take so many factors into account (speed of traffic, bottlenecks, accidents, etc.) that any conclusions we may draw from our model may be inappropriate for the problems we are dealing with.

It is also important to realize that the usefulness of a mathematical model may change with time. For example, signal-flow graphs, such as those discussed in Chapter 5, were used extensively in the 1950s and 1960s to solve systems of simultaneous linear equations arising in practice. However, since the advent of high-speed electronic computers which can solve simultaneous equations extremely quickly, the use of signal-flow graphs has declined considerably. It remains to be seen how much impact the use of high-speed computation will have on the design and analysis of large-scale networks.

15.2 FOUR TYPES OF PROBLEMS

Most problems in graph theory can be described under one or more of the following interrelated headings:

existence problems does there exist...? is it possible to...?
construction problems if...exists, how can you construct it?
enumeration problems how many...are there, and can you list them all?
optimization problems if there are several..., which one is the best?

For example, in investigating the bracing of frameworks, we considered the following questions:

existence problem: is it possible to brace the framework so as to make it rigid?
construction problem: if such a bracing exists, how can you construct one?
enumeration problem: how many rigid bracings are there, and can you list them?
optimization problem: which rigid bracings involve fewest braces?

Let us look at each type of problem in turn.

Existence Problems

From a historical point of view, many of the existence problems which we now regard as part of graph theory arose as recreational puzzles. For example:

> *the Königsberg bridges problem* (Chapter 6): does there exist a closed trail crossing each of the seven bridges exactly once?
>
> *the knight's-tour problem* (Chapter 7): does there exist a sequence of knight's moves visiting each square of an 8 × 8 chessboard exactly once and returning to the starting point?
>
> *the four-color problem* (Chapter 13): does there exist a map which requires five colors to color it, so that neighboring countries are differently colored?

the utilities problem (Chapters 1 and 11): does there exist a way of connecting the three neighbors to the three utilities in such a way that no two connections cross?

the queens-on-a-chessboard problem (Chapter 14): does there exist an arrangement of five queens on an 8×8 chessboard so that every non-occupied square is attacked?

The methods used to answer such questions vary considerably from problem to problem. For example, if the answer is **yes**, as in the *knight's tour problem* and the *queens-on-a-chessboard problem,* then it is sufficient to produce a single example to substantiate the answer. This may not be easy to do in practice—for example, it may take a lot of trial-and-error to find a knight's tour—but once a single solution is found, the question has been completely answered.

If the answer is **no**, then a completely different approach is needed so as to ensure that a solution cannot possibly exist. In the case of the *Königsberg bridges problem,* it is enough to notice that when we enter part of the city we must be able to leave it again, so that every vertex of the corresponding graph must have even degree; but the corresponding graph has four vertices of odd degree (see page 123), so a solution cannot possibly exist. For the *utilities problem,* we need to show that the complete bipartite graph $K_{3,3}$ is non-planar, and this can be done either directly (see page 217) or by using Euler's polyhedral formula (see page 220). Finally, in the case of the *four-color problem,* it was a major task lasting many years to show that no map needing five colors can be constructed.

It is instructive to generalize such problems. For example, instead of solving the Königsberg problem for the given layout of islands and bridges, we can ask whether *any* given graph has an Eulerian trail. We answered this question completely in Theorem 6.1, in the form of a simple test which can be used to determine very quickly whether a given connected graph is Eulerian:

a connected graph is Eulerian if and only if every vertex has even degree.

In contrast, we may generalize the knight's-tour problem and ask whether any given graph has a Hamiltonian cycle. Unlike the Eulerian problem, no useful test is known for determining whether a given graph is Hamiltonian, although there are some sufficient conditions, such as those given in Dirac's theorem and Ore's theorem (Theorems 7.1 and 7.2), which work well in particular cases.

Lying between these extremes are the problems of determining the chromatic number of a given graph and deciding whether it is planar; these generalize the four-color problem and the utilities problem. In the case of the chromatic number, there is *no* simple method for determining the chromatic number of a given graph in general. We usually have to resort to other means, such as a trial-and-error approach or using the deletion-contraction theorem (Theorem 12.3) to find the chromatic polynomial and deducing the chromatic number from this. In the case of planarity, we have a test which (in principle, at least) gives us a complete answer to the question of whether a given graph is planar—namely, Kuratowski's theorem (Theorem 11.3):

a graph is planar if and only if it contains no subdivision of K_5 *or* $K_{3,3}$.

Unfortunately, it is usually very difficult to recognize subdivisions of K_5 and $K_{3,3}$ in a given graph, and so this test is almost useless in practice. We therefore have to resort to other means, such as using Euler's formula to show that a particular graph is non-planar. Alternatively, there are a number of 'planarity algorithms' which can be used and are generally quick and easy to apply.

We note, finally, that for every property that a graph G may have (planar, Eulerian, 2-connected, 3-colorable, etc.), there is a corresponding existence problem; for example:

planar: does there exist a plane drawing of G?

Eulerian: does there exist an Eulerian trail in G?

2-connected: does there exist a vertex whose removal disconnects G?

3-colorable: does there exist a 3-coloring of the vertices of G?

Construction Problems

The construction problems occurring in this book are of three types:

type 1:   problems for which solutions are known to exist, and we wish to find one;

type 2:   problems for which solutions may or may not exist, and we find out by trying to construct them;

type 3:   problems for which solutions are known to exist, and we wish to find the 'best' one.

For each type of problem, we may be able to construct the required solutions by trial-and-error methods; and if the graphs involved are small, this may be the best way. For example, if we are given a graph with just six vertices, it is probably as easy to determine by inspection whether it is Eulerian, or planar, or 3-chromatic, than to apply any systematic procedure. On the other hand, many graphs which arise in practical situations may have hundreds or thousands of vertices; and for such large graphs, we need to use an *algorithm*. We have met several graphical algorithms in this course, some of which are extremely efficient. Those relating to problems of *type 3* we consider below, under the heading of *Optimization problems;* those relating to problems of *type 1* and *type 2* we consider here. But first we need to introduce some terminology which will be useful when we discuss the efficiency of a given algorithm.

When we say that a graph algorithm involves $O(m)$ operations, it means that the number of operations a computer uses in applying the algorithm to a given graph is at most Cm, where C is a fixed constant (which changes from algorithm to algorithm) and m is the number of edges in the graph. Similarly, if a graph algorithm involves $O(n^2)$ operations, then the number of operations a computer uses in applying it is at most Cn^2, where n is the number of vertices in the graph. An algorithm which can always be completed in $O(n^k)$ or $O(m^k)$ operations, for some fixed number k, is called a **polynomial algorithm**; such algorithms are usually regarded as being **efficient algorithms**, even if k is large—for example, an algorithm involving $O(n^{100})$ is, in this sense, an efficient algorithm. If no polynomial algorithm exists for a given problem, then the problem is called **NP-hard**; all algorithms used to solve such a problem will be **inefficient algorithms**. Finally, there is a large class of important problems for which no polynomial algorithm has ever been discovered, but nor has it ever been proved that such a polynomial algorithm does not exist. Such problems are known as **NP-complete problems** and have the property that if a polynomial algorithm can be found for any *one* of these problems, then polynomial algorithms will be known to exist for *all* of them.

We now return to our three types of problem, starting with those of *type 1*.

Type 1 Problems

We discuss three *type 1* problems—finding an Eulerian trail in a given graph, getting out of a maze, and constructing a spanning tree in a graph.

Fleury's algorithm   We saw above that there is a simple test for determining whether a given graph is Eulerian—namely, look at the vertex-degrees and see whether they are all even. If they are, then the graph is Eulerian, and the problem becomes that of finding an Eulerian trail in the graph. In Chapter 6 we described an algorithm (Fleury's algorithm) for finding such a trail. This algorithm can easily be applied by hand or by machine and is an efficient algorithm involving $O(m)$ operations, where m is the number of edges in the graph.

Tarry's algorithm   Also discussed in Chapter 6 was the problem of getting out of a maze. This is also an Eulerian-type problem, and we know that a solution must exist (since otherwise we could not have become stuck in the maze to begin with!). As with the Eulerian problem, an algorithm (Tarry's algorithm) exists for solving it; like Fleury's algorithm, it is an efficient algorithm involving $O(m)$ operations, where m is the number of edges in the corresponding graph.

The spanning tree algorithm   In Chapter 10, we described two algorithms for constructing a spanning tree in a given connected graph. In one of these algorithms, we start with no edges and add edges one at a time in such a way that no cycles are created; in the other algorithm, we start with the graph and remove edges one at a time in such a way that the resulting graphs are never disconnected. These algorithms are easy to apply by hand, or to adapt for computer use, and are efficient algorithms involving $O(n^2)$ steps, where n is the number of vertices in the graph.

Type 2 Problems

We discuss two *type 2* problems—determining whether a given graph is planar and finding its chromatic number.

A planarity algorithm   As mentioned above, the best way of determining whether a given graph is planar is often simply to try to construct a plane drawing of it. Another method is essentially to choose a cycle in the graph and to construct a bipartite graph whose two sets of vertices correspond to those edges of the graph which can occur together *inside* the chosen cycle and those parts which must then lie *outside* the cycle. If we can construct such a bipartite graph, then the original graph is planar; if we cannot, then it is non-planar.

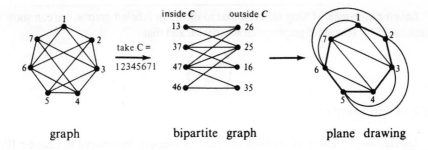

| | inside C | outside C | |
| graph | bipartite graph | | plane drawing |

This algorithm is very efficient—if the graph in question has n vertices, then the corresponding algorithm is a polynomial algorithm involving $O(n^3)$ operations. However, even more efficient planarity algorithms exist; in 1974, J.E. Hopcroft and R.E. Tarjan constructed one which involves only $O(n)$ operations.

Chromatic polynomials   In Chapter 12 we discussed the problem of finding the chromatic number of a given graph G. One way of doing this is to start by finding the chromatic polynomial $P_G(k)$, and then determining the smallest value of k for which $P_G(k)$ is non-zero. In order to obtain the chromatic polynomial of G, we apply the deletion-contraction algorithm, successively replacing G by a number of smaller and smaller graphs whose chromatic polynomials we can eventually find by inspection. This algorithm is not, however, an efficient algorithm—indeed, *most* problems involving chromatic numbers or chromatic polynomials come under the heading of NP-complete problems.

Further graph algorithms are discussed later in the chapter, where we consider *type 3* problems.

Enumeration Problems

The subject of graphical enumeration is a major one, although it has not featured prominently in this book. However, we have looked at a few important problems, which we now summarize.

Labeled graphs   The simplest graphical enumeration problem is that of determining the number of labeled graphs with n vertices. Since each of the $\frac{1}{2}n(n-1)$ possible edges is either present or absent, there are $2^{n(n-1)/2}$ such graphs altogether. The number of labeled graphs with n vertices and m edges is then

$$\binom{\frac{1}{2}n(n-1)}{m},$$

since each choice of m of the $\frac{1}{2}n(n-1)$ possible edges determines a different labeled graph with exactly m edges.

Labeled digraphs Using ideas similar to those for labeled graphs, we can show that there are $2^{n(n-1)}$ labeled digraphs with n vertices, and that

$$\binom{n(n-1)}{m}$$

of these have exactly m arcs.

Labeled trees Using the method of Prüfer sequences, introduced in Chapter 10, we proved *Cayley's theorem,* that the number of labeled trees with n vertices is n^{n-2}. The proof involved constructing a one-to-one correspondence between labeled trees and sequences of $n-2$ integers, each of which is one of the numbers $1, 2, \ldots, n$. In contrast, the corresponding problems for *unlabeled* graphs are far more difficult and are usually solved using Pólya's theorem, which lies outside the scope of this book. The numbers of simple graphs of various types are:

number of vertices	1	2	3	4	5	6	7	8
labeled graphs	1	2	8	64	1024	32768	2097152	268435456
unlabeled graphs	1	2	4	11	34	156	1044	12346
unlabeled connected graphs	1	1	2	6	21	112	853	11117
unlabeled regular graphs	1	2	2	4	3	8	6	20
unlabeled Eulerian graphs	1	0	1	1	4	8	37	184
unlabeled hamiltonian graphs	1	0	1	3	8	48	383	6020
labeled trees	1	1	3	16	125	1296	16807	262144
unlabeled trees	1	1	1	2	3	6	11	23
labeled digraphs	1	4	64	4096	2^{20}	2^{30}	2^{42}	2^{56}
unlabeled digraphs	1	3	16	218	9608	1540944	$\sim 9 \times 10^9$	$\sim 2 \times 10^{12}$

Optimization Problems

We now turn our attention to those problems for which solutions clearly exist, and we want to find the best one—such problems were called *type 3* problems above. We discuss algorithms for four of these problems—the *shortest path problem,* the *scheduling problem,* the *minimum connector problem,* and the *traveling salesman problem;* many further *type 3* problems will be found in the companion book on *Networks.*

The shortest path algorithm In Chapter 8, we discussed the problem of finding the shortest path between two vertices in a weighted digraph. The algorithm we used involved a breadth-first search of the graph or digraph, and proceeded step by step from the initial vertex to the final vertex. The shortest distance from the initial vertex to each of the intermediate vertices also emerged from these calculations. This algorithm can easily be applied by hand or by machine and is an efficient algorithm involving $O(n^2)$ operations, where n is the number of vertices of the graph or digraph.

The scheduling algorithm In Chapter 8 we also showed how to obtain the *longest* path between two vertices in a weighted digraph. If the digraph is an activity network, then this longest path is a *critical path,* involving the activities which must be completed on time if the entire job is not to be delayed. As with the shortest path algorithm, the finding of a critical path involves $O(n^2)$ operations, where n is the number of vertices in the digraph.

The minimum connector problem The problem of finding a minimum connector (that is, a minimum-weight spanning tree) in a given connected graph is one which we discussed in Chapter 10. We gave an easy-to-apply algorithm for solving this problem—the so-called *greedy algorithm*—and presented a variation of it (Prim's algorithm) which is more suitable for computer implementation. In each case, the algorithm is an efficient one, involving $O(n^2)$ operations, where n is the number of vertices in the graph.

The traveling salesman problem In contrast to the minimum connector problem, there is no efficient algorithm known for solving the traveling salesman problem. As we saw in Chapter 10, lower and upper bounds for the solution of the traveling salesman problem can easily be derived from the solution of the minimum connector problem. However, no algorithm for determining the *exact* solution of the traveling salesman problem is known—the problem is in fact an NP-complete problem.

15.3 THE FUTURE

Current research in graph theory is extremely active. In the 1970s and 1980s, several advances were made, including the development of an $O(n)$ algorithm for planarity, the introduction of the term NP-*complete,* the determination of the thickness of the complete graph K_n, the discovery of Kuratowski-type theorems for graphs of any given genus, and, of course, the proof of the four-color theorem. What important results will emerge from the 1990s remains to be seen.

Of some interest are various generalizations of the notion of a graph. One such generalization starts with the idea of a graph as a *one-dimensional complex,* consisting of points and lines in space. By adding triangles and tetrahedra, we can construct two-dimensional and three-dimensional complexes, and we can extend these ideas to yet higher dimensions. Such **simplicial complexes,** as they are called, are of importance in an area of mathematics known as *combinatorial topology,* and occur in the modeling of certain physical theories—in particular, those concerning electromagnetic phenomena and elastic bodies.

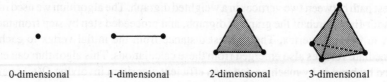

0-dimensional   1-dimensional   2-dimensional   3-dimensional

Another generalization of the concept of a graph is that of a **hypergraph**. Instead of taking *pairs* of vertices as the edges of a graph, we take arbitrary subsets. For example, we can take the vertices of a hypergraph to be a, b, c, and d, and the edges to be the subsets abc, bd, cd, and c. The resulting hypergaph would then look something like this

Hypergraphs have already proved to be of great interest, both theoretically and in their practical applications to a number of different areas. It will be interesting to see what role they play in the coming years.

15.4 SUGGESTIONS FOR FURTHER READING

There are many books on graphs and digraphs and their applications. Two books at an elementary level are

G. Chartrand, *Introductory Graph Theory,* Dover, New York, 1985.

O. Ore, *Graphs and their Uses,* 2nd ed., New Mathematical Library **10**, Mathematical Association of America, Washington, D.C., to be published in 1990.

Standard texts in graph theory include

C. Berge, *Graphs,* North–Holland, Amsterdam–New York, 1985.

B. Bollobás, *Graph Theory: An Introductory Course,* Graduate Texts in Mathematics **63**, Springer-Verlag, New York, 1979.

J. A. Bondy and U. S. R. Murty, *Graph Theory with Applications,* American Elsevier, New York, 1979.

G. Chartrand and L. Lesniak, *Graphs & Digraphs,* 2nd ed., Wadsworth & Brooks/Cole, Monterey, California, 1986.

F. Harary, *Graph Theory,* Addison–Wesley, Reading, Massachusetts, 1969.

W. T. Tutte, *Graph Theory,* Encyclopedia of Mathematics **21**, Addison–Wesley, Reading, Massachusetts, 1984.

R. J. Wilson, *Introduction to Graph Theory,* 3rd ed., Longman, Harlow, Essex, 1985.

A historical approach to graph theory can be found in

N. L. Biggs, E. K. Lloyd, and R. J. Wilson, *Graph Theory 1736–1936,* paperback ed., Clarendon Press, Oxford, 1986.

Applications of graph theory, and the use of algorithms, are discussed in

A. K. Dolan and J. Aldous, *Networks—An Introductory Approach,* John Wiley & Sons, New York, 1990.

T. B. Boffey, *Graph Theory in Operations Research,* Macmillan, London, 1982.

S. Even, *Graph Algorithms,* Computer Science Press, Potomac, Maryland, 1979.

M. R. Garey and D. S. Johnson, *Computers and Intractability. A Guide to the Theory of NP-Completeness,* W. H. Freeman, San Francisco, 1979.

A. Gibbons, *Algorithmic Graph Theory,* Cambridge University Press, Cambridge, 1985.

M. C. Golumbic, *Algorithmic Graph Theory and Perfect Graphs,* Academic Press, New York, 1980.

E. L. Lawler, J. K. Lenstra, A. H. G. Rinnooy Kan, and D. B. Shmoys, eds., *The Traveling Salesman Problem,* John Wiley & Sons, New York, 1985.

K. Lockyer, *Critical Path Analysis and Other Project Network Techniques,* Pitman, London, 1984.

F. Roberts, *Discrete Mathematical Models, with Applications to Social, Biological and Environmental Problems,* Prentice–Hall, Englewood Cliffs, New Jersey, 1976.

M. N. Swamy and K. Thulasiraman, *Graphs, Networks and Algorithms,* John Wiley & Sons, New York, 1981.

H. N. V. Temperley, *Graph Theory and Applications,* Halsted Press, John Wiley & Sons, New York, 1981.

H. Walther, *Ten Applications of Graph Theory,* D. Reidel, Dordrecht, 1984.

R. J. Wilson and L. W. Beineke, eds., *Applications of Graph Theory,* Academic Press, London, 1979.

Specialist texts on some of the topics in this book include

D. Barnette, *Map Coloring, Polyhedra and the Four-color Problem,* Dolciani Mathematical Expositions **8,** Mathematical Association of America, Washington, D.C., 1983.

L. W. Beineke and R. J. Wilson, eds., *Selected Topics in Graph Theory,* Academic Press, London, Vol. 1, 1978, Vol. 2, 1983, Vol. 3, 1988.

M. Capobianco and J. C. Molluzzo, *Examples and Counterexamples in Graph Theory,* American Elsevier, New York, 1978.

J. L. Gross and T. W. Tucker, *Topological Graph Theory,* John Wiley & Sons, New York, 1987.

E. M. Palmer, *Graphical Evolution,* John Wiley & Sons, New York, 1985.

G. Ringel, *Map Color Theorem,* Springer–Verlag, New York, 1974.

T. L. Saaty and P. C. Kainen, *The Four-color Problem,* 2nd ed., Dover, New York, 1986.

A. T. White, *Graphs, Groups and Surfaces,* 2nd ed., Mathematical Studies **8**, North-Holland, Amsterdam, 1984.

SOLUTIONS TO SELECTED PROBLEMS

CHAPTER 1

1.1. (a) *vertex-set:* {London, Oslo, New York, Sydney}
edge-list: (London–Oslo, London–New York, London–Sydney, Oslo–New York, Oslo–Sydney, New York–Sydney)
(b) *vertex-set:* {*u,v,w,x,y,z*}
edge list: (*uv,uw,vw,vw,yx*)
(c) *vertex-set:* {1,2,3,4,5,6}
edge-list: (12,22,23,24,24,24,45,46).

1.3. There are many possible drawings of these graphs—for example:

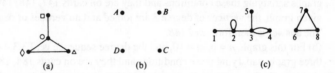

1.4. (a) (1) and (5); (b) (3); (c) (2) and (4); (d) (1), (2), and (3).

1.6. Graphs (a), (b), and (d) are subgraphs of *G*. [Note that graph (d) is *G* itself.] Graphs (c) and (e) are not subgraphs of *G* since they contain the edge *vz* which is not contained in *G*.

1.8. *graph (1):* deg 1 = 1, deg 2 = 1, deg 3 = 4, deg 4 = 4, deg 5 = 1, deg 6 = 1; the degree-sequence is (1,1,1,1,4,4);
graph (2): deg *a* = 4, deg *b* = 4, deg *c* = 4, deg *d* = 4, deg *e* = 4; the degree sequence is (4,4,4,4,4);
graph (3): deg *u* = 3, deg *v* = 1, deg *z* = 3, deg *w* = 1; the degree-sequence is (1,1,3,3);
graph (4): deg *A* = 0, deg *B* = 0, deg *C* = 0, deg *D* = 0; the degree-sequence is (0,0,0,0);
graph (5): deg 1 = 1, deg 2 = 2, deg 3 = 4, deg 4 = 2, deg 5 = 1, deg 6 = 2, deg 7 = 2, deg 8 = 2; the degree-sequence is (1,1,2,2,2,2,2,4).

1.11. (a) (*i*) (1,1,1,1,1,1,2,4,4); (*ii*) (4,4,4,4,4); (*iii*) (0,1,3,4,4,5,5).
(b) In *graph (i)*, the sum of the degrees is 16 and the number of edges is 8; in *graph (ii)*, the sum of the degrees is 20 and the number of edges is 10; in *graph (iii)*, the sum of the degrees is 22 and the number of edges is 11. In each case the sum of the degrees is exactly twice the number of edges.

1.12. (a) *n* = 5, *r* = 2, so the number of edges is $\frac{1}{2}(5)(2) = 5$;
(b) *n* = 10, *r* = 3, so the number of edges is $\frac{1}{2}(10)(3) = 15$;
(c) *n* = 12, *r* = 5, so the number of edges is $\frac{1}{2}(12)(5) = 30$.

1.14. *Consequence 1:* Since the sum of all the vertex-degrees is twice the number of edges, it must be an even number.
Consequence 2: If the number of vertices of odd degree were odd, then the sum of all

the vertex-degrees would be an odd number, contradicting Consequence 1. So the number of vertices of odd degree must be even.

Consequence 3: Since G has n vertices each of degree r, the sum of all the vertex-degrees is nr. By the handshaking lemma, the number of edges is half this sum—that is, $\frac{1}{2}nr$.

1.16. (a) the last one; (b) the middle one; (c) the last one.

1.17. There are several possible relabelings—for example,
(a) $1 \leftrightarrow A$, $2 \leftrightarrow B$, $3 \leftrightarrow C$, $4 \leftrightarrow D$, $5 \leftrightarrow E$, $6 \leftrightarrow F$;
(b) $a \leftrightarrow 1$, $b \leftrightarrow 4$, $c \leftrightarrow 7$, $d \leftrightarrow 3$, $e \leftrightarrow 6$, $f \leftrightarrow 2$, $g \leftrightarrow 5$.

1.18. Graphs (a) and (c) are the same; graph (d) is isomorphic to (a) and (c), as can be seen by interchanging the labels 3 and 6; graph (b) is not isomorphic to any of the other three, since it contains no 'triangles'.

1.21. No. To see this, look at the four vertices of degree 2. In the first graph they are joined in pairs, whereas in the second graph none of them is joined to any other.

1.25. (a) For this graph, $n = 6$, $m = 8$, and the degree sequence is (2,2,2,3,3,4). There are four graphs satisfying these conditions and they are on cards 147, 148, 149, and 150. In the given graph, the vertices of degree 3 are joined and no vertices of degree 2 are joined. The answer is therefore *card 148*.
(b) For this graph, $n = 6$, $m = 10$, and the degree sequence is (2,3,3,4,4,4). There are three graphs satisfying these conditions and they are on cards 184, 185, and 186. In the given graph, the vertex of degree 2 is joined to one vertex of degree 3 and one vertex of degree 4. The answer is therefore *card 186*.

CHAPTER 2

2.1. (a), (d), (g), and (h) are TRUE; (b), (c), (e), and (f) are FALSE.

2.4 (a)
$$\begin{pmatrix} 0 & 1 & 0 & 0 & 1 \\ 1 & 0 & 1 & 3 & 0 \\ 0 & 1 & 0 & 1 & 0 \\ 0 & 3 & 1 & 0 & 1 \\ 1 & 0 & 0 & 1 & 0 \end{pmatrix}$$

2.5 (a)

2.6. The sum of the numbers is the degree of the vertex corresponding to the particular row or column.

2.7.
$$\begin{pmatrix} 0 & 2 & 1 & 0 \\ 2 & 0 & 1 & 0 \\ 1 & 1 & 0 & 1 \\ 0 & 0 & 1 & 0 \end{pmatrix} \quad \begin{pmatrix} 0 & 2 & 0 & 1 \\ 2 & 0 & 0 & 1 \\ 0 & 0 & 0 & 1 \\ 1 & 1 & 1 & 0 \end{pmatrix} \quad \begin{pmatrix} 0 & 2 & 0 & 1 \\ 2 & 0 & 0 & 1 \\ 0 & 0 & 0 & 1 \\ 1 & 1 & 1 & 0 \end{pmatrix}$$
$$\qquad\qquad (a) \qquad\qquad\qquad\quad (b) \qquad\qquad\qquad\quad (c)$$

Since graph *(b)* is obtained from graph *(a)* by interchanging the labels 3 and 4, it follows that matrix *(b)* is obtained from matrix *(a)* by interchanging the third and fourth rows, and the third and fourth columns. Similarly, matrix *(c)* is obtained from matrix *(b)*

by interchanging the first and second rows, and the first and second columns. The fact
that matrix *(b)* and matrix *(c)* are identical follows from the symmetry of this graph—interchanging the labels 1 and 2 leaves it unaltered.

2.8   (a)
$$\begin{pmatrix} 1 & 0 & 0 & 0 & 1 & 0 & 0 & 0 \\ 1 & 1 & 0 & 0 & 0 & 1 & 1 & 1 \\ 0 & 1 & 1 & 0 & 0 & 0 & 0 & 0 \\ 0 & 0 & 1 & 1 & 0 & 1 & 1 & 1 \\ 0 & 0 & 0 & 1 & 1 & 0 & 0 & 0 \end{pmatrix}$$

2.9.

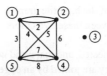

2.13.   (a) trail, 5, *x, y*; (b) walk, 4, *v, v*; (c) path, 1, *v, w*; (d) trail, 6, *u, u.*
[Note that alternative answers are possible in parts (a), (c), and (d); for example, we
could have given the answer *walk* in each case, since every trail is a walk. In each case
we have chosen the most restrictive term.]

2.15.   *length 3: svwz*
length 4: stvwz and *svwyz*
length 5: stuvwz, stvwyz, and *svwxyz*
length 6: stuvwyz and *stvwxyz*
length 7: stuvwxyz.

2.17

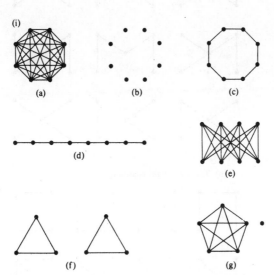

2.18

	K_9	N_9	C_9	$K_{9,9}$	Q_5	tetra-hedron	cube	octa-hedron	dodeca-hedron	icosa-hedron	Petersen
number of vertices	9	9	9	18	32	4	8	6	20	12	10
number of edges	36	0	9	81	80	6	12	12	30	30	15
degree of each vertex	8	0	2	9	5	3	3	4	3	5	3

2.23. If we color the vertices of the bipartite graph black and white, then the vertices in each cycle must alternate between these two colors. This implies that the number of edges in each cycle must be even.

2.30. Assume that G is disconnected, and that v and w are vertices of G. If v and w lie in different components of G, they are joined by an edge in $\overline{G}$. If v and w lie in the same component of G, and z is any vertex in another component of G, then vzw is a path in $\overline{G}$. It follows that any two vertices can be connected by a path in $\overline{G}$, and hence that $\overline{G}$ is connected.

2.32. They are depicted on graph cards 1, 3, 6, 13, 14, 29, 30, 32, 77, 78, 79, 81, 82, and 85.

2.34. Every tree can be built up from a single vertex by successively adding an edge and a new vertex, as many times as necessary. At each stage we increase the number of vertices by 1 and the number of edges by 1. Since we start with 1 vertex and 0 edges, we must end up with n vertices and $n-1$ edges.

2.37.

(a) There are nine spanning trees:

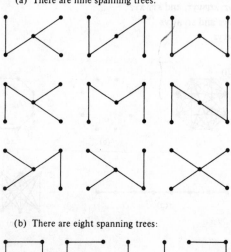

(b) There are eight spanning trees:

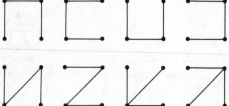

CHAPTER 3

3.1.

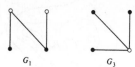

3.3.   There are six trees with six vertices—namely,

The first five of these are the carbon-graphs of alkanes with the chemical formula C_6H_{14}. (They are, respectively, n-hexane, 2-methyl pentane, 3-methyl pentane, 2,3-dimethyl butane, and 2,2-dimethyl butane.) The last one must be excluded since it contains a vertex of degree 5.

3.4.   (a) The number of vertices is

$$n + (2n + 2) = 3n + 2;$$

the number of edges is half the sum of the vertex-degrees (by the handshaking lemma), and is therefore $\frac{1}{2}\{4n + 1(2n + 2)\} = 3n + 1$.

(b) By part (a), the number of vertices of an alkane exceeds the number of edges by 1, and so the graph must be a tree.

3.7. G_1 and G_3 are balanced. The corresponding bipartite graphs are

$$G_1 \qquad\qquad G_3$$

Note that in G_2 and G_4 the cycle $ABCA$ has just one negative edge. These graphs are therefore not balanced.

3.10.   (a) Since the signed graph is balanced, we can color its vertices black and white so that every negative edge has a black end and a white end. If we now proceed around any cycle, there is a change of color whenever we use a negative edge. Since the final color must be the same as the first one, there must be an even number of color-changes, and hence an even number of negative edges.

(b) There are three cycles—$ABCA$, $ACDA$, and $ABCDA$. The number of negative edges in each is as follows:

$$G_1\!: ABCA\!:2, \ ACDA\!:2, \ ABCDA\!:2;$$
$$G_3\!: ABCA\!:2, \ ACDA\!:2, \ ABCDA\!:2.$$

3.11.

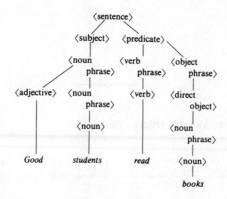

3.15. The branching tree is

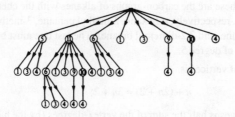

There are therefore *five* decreasing sequences of maximum length: 11,6,1; 11,6,3; 11,6,4; 11,9,4; 11,10,4.

3.17. Subsets of a set:

nested parentheses:

$$((( )( )( ))(( )(( ))))$$

3.20. (a) The corresponding bipartite graph is

which is not connected. The bracing is therefore a non-rigid bracing, and can be distorted as shown:

(b) The bracing is a rigid bracing since its bipartite graph is connected:

It is not a minimum bracing, since the bipartite graph contains a cycle.

3.24. Since a minimum bracing corresponds to a tree with $r+s$ vertices and $r+s-1$ edges, the number of braced cells is $r+s-1$.

3.26. (a)

(b) There are several possibilities—for example,

$$\{abf, abc, ace, cde, cg\} \text{ and } \{abf, abc, cde, cg\}.$$

(c) Again, there are several possibilities. The solutions arising from the complete graphs in part (b) are

0–12 seconds: a, b, and f
12–24 seconds: a, b, and c
24–36 seconds: a, c, and e
36–48 seconds: c, d, and e
48–60 seconds: c and g

Total waiting time: 252 seconds

0–15 seconds: a, b, and f
15–30 seconds: a, b, and c
30–45 seconds: c, d, and e
45–60 seconds: c and g

Total waiting time: 255 seconds

3.27. (a)

(b) There are several possibilities—for example,

$$\{AC, DE, BD, DF\} \text{ and } \{AD, BD, CE, CF\}.$$

(c) Again, there are several possibilities. The solutions arising from the complete graphs in part (b) are:

99–99.5	MHz:	A and C	and	99–99.5	MHz:	A and D
99.5–100	MHz:	C and E		99.5–100	MHz:	B and D
100–100.5	MHz:	B and D		100–100.5	MHz:	C and E
100.5–101	MHz:	D and F		100.5–101	MHz:	C and F

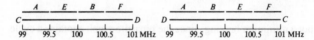

3.28.

Note that this interval graph is not the same as the compatibility graph in Problem 3.27, although they both arise from the same set of intervals [the first set of intervals in the solution of Problem 3.27(c)]. The reason for this difference is that *in a compatibility graph non-overlapping intervals* (such as A and D, or C and F) *can sometimes give rise to adjacent vertices, whereas in an interval graph non-overlapping intervals must always give rise to non-adjacent vertices.*

3.31. Checking properties (a), (b), and (c) for the subgraphs H_1 and H_2 should cause you no difficulty.
Property (a) tells us that each cube has a front and a back, and a left side and a right side, and the subgraphs H_1 and H_2 tell us which pairs of colors appear on these faces. Property (b) tells us that each color appears exactly twice on the sides of the stack, and exactly twice on the front and back (that is, once on the front and once on the back). Property (c) tells us that the faces appearing on the front and back of a cube cannot be the same as those appearing on the sides.

3.32. If one of the subgraphs, H_1 say, contains the loop at R, then it cannot contain any other edge incident with R, by property (b). It follows from property (a) that H_1 must contain the 2-edge joining G and Y, the 3-edge joining B and Y, and one of the 4-edges incident with Y. But this means that Y has degree 3, contradicting property (b). It follows that neither subgraph can contain the loop at R, and a similar argument shows that neither subgraph can contain the loop at G. If one of the subgraphs contains the 2-edge joining R and Y, then R cannot be incident with both edges joining R and G, by property (b), and so the two edges incident with G must be the 4-edge joining G and Y and the 1-edge joining G and R. But this means that neither R nor Y can be incident with a 3-edge, contradicting property (a). It follows that neither subgraph can contain the 2-edge join-ing R and Y, and so both H_1 and H_2 must be subgraphs of the following graph:

The result now follows easily by considering the possible cases that can arise.

3.35. The lengths of the corresponding paths are (a) 3; (b) 4; (c) 3; (d) 2. Thus, key change (d) is the least 'remote.'

CHAPTER 4

4.1. (a) *vertex-set:* $\{1, 2, 3, 4, 5\}$
arc-list: (21, 25, 42, 43, 51, 52, 54)

(b) *vertex set:* $\{a, b, c, d, e, f, g\}$
arc-list: (ab, bb, bb, cd, cf, dd, ed, ef, ef, fc, fc).

4.2. (a) is a subdigraph—for example, the subdigraph whose arcs are 42, 43, 52, and 54;

(b) is a subdigraph—for example, the subdigraph whose arcs are 21, 51, 52, and 54;

(c) is not a subdigraph.

4.4. Digraphs (b) and (d) are the same;

digraph (c) is isomorphic to (b) and (d), as can be seen by interchanging the labels 1 and 4;

digraph (a) is not isomorphic to any of the other three, since it contains a vertex (2) with out-degree 3.

4.10. (a) and (d) are TRUE; (b), (c), (e) and (f) are FALSE.

4.11. (a) *out-degree sequence:* (0,1,1,1,1,1,1,1,1,1),
in-degree sequence: (0,0,0,0,0,0,1,3,4);

(b) *out-degree sequence:* (1,2,2,2,3),
in-degree sequence: (1,2,2,2,3);

(c) *out-degree sequence:* (1,1,2,2,2,3),
in-degree sequence: (0,0,2,3,3,3).

4.12.

	digraph (a)	digraph (b)	digraph (c)
number of arcs	8	10	11
sum of out-degrees	8	10	11
sum of in-degrees	8	10	11

In each case, the sum of the out-degrees and the sum of the in-degrees are both equal to the number of arcs.

4.16.

4.17.   (a) The sum of the numbers in any row is the out-degree of the vertex corresponding to that row.

(b) The sum of the numbers in any column is the in-degree of the vertex corresponding to that column.

4.19.

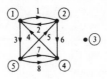

4.22.   (a) *length 5: stvwyz*
            length 6: stuvwyz and stvwxyz
            length 7: stuvwxyz;

(b) *length 3: zuvs and zwxs*
            length 5: zuvwxs;

(c) *stvwyzuvs and stvwyzwxs.*

Any cycle containing both *s* and *z* must consist of a path from *s* to *z* followed by a path from *z* to *s*. However, all paths from *s* to *z* contain both *v* and *w* [by part (a)], and all paths from *z* to *s* contain *v* or *w* [by part (b)], so either *v* or *w* must occur twice. Since this is not allowed, there can be no cycle containing both *s* and *z*.

4.23.   (a) connected, but not strongly connected (since there are no paths from the center vertex to any other);

(b) strongly connected;

(c) disconnected;

(d) connected, but not strongly connected (since there are no paths from the top right-hand vertex to any other).

CHAPTER 5

5.1.   (a) and (b) negative feedback cycles; (c) positive feedback cycle.

5.3.   *Positive feedback cycle: cefhgc; negative feedback cycles; ghg, ahga, abdfhga, ceifhgc.*

5.7.   (a)

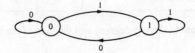

(b)

	number of states	out-degree of each vertex	in-degree of each vertex
one-moment delay machine	2	2	2
two-moment delay machine	4	2	2
three-moment delay machine	8	2	2

For an n-moment machine, there are 2^n states, each with out-degree and in-degree 2.

5.10. Applying reduction (v), we eliminate the cycle of length 2:

Applying reduction (ii), we eliminate the vertex x_4:

$$\underset{x_1}{\bullet} \xrightarrow{a} \underset{x_2}{\bullet} \underset{\frac{bcd}{1-cf}}{\xrightarrow{\hspace{1cm}}} \underset{x_5}{\bullet}$$

with an arc e from x_2 to x_5.

Applying reduction (i), we eliminate the multiple arcs:

$$\underset{x_1}{\bullet} \xrightarrow{a} \underset{x_2}{\bullet} \xrightarrow{e+\frac{bcd}{1-cf}} \underset{x_5}{\bullet}$$

Applying reduction (ii), we eliminate the vertex x_2:

$$\underset{x_1}{\bullet} \xrightarrow{a\left(e+\frac{bcd}{1-cf}\right)} \underset{x_5}{\bullet}$$

It follows that

$$x_5 = (ae - acef + abcd)\, x_1 / (1 - cf).$$

CHAPTER 6

6.1.

	Eulerian	Eulerian trail
(a)	no	...
(b)	yes	ABCDEACEBDA
(c)	no	...
(d)	yes	ABCADCFBEFDEA
(e)	no	...
(f)	no	...
(g)	no	...

	Hamiltonian	Hamiltonian cycle
(a)	yes	ABCDA
(b)	yes	ABCDEA
(c)	yes	ABCDHGFEA
(d)	yes	ABCDFEA
(e)	no	...
(f)	yes	ADBECFA
(g)	yes	ACDBA

6.3.   Strictly speaking, the answer is *no*, since (according to Saalschütz) the new bridge was a railway bridge! If we ignore that fact, the answer is *yes*, since A and D are now the only vertices of odd degree. A suitable open trail is *ABACADBCD*, crossing the bridges in the order *abcdefhg*.

6.5.   (a) K_n is Eulerian when n is odd (since K_n is regular of degree $n-1$);

   (b) $K_{r,s}$ is Eulerian when r and s are both even (since each of the vertex-degrees is either r or s);

   (c) C_n is Eulerian for all values of n (since C_n is regular of degree 2);

   (d) the octahedron graph is Eulerian (since it is regular of degree 4); the other Platonic graphs are not Eulerian (since they are regular of degree 3 or 5);

   (e) Q_n is Eulerian when n is even (since Q_n is regular of degree n);

   (f) the Petersen graph is not Eulerian (since it is regular of degree 3).

6.8.   There is only one possibility—the cycles C_1, C_2, C_3, and C_4 shown below:

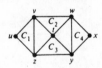

If we trace around C_1, 'picking up' C_2 and C_3 as we go, we get the closed trail

$$u(vwtv)(ztyz)u.$$

This trail misses C_4, which can be inserted at the vertex w to give the Eulerian trail

$$uv(wxyw)tvztyzu.$$

6.9.   Removing the edges uv and vz, we obtain the following graph:

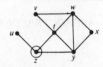

We cannot use the edge uz (which is a bridge), so we must use either zt or zy. There are now several possibilities. For example, we can traverse the edges *zt, tv, vw,* and *wy,* giving the following graph:

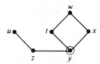

At this stage, we cannot use the edge *yz* (which is a bridge), so we traverse the cycle *ytwxy,* returning (since there is no alternative) by the bridges *yz* and *zu.* Thus we obtain the Eulerian trail *uvztvwytwxyzu.*

6.10. (a) is edge-traceable, since *A* and *B* are the only vertices of odd degree; a suitable open trail is *ACBDAEB,* starting at *A* and ending at *B.*
  (b) is not edge-traceable, since it has four vertices of odd degree.
  (c) is edge-traceable, since the only vertices of odd degree are *u* and *x;* a suitable open trail is *uvwxyzuwyuxvzx.*

6.12. Such graphs do not exist, since the number of vertices of odd degree is always even, by the handshaking lemma.

6.15. If we add *k* edges to *G,* joining the *k* vertices of odd degree in pairs, we get a new graph *G'* in which every vertex has even degree. It follows that *G'* has an Eulerian trail. If we now write out this trail, and then omit the added edges, we get the required *k* pen-strokes.

6.18.

Edge	AB	BC	CB	BD	DE	EF	FD
Markers at beginning	2	2	0	2	2	2	2
Markers at end	3	3	0	3	3	3	1

Edge	DF	FG	GH	HI	IH	HJ	JM
Markers at beginning	1	2	2	2	0	2	2
Markers at end	0	3	3	3	0	3	3

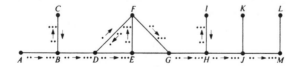

6.19. There are exactly two vertices of odd degree, *b* and *c,* and the shortest path between them is *bedc,* of length 6. Doubling up the edges in this path, we obtain the following Eulerian graph:

An Eulerian trail is *abcdedcebea*, of total length 27.

6.22. (a) Since there is no vertex whose in-degree and out-degree are equal, this digraph is neither Eulerian nor arc-traceable.

(b) In this digraph, the in-degree and out-degree of each vertex are equal, and the digraph is therefore Eulerian: an Eulerian trail is *ABDECDACBEA*.

(c) In this digraph,

$$\text{indeg } B = \text{outdeg } B, \quad \text{indeg } C = \text{outdeg } C,$$
$$\text{indeg } D = \text{outdeg } D, \quad \text{outdeg } A - \text{indeg } A = 1,$$
$$\text{indeg } E - \text{outdeg } E = 1;$$

the digraph is therefore arc-traceable: a suitable trail is *ABDECDACBE*. Note that any such trail must start at *A* and finish at *E*.

CHAPTER 7

7.2. (a) There are two Hamiltonian cycles:

JVTSRWXZQPNMLKFDCBGHJ and *JVTSRWXHGFDCBZQPNMLKJ*.

(Note that the letter after *R* must be *W*, since otherwise *W* would have to be omitted.)

(b) There is only one such path—*BCDFGHXZQPNMLKJVWRST*.

7.5. (a) K_n is Hamiltonian if $n \geq 3$; if the vertices are denoted by $1,2,...,n$, then a Hamiltonian cycle is $123 \cdots n1$.

(b) $K_{r,s}$ is Hamiltonian whenever $r = s$ and $r \geq 2$.

(c) Since a tree contains no cycles, no tree can be Hamiltonian.

(d) All five Platonic graphs are Hamiltonian.

(Hamiltonian cycles for the tetrahedron, cube and octahedron were given in parts (a), (c), and (d) of Problem 6.1. Several Hamiltonian cycles for the dodecahedron were given in our discussion of the Icosian game, and a Hamiltonian cycle for the icosahedron is as follows:

7.12. The vertices of any bipartite graph can be split into two sets *A* and *B* in such a way that each edge has one end in *A* and one end in *B*. Any Hamiltonian cycle must alternate between these two sets, ending in the same set as it started. It follows that if a bipartite graph is Hamiltonian then the sets *A* and *B* must have the same number of vertices. This is impossible if the total number of vertices is odd.

(a) This graph is a bipartite graph with an odd number of vertices, and so cannot be

Hamiltonian. (You can check that the graph is bipartite by writing down the sets A and B. They are

$$\{a,c,e,h,j,l,m\} \quad \text{and} \quad \{b,d,f,g,i,k\},$$

containing seven and six vertices, respectively.)

(b) The graph associated with any chessboard is bipartite, since a knight's move always takes a knight to a square of a different color. So

$$A = \{\text{black squares}\} \quad \text{and} \quad B = \{\text{white squares}\}.$$

The result now follows immediately from the above. (All we are saying is that, since a knight always moves from a black square to a white square, or *vice versa*, the number of black squares must equal the number of white squares. However, this is impossible for any board with an odd number of squares.)

7.14.   (a) Any of the cycle graphs C_n, where $n \geq 5$.

(b) The complete bipartite graph $K_{r,s}$, where $r = \frac{1}{2}(n-1)$, $s = \frac{1}{2}(n+1)$, and n is odd.

[Note that, if n is even, then deg $v \geq \frac{1}{2}n$ for each vertex v, and so the graph is Hamiltonian, by Dirac's theorem.]

7.15.   (a) A Hamiltonian cycle is $ABDA$;

(b) a Hamiltonian cycle is $ABECDA$:

(c) a Hamiltonian cycle is $ABECDA$.

7.19.   Since the number of cities is small, we can solve this problem by trial and error. The two shortest routes are $AECBDA$ and $AEDBCA$ (and their reverses). The total distance traveled in each case is $20+30+50+80+80 = 260$. The reverses of these routes are equally short, so the king has a choice of four routes.

7.20.   Since the number of possible routes is enormous (about 6.08×10^{62}), there is no possibility of sorting through all of them, even on the fastest computer. We are therefore forced to make certain simplifications based on the particular layout of the map in question. For example, since Florida and Georgia are neighboring states in the Southeast, whereas Oregon is a long way away on the West Coast, it is unlikely that our route will take us from Florida to Georgia via Oregon. We can therefore simplify the problem considerably by leaving out connections between pairs of cities which are more than (say) 1000 miles apart, since it is unlikely that any such connection will appear on the shortest route. We might go even further and ignore all connections between pairs of states which do not meet. This would simplify the problem considerably, and although the solution of the new problem may not be exactly the same as that of the original problem, it will probably be a good approximation to it. Finally, we might try a regional approach to the problem in which we break the original problem into much smaller ones involving the various regions of the United States (such as the Northeast, the Midwest, the Southwest, and so on). If we can solve the shortest route problem for the different regions, we may be able to combine these solutions so as to give a solution (possibly approximate) for the original shortest route problem.

CHAPTER 8

8.1   We obtain the following table:

Vertices	S	A	B	C	D	E	T
S	[0]	7	13	28	...	...	...
A		[7]	11	28	32	17	...
B			[11]	16	17	17	...
C				[16]	17	17	...
D, E					[17]	[17]	22
T							[22]

Thus, the shortest distance from S to T is 22. Tracing back through the network, we obtain the shortest path $SABDT$.

8.5.   The graph representing the problem is

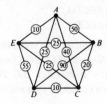

The cheapest routes are as follows:

	A	B	C	D	E
A	—	35	35	25	10
B	35	—	20	30	25
C	35	20	—	10	25
D	25	30	10	-·	35
E	10	25	25	35	—

8.6.   We obtain the following table:

Vertices	S	A	B	C	D	E	T
	–	(S)	(S,A)	(S,B)	(A,B)	(A,C)	(D,E)
S	[0]	[7]	...	...	...	...	...
S, A			[13]	...	...	...	...
S, A, B				[28]	[32]	...	...
S, A, B, C, D						[31]	...
S, A, B, C, D, E							[43]

Thus, the longest distance from S to T is 43. Tracing back through the network, we obtain the longest path $SCET$.

8.9.

Activity	SA	SB	SC	AB	AD	AE	BC	BD	CE	DT	ET
Earliest starting time	0	0	0	7	7	7	13	13	28	32	31
Latest starting time	6	10	0	19	13	21	23	32	28	38	31
Float time	6	10	0	12	6	14	10	19	0	6	0

8.12.   The activity network is

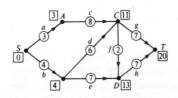

The critical path is *SACDT*, with length 20. We obtain the following table:

Activity	SA	SB	AC	BC	BD	CD	CT	DT
Earliest starting time	0	0	3	4	4	11	11	13
Latest starting time	0	1	3	5	6	11	13	13
Float time	0	1	0	1	2	0	2	0

CHAPTER 9

9.1.   (a) $\kappa(G) = 2$, G is 2-connected, but not 3-connected.
         $\lambda(G) = 2$; G is 2-edge connected, but not 3-edge connected.
         (b) $\kappa(G) = 1$; G is neither 2-connected nor 3-connected.
         $\lambda(G) = 1$; G is neither 2-edge connected nor 3-edge connected.
         (c) $\kappa(G) = 2$; G is 2-connected, but not 3-connected.
         $\lambda(G) = 3$; G is both 2-edge connected and 3-edge connected.

9.4.   (a), (c), (d), and (f) are cutsets; (b) is not a cutset, since its removal does not disconnect the graph; (e) is not a cutset, since we can disconnect the graph by removing just *xz* and *yz*.

9.6.   (a) and (d) are vertex-cutsets; (b) is not a vertex-cutset, since its removal does not disconnect the graph; (c) is not a vertex-cutset, since we can disconnect the graph by removing just *u* and *x*, or just *y*.

9.9.   In each case there are several possibilities—for example:
         (a) *saet, sbdt, sceft;*
         (b) *sbet, sabdt;*
         (c) *saet, sbft.*
         This graph does not contain three vertex-disjoint *st*-paths, since every *st*-path must pass through at least one of the two vertices *b* and *e*.

9.11.   (a) If the two st-paths were not edge-disjoint, then they would have an edge in common. But this would mean that they had at least one vertex (other than s and t) in common, contradicting the fact that they are vertex-disjoint.

      (b) There are many possibilities—for example,

In the above graph the only pairs of edge-disjoint st-paths are $savct$ and $sbvdt$, and $savdt$ and $sbvct$. In neither case are the paths vertex-disjoint, since they all pass through the vertex v.

9.12.   (a) In this case, $k = 2$; two edge-disjoint st-paths are $sact$ and $sbdt$, and two edges separating s from t are sa and sb. Thus the maximum number of edge-disjoint st-paths and the minimum number of edges separating s from t are both equal to 2.

      (b) Again, $k = 2$; two edge-disjoint st-paths are $svxt$ and $swyt$, and two edges separating s from t are vx and wy. Thus the maximum number of edge-disjoint st-paths and the minimum number of edges separating s from t are both equal to 2.

      (c) In this case, $k = 3$; three edge-disjoint st-paths are $suwzt$, syt, and $svxt$, and three edges separating s from t are su, sv, and sy. Thus the maximum number of edge-disjoint st-paths and the minimum number of edges separating s from t are both equal to 3.

9.18.   (a) 5; (b) 5.

CHAPTER 10

.10.1.   There are eleven non-isomorphic trees with seven vertices:

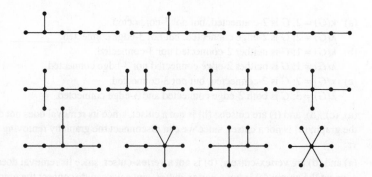

10.4.   (a) For each component of G, the number of vertices exceeds the number of edges by 1. Since there are k components, the total number of edges is $n - k$.

      (b) By the result of part (a), any forest with 12 vertices and 9 edges has exactly three components. An example of such a forest is

(c) If each component has at least two vertices, then the result is true, since each component would then have at least two vertices of degree 2. (This can be seen by applying the handshaking lemma to each component.) However, the result is not true, in general—for example, the following forest has eight components, but only two vertices of degree 1:

10.8.

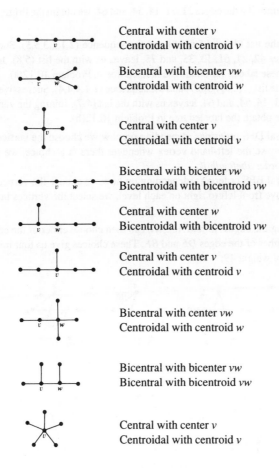

Central with center v
Centroidal with centroid v

Bicentral with bicenter vw
Centroidal with centroid w

Central with center v
Centroidal with centroid v

Bicentral with bicenter vw
Bicentroidal with bicentroid vw

Central with center w
Bicentroidal with bicentroid vw

Central with center v
Centroidal with centroid v

Bicentral with center vw
Centroidal with centroid w

Bicentral with bicenter vw
Bicentral with bicentroid vw

Central with center v
Centroidal with centroid v

10.10. The 16 labeled trees are as follows. Note that the first four are obtained by labeling the star graph $K_{1,3}$, whereas the other 12 arise from labeling the path graph P_4.

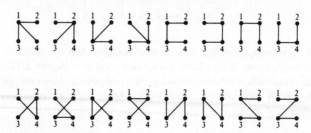

10.12. (a) Successively removing the edges 42, 21, 61, 13, 35, and 75, we obtain the Prüfer sequence **(2,1,1,3,5,5)**.

   (b) Successively removing the edges 21, 31, 14, 54, and 64, we obtain the Prüfer sequence **(1,1,4,4,4)**.

10.14. (a) We start with the list $(1,2,3,4,5,6,7,8)$ and the sequence **(2,1,1,3,5,5)**. Successively adding the edges 42, 21, 61, 13, 35, and 75, leaves us with the list (5,8). Joining the vertices with these labels, we obtain the labeled tree in Problem 10.12(a).

   (b) We start with the list (1,2,3,4,5,6,7) and the sequence **(1,1,4,4,4)**. Successively adding the edges 21, 31, 14, 54, and 64, leaves us with the list (4,7). Joining the vertices with these labels, we obtain the labeled tree in Problem 10.12(b).

10.16. (a) There are several DFS orderings, depending on how we choose the vertices at each stage. If we choose the left-hand vertex whenever there is a choice, we select the vertices in the order *abefcgdhijk*.

   (b) There are several BFS orderings, depending on how we choose the vertices at each stage. If we move from left to right on each level, we select the vertices in the order *abcdefghijk*.

10.20. We start by choosing the edges AB and AC. We can then choose either of the edges AD and CD, and then either of the edges DE and BE. These choices give us four minimum spanning trees, all of weight 49:

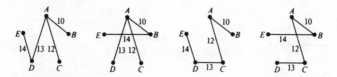

10.24. (a)

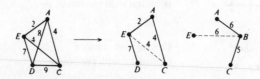

The minimum-weight spanning tree joining the vertices A, C, D, and E is the tree with edges AE, DE, and AC or CE, with total weight 13. The two edges of smallest weight incident to B are BC and BA or, BE with total weight 11. The lower bound is therefore $13 + 11 = 24$.

(b)

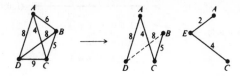

The minimum-weight spanning tree joining the vertices $A, B, C,$ and D is the tree with edges $AC, BC,$ and AD or BD with total weight 17. The two edges of smallest weight incident to E are EA and EC, with total weight 6. The lower bound is therefore $17 + 6 = 23$.

10.32. First, we order the items in decreasing order of value per unit weight, as shown below. (In this case, the weight of an item is the time needed to produce that item.)

Order number i	1	2	3	4	5
Item	B	E	D	C	A
Weight w_i	7	4	4	2	3
Value v_i	14	8	7	3	3
Value per unit weight	2	2	1.75	1.5	1

We begin by branching out from the null solution:

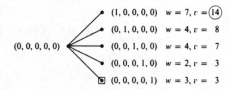

STORE $v = 14$, solution $= (1,0,0,0,0)$
Next we branch out from the solution $(1,0,0,0,0)$:

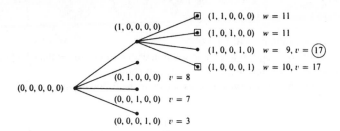

STORE $v = 17$, solution $= (1,0,0,1,0)$
We delete the marked vertices and continue the branching process from vertex $(1,0,0,1,0)$.

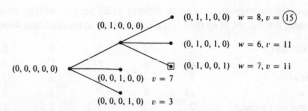

STORE $v = 17$, solution = $(0,1,0,0,0)$
The new solution is infeasible, so we continue the branching process from the current feasible solution with the highest value—namely, $(0,1,0,0,0)$.

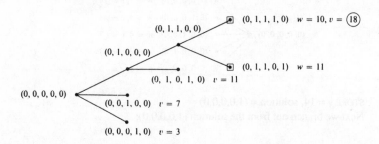

STORE $v = 17$, solution = $(1,0,0,1,0)$
We continue the branching process from vertex $(0,1,1,0,0)$.

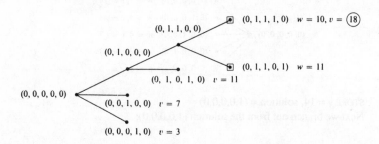

STORE $v = 18$, solution = $(0,1,1,1,0)$
The solution $(0,1,1,1,0)$ is a feasible solution with a value greater than the previous stored value, so we update the stored value, as shown above.
We continue the branching process as shown in the following diagrams.

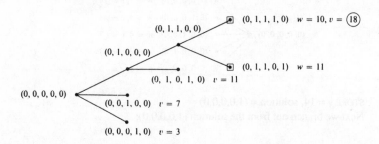

STORE $v = 18$, solution = $(0,1,1,1,0)$

(0, 0, 1, 0, 0)

(0, 0, 1, 1, 0) $w = 6, v = \textcircled{10}$

(0, 0, 0, 0, 0)

(0, 0, 1, 0, 1) $w = 7, v = 10$

(0, 0, 0, 1, 0) $v = 3$

STORE $v = 18$, solution = (0,1,1,1,0)

(0, 0, 0, 0, 0)   (0, 0, 1, 0, 0)   (0, 0, 1, 1, 0)   (0, 0, 1, 1, 1) $w = 9, v = \textcircled{13}$

(0, 0, 0, 1, 0) $v = 3$

STORE $v = 18$, solution = (0,1,1,1,0)

(0, 0, 0, 0, 0)   (0, 0, 0, 1, 0)   (0, 0, 0, 1, 1) $w = 5, v = \textcircled{6}$

STORE $v = 18$, solution = (0,1,1,1,0)

The branch-and-bound procedure has now been completed, so the optimum solution vector is (0,1,1,1,0), corresponding to items E, D, and C, with a total value of 18.

CHAPTER 11

11.2.

 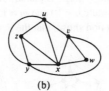

(a)   (b)   (c)

11.4. In any plane drawing of K_5, the cycle $uvwxyu$ must appear as a pentagon. The edge vy must lie either inside or outside this pentagon. Since the argument is similar in each case, we shall assume that vy lies *inside* the pentagon, as in diagram (b).

(a)   (b)   (c)

Since the edges ux and uw cannot cross vy, they must lie outside the pentagon, as in diagram (c). But the edge vx cannot cross uw, and the edge wy cannot cross ux, so both vx and wy must lie inside the pentagon, and must therefore cross. Since this is not allowed, we deduce that K_5 has no plane drawing—that is, K_5 is non-planar.

11.5. (a) TRUE, since if G is planar, we can draw G without crossings. If we now omit the vertices and edges not contained in the subgraph, we get a plane drawing of the subgraph.

(b) FALSE—for example, $K_{3,3}$ is not planar, whereas the cycle graph C_6 (a subgraph of $K_{3,3}$) is planar.

(c) FALSE—for example, C_6 is planar, whereas $K_{3,3}$ (which contains C_6) is not.

(d) TRUE, since if G is planar, then G cannot have a non-planar subgraph (by the result of part (a)).

11.8. For graph (a), there are 9 edges, the face-degrees are 3, 3, 4, 4, and 4, and

$$3 + 3 + 4 + 4 + 4 = 2 \times 9;$$

for graph (b), there are 11 edges, the face-degrees are 3, 3, 3, 3, 3, 3, and 4, and

$$3 + 3 + 3 + 3 + 3 + 3 + 4 = 2 \times 11;$$

for graph (c), there are 11 edges, the face-degrees are 3, 3, 3, 3, 3, 3, and 4, and

$$3 + 3 + 3 + 3 + 3 + 3 + 4 = 2 \times 11;$$

The handshaking lemma is therefore verified in each case.

11.9. For graph (a), $n = 6, m = 9, f = 5$, so $n - m + f = 2$;
For graph (b), $n = 6, m = 11, f = 7$, so $n - m + f = 2$;
For graph (c), $n = 6, m = 11, f = 7$, so $n - m + f = 2$.
Euler's formula is therefore verified in each case.

11.12. (a) Since the shortest cycle length in G is 5, the degree of each face in a plane drawing is at least 5, so that $2m \geq 5f$ and we have $f \leq \frac{2}{5} m$. Combining this with Euler's formula, $f = m - n + 2$, we get $m - n + 2 \leq \frac{2}{5} m$, and hence $m \leq \frac{5}{3} (n-2)$.

(b) Suppose that the Petersen graph is planar. Since it contains no triangles or cycles of length 4, we can substitute $n = 10$ and $m = 15$ into the result of part (a) to give $15 \leq \frac{40}{3}$. This contradiction shows that the Petersen graph is not planar.

11.14.

icosahedron   dodecahedron C_6

   (a)   (b)   (c)   (d)

11.15. (a) Since G is simple, we can apply Corollary 1 to deduce that $m \leq 3n-6$, where m is the number of edges of G. *If every vertex has degree 5 or more*, we have (on counting the edges around each vertex) $2m \geq 5n$. Thus $\frac{5}{2}n \leq m \leq 3n-6$, giving $n \geq 12$. This contradiction establishes the result.

(b) Since G has no vertices of degree 1 or 2, we have (on counting the edges around each vertex) $2m \geq 3n$. *If every face has degree 5 or more*, we have (on counting the edges around each face) $2m \geq 5f$. Combining these two inequalities with Euler's formula yields $f \geq 12$. This contradiction establishes the result.

[Note that either of these results can be deduced from the other by duality.]

11.20. Deletion of the edge vw gives the following subgraph, which is a subdivision of $K_{3,3}$:

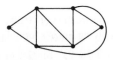

It follows from Kuratowski's theorem that the given graph is non-planar.

11.22. (a) Planar: a plane drawing is as follows:

For this graph, $n = 6$, $m = 10$, and $f = 6$, so $n - m + f = 2$.

(b) Planar: a plane drawing is as follows:

For this graph, $n = 6$, $m = 11$, and $f = 7$, so $n - m + f = 2$.

(c) Non-planar: this graph clearly contains $K_{3,3}$ as a subgraph, as can be seen by comparing it with card 175; it also contains a subdivision of K_5, as can be seen by removing the vertical edge in the center.

(d) Non-planar: this graph contains $K_{3,3}$ as a subgraph (the two vertices of degree 4 and any vertex of degree 5 form one set, the remaining three vertices of degree 5 form the other); it also contains K_5 as a subgraph, as can be seen by removing one of the vertices of degree 4 and its incident edges.

[Note that in parts (c) and (d), K_5 and $K_{3,3}$ are regarded as subdivisions of themselves.]

11.25. Three planar subgraphs which can be superimposed to form K_9 are shown on page 227. It follows that $t(K_9) \leq 3$.

11.27. Since the graph $K_{2,s}$ is planar for any given value of s, we can split $K_{r,s}$ into $\frac{1}{2}r$ planar subgraphs, each of which is isomorphic to $K_{2,s}$. Thus $t(K_{r,s}) \leq \frac{1}{2}r$. Combining this with the lower bound for $t(K_{r,s})$ given on page 226, we get

$$\lceil rs / (2r + 2s - 4) \rceil \leq t(K_{r,s}) \leq \tfrac{1}{2}r.$$

These two bounds are equal if

$$\tfrac{1}{2}r - \frac{rs}{2r+2s-4} < 1.$$

Rearranging this inequality gives

$$s > \tfrac{1}{2}(r - 2)^2.$$

Thus, if $s > \frac{1}{2}(r - 2)^2$, then $t(K_{r,s}) = \frac{1}{2}r$.

11.32. (a) card 50; (b) card 51; (c) card 189.

11.34. The dual graphs are as follows. Since their degree-sequences are (3,3,3,3,3,5) and (3,3,3,3,4,4), they are clearly not isomorphic.

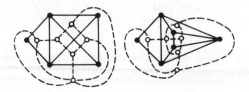

11.36. It follows directly from the construction of G^*, that G^* has f vertices and m edges. If G^* has f^* faces, then, by applying Euler's formula to both G and G^*, we obtain

$$\text{for } G: n - e + f = 2; \quad \text{for } G^*: f - e + f^* = 2.$$

Comparing these gives $f^* = n$, as required.

11.37. If G is bipartite, then every cycle of G has even length, by the result of Problem 2.23. By duality, every cutset of G^* has an even number of edges. In particular, every vertex of G^* has even degree. Thus, G^* is Eulerian, by Theorem 6.1. Conversely, if G^* is Eulerian, then every vertex of G^* has even degree. By duality, every face of G has even degree. In particular, every cycle of G has even length. Thus, G is bipartite.

CHAPTER 12

12.1.

12.4. (a) 7; (b) 2; (c) 3: (d) 2: (e) 4.

12.5. (a) The only graphs with $\chi(G) = 1$ are the graphs with no edges—that is, the null graphs N_n.

   (b) The graphs with $\chi(G) = 2$ are the bipartite graphs (other than N_n), since we can color their vertices black and white so that each edge has a black end and a white end.

12.6. a. TRUE, because if G contains K_r as a subgraph, then G contains r mutually adjacent vertices which require r colors. So $\chi(G) \geq r$.

   b. FALSE—for example, the cycle graph C_5 has chromatic number 3, but contains no triangle.

12.12. (a) $k(k-1)(k-2)(k-3)(k-4)$; (b) $k(k-1)^4$.

12.15. (a) $k(k-1)^2(k-2)$, since we can assign k colors to v, $k-1$ colors to u and x, and $k-2$ colors to w;

   (b) $k(k-1)^3(k-2)$, since we can assign k colors to v, $k-1$ colors to u and x, $k-2$ colors to w, and $k-1$ colors to y;

(c) $k(k-1)(k-2)^2$, since we can assign k colors to v, $k-1$ colors to w, and $k-2$ colors to u and x;

(d) $k^2(k-1)^2(k-2)$, since we can color K_3 with $k(k-1)(k-2)$ colors and K_2 with $k(k-1)$ colors;

(e) the number of colorings in which v and w are colored the same is $k(k-1)^2$, since we can assign k colors to v, 1 color (that used for v) to w, $k-1$ colors to u, and $k-1$ colors to x; the number of colorings in which v and w are colored differently is $k(k-1)(k-2)^2$, since we can assign k colors to v, $k-1$ colors to w, $k-2$ colors to u, and $k-2$ colors to x. The total number of colorings is therefore

$$k(k-1)^2 + k(k-1)(k-2)^2 = k(k-1)(k^2-3k+3).$$

12.16. The polynomials in parts (a) and (b) of Problem 12.15 are, respectively,

$$k^4 - 4k^3 + 5k^2 - 2k$$

and

$$k^5 - 5k^4 + 9k^3 - 7k^2 + 2k.$$

These polynomials clearly satisfy the given properties.

12.18. (a)

$$P_G(k) = \{k(k-1)(k-2)\}^2 - k(k-1)^2(k-2)^2 = k(k-1)^3(k-2)^2.$$

(b)

$$P_G(k) = k(k-1)^4 - k(k-1)(k^2-3k+3) \quad \text{[by Problem 12.15(e)]}$$
$$= k(k-1)(k^3-4k^2+6k-4)$$
$$= k(k-1)(k-2)(k^2-2k+2).$$

12.20. (a) Since the graph G contains vertices of degree 3, we have $\chi'(G) \geq 3$. The following diagram illustrates a 3-edge-coloring of G. So $\chi'(G) = 3$.

(b) Since the graph G contains vertices of degree 4, we have $\chi'(G) \geq 4$. The following diagram illustrates a 5-edge-coloring of G. So $\chi'(G) = 4$ *or* 5. A little trial and error will convince you that no 4-edge-coloring is possible, so $\chi'(G) = 5$.

12.23. (a) The only graphs with $\chi'(G) = 1$ are the graphs whose components are either single edges or isolated vertices. (At least one edge must be included.)

(b) The only graphs with $\chi'(G) = 2$ are the graphs whose components are either path graphs, cycles of even length, or isolated vertices. (At least one path of length 2 or more, or cycle of even length, must be included.)

12.24. (a) TRUE, because if G contains a vertex of degree r, then G contains r edges all of which must be differently colored. So $\chi'(G) \geq r$.

    (b) FALSE—for example, the cycle graph C_5 has chromatic index 3, but contains no vertex of degree 3.

12.25. 1. (a) $2 \leq \chi'(C_7) \leq 3$;   (b) $\chi'(C_7) = 3$;

    2. (a) $5 \leq \chi'(K_6) \leq 6$;   (b) $\chi'(K_6) = 5$;

    3. (a) $4 \leq \chi'(K_{3,4}) \leq 5$;   (b) $\chi'(K_{3,4}) = 4$.

    A 5-edge-coloring of K_6, and a 4-edge-coloring of $K_{3,4}$, are

12.30. The graphs on cards 7, 38, 48, 51, and 52.

12.35. We can represent this situation by a complete graph K_n, and the solution is given by $\chi'(K_n)$. Thus the number of matches necessary is $n - 1$ if n is even, and n if n is odd.

12.36. Most of the information is irrelevant! The maximum degree of a student-vertex is 3, and that of a tutor-vertex is 15; thus the maximum vertex-degree in the bipartite graph is 15. It follows from König's theorem that the number of periods needed is 15.

CHAPTER 13

13.1.

13.4. If there were a map in the plane with five mutually adjacent regions, it would then follow by duality that the complete graph K_5 could be drawn in the plane without crossings. Since K_5 is non-planar, no such map can exist. Note that if such a map were to exist, then the four-color theorem would be false. However, the converse is not true: the fact that no such map exists does not imply the four-color theorem.

13.6. (a) For any vertex v, the faces surrounding v must be even in number since they can be colored with two colors. It follows that every vertex of G has even degree, and so G is Eulerian.

    (b) For any face F, the faces surrounding F must alternate in color, and so there must be an even number of them. It follows that every face of G has even degree.

13.11. From Theorem 13.7, we obtain $g(K_7) = 1$ and $g(K_{11}) = 5$.

13.15. For graphs of genus 1 embedded on the torus, we have $g = 1$, and hence

$$n - m + f = 0.$$

For K_5, $n = 5$, $m = 10$, $f = 5$, and thus

$$n - m + f = 0;$$

for $K_{3,3}$, $n = 6$, $m = 9$, $f = 3$, and thus

$$n - m + f = 0.$$

Drawings of K_5 and $K_{3,3}$ with the requisite number of faces are

K_5　　　　　$K_{3,3}$

13.16. By Theorem 13.6, $n - m + f = 2 - 2g$. However, each face is bounded by at least three edges, and thus $3f \leq 2m$. It follows that

$$2 - 2g \leq n - m + \tfrac{2}{3}m,$$

and thus

$$g \geq \tfrac{1}{2}\left(\tfrac{1}{3}m - n + 2\right) = \tfrac{1}{6}(m - 3n) + 1.$$

Since g is an integer, the result follows.

CHAPTER 14

14.2. (a) There are many possibilities—for example:

(b) The corresponding graph is

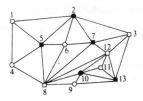

The coloring in part (a) leads to a vertex decomposition of the required type—namely,

$$\{1,3,8,11\}, \{2,10\}, \{4,6,9,12\}, \{5,7,13\}.$$

14.5.   The tour graph is

Since vertices 1, 2, 3, and 4 are mutually adjacent, at least four colors are needed to color the vertices of this graph so that neighboring vertices are colored differently. This means that at least four days are needed to schedule the various tours. In fact, four days are sufficient, as the following vertex decomposition shows:

Monday:	tours 1, 5, and 7;
Tuesday:	tours 2, 9, and 12;
Wednesday:	tours 3, 6, and 11;
Thursday:	tours 4, 8, and 10.

(Several other vertex decompositions are possible.)

14.6.   There are many possibilities—for example,
   (a) $\{A, C\}$ and $\{B, E\}$ are minimum dominating sets, giving rise to the vertex decompositions $\{A, B, E\}$, $\{C, D\}$ and $\{B, A, C\}$, $\{E, D\}$, respectively.
   (b) $\{A, G\}$ is a minimum dominating set, giving rise to the vertex decomposition $\{A, B, D, E\}$, $\{G, F, H, C\}$.

14.7.

There are no minimum dominating sets with three vertices. A minimum dominating set with four vertices is $\{1,2,3,5\}$, giving rise to the vertex decomposition

$$\{1,6,8\}, \{2,7,9\}, \{3,4\}, \{5\}.$$

(Several other solutions are possible.) Hence the smallest number of knights is 4.

14.13.   Since the edges incident to the vertex of degree k must all appear in different matchings, the number of matchings is at least k.

14.14.   By Problem 14.13, at least three matchings are needed for each graph, since each graph has maximum vertex-degree 3. For graph (1), three matchings are sufficient; a corresponding edge decomposition is

$$\{AB, DE\}, \{AE, BC\}, \{BE, CD\}.$$

However, for graph (2), four matchings are needed; a corresponding edge decomposition is

$$\{AB, CE\}, \{AE, BD\}, \{BC, DE\}, \{CD\}.$$

14.16. The corresponding bipartite graph is

We can decompose this graph into four matchings, giving the following schedule:

9 *am* – 10 *am*:	1–A,	2–C,	3–B
10 *am* – 11 *am*:	1–B,	4–A,	5–C
11 *am* – 12 *noon*:	2–A,	3–C,	4–B
12 *noon* – 1 *pm*:	5–B		

Several other schedules are possible.

14.19. (a) Each bus company needs a network which connects all the *n* towns, and so must have at least *n* – 1 interconnected roads. It follows that if there are *k* companies, then the total number of roads is at least $k(n-1)$; that is $m \geq k\,(n-1)$. It follows that $k \leq m/(n-1)$.

(b) This network has 13 towns and 28 roads, and so $k \leq \frac{28}{12}$; it follows that $k = 1$ or 2.

The following diagram shows that $k = 2$:

14.20. There are several possibilities—for example:

Note that in this example, $n = 9$ and $m = 24$, so *m* is a multiple of $n - 1$.

INDEX